Contemporary
New Zealand Cinema

TAURIS WORLD CINEMA SERIES

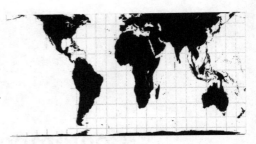

Series Editor: Lúcia Nagib
Advisory Board: Laura Mulvey (UK), Donald Richie (Japan), Robert Stam (USA), Ismail Xavier (Brazil)

The aim of the **Tauris World Cinema Series** is to reveal and celebrate the richness and complexity of film art across the globe. A wide variety of cinemas will be explored, both in the light of their own cultures and in the ways they interconnect with each other in a global context.

The books in the series will represent innovative scholarship, in tune with the multicultural character of contemporary audiences and designed to appeal to both the film expert and the general interest reader. It will draw upon an international authorship, comprising academics, film writers and journalists.

Prominent strands of the Series will include **World Film Theory**, offering new theoretical approaches as well as re-assessments of major movements, filmmakers, genres, technologies and stars; **New Cinemas,** focusing on recent film revivals in different parts of the world; and **new translations** into English of international milestones of film theory and criticism.

Books in the Series include:

Brazil on Screen: Cinema Novo, New Cinema, Utopia
Lúcia Nagib

East Asian Cinemas: Exploring Transnational Connections on Film
Edited by Leon Hunt and Leung Wing-Fai

Lebanese Cinema: Imagining the Civil War and Beyond
Lina Khatib

Contemporary New Zealand Cinema: From New Wave to Blockbuster
Edited by Ian Conrich and Stuart Murray

Queries, ideas and submissions to:
Series Editor, Professor Lúcia Nagib – l.nagib@leeds.ac.uk
Cinema Editor at I.B.Tauris, Philippa Brewster – p.brewster@blueyonder.co.uk

Contemporary
New Zealand Cinema

From New Wave to Blockbuster

Edited by Ian Conrich and Stuart Murray

I.B. TAURIS
LONDON · NEW YORK

Published in 2008 by I.B.Tauris & Co Ltd
6 Salem Road, London W2 4BU
175 Fifth Avenue, New York NY 10010
www.ibtauris.com

In the United States of America and Canada distributed by
Palgrave Macmillan, a division of St. Martin's Press,
175 Fifth Avenue, New York NY 10010

ISBN: 978 1 84511 837 2

A full CIP record for this book is available from the British Library
A full CIP record is available from the Library of Congress

Library of Congress Catalog Card Number: available

Printed and bound in Great Britain by CPI Antony Rowe, Chippenham,
from camera-ready copy edited and supplied by the author with the assistance of
Opuscule

Contents

Illustrations

Acknowledgements

The editors would like to thank Jodie Robson and the contributors for their help with the completion of this collection, Lindsay Shelton, Kathleen Drumm, and the staff of the New Zealand Film Commission for their generosity in supplying many illustrations, as well as the staff at the New Zealand Film Archive. Philippa Brewster and Jayne Hill at I.B.Tauris were invaluable in their commitment to seeing this book through to publication. Lastly, we would like to thank The British Academy for its assistance with travel and research.

Foreword

Lindsay Shelton

It is exciting to experience how New Zealand's national cinema is changing New Zealanders' perceptions, by giving us new confidence in who we are, and encouraging our awareness and understanding of our different communities. At a 2005 preview screening of Taika Waititi's *Tama Tu*, a short film about young Maori soldiers in Italy during the Second World War, I realised that most of the audience were Maori war veterans who had fought in Italy. Members of a generation who have generally kept silent about the war, their response to the film was anything but silent and the atmosphere in the cinema was electric with recognition. A year later, I sat with a general audience at one of the first screenings of Chris Graham's *Sione's Wedding*, a comedy which tells its story of a group of young Samoan New Zealanders with warmth and good humour. In a different way, this film also offered the shared pleasure of recognition, and in doing so it earned substantial popular success with local audiences.

Gordon Mirams said that if there was any New Zealand culture, it was to a large extent the creation of Hollywood. The campaign which changed this, and which proclaimed the need for New Zealanders to see their own films, did not begin until 1970, and Gregory A. Waller's article in this collection describes how it took seven years to achieve its goal. Of course, Hollywood films never disappeared from New Zealand screens. However, for the last thirty years there has been a difference: we have been seeing our own films every year, as well.

There is another difference. Since the early 1980s, New Zealand movies have been sold for screening in more than sixty other countries. Local audiences had been Geoff Murphy's sole target when he made *Goodbye Pork Pie* in 1980. I remember his surprise and pleasure when we came back from New Zealand's first international film market with the news that his movie would be screening in twenty countries. And when Murphy's 1983 film *Utu* was praised by Pauline Kael in the *New Yorker* and Vincent Canby in the *New York Times*, this was a new level of international recognition not only for the director but also on a broader level for New Zealand. We were no longer only a beautiful country. Now our films were making us known as a creatively talented one as well.

It is amazing to realise the speed with which New Zealand cinema established itself. Mark Williams's article considers the achievements of

Peter Jackson, and tracks the establishment of his international reputation only six years after he made his first feature. With his four most recent New Zealand films, Jackson has dominated the world's box office. His popularity with audiences at home has been equally extraordinary. Only four features have grossed more than $NZ12million in New Zealand. One was *Titanic*. The other three were *The Lord of the Rings*.

Less than ten years earlier, the box office record was $6.7 million, set by *Once Were Warriors*. Seen by more than a million New Zealanders (in a population of less than four million), it grossed more than *Jurassic Park*. Such statistics—there are many of them—help to demonstrate the high achievements of New Zealand's small film industry. Ian Conrich and Stuart Murray put things into perspective when they count a total of only 260 New Zealand features since 1977. The United States or Japan or India have each produced many more than that number in any one year. The comparison is clear. New Zealand films and filmmakers have earned successes quite disproportionate to the size of their industry.

The different narratives in this book all fit into what Nick Roddick calls the 'endlessly fascinating' history of cinema. New Zealand's cinema history is as fascinating as any, but its story has so far been told by very few. This book's perspectives and analysis are an important addition to the small collection of writing which explores how New Zealand has belatedly earned such a prominent place in the international cinema world.

Wellington, 2008

Lindsay Shelton was founding director of the Wellington Film Festival from 1972 to 1979, and the first Marketing Director of the New Zealand Film Commission from 1979 until 2001. He is the author of *The Selling of New Zealand Movies* (Awa Press, 2005).

Introduction

Ian Conrich and Stuart Murray

As a contemporary national cinema competing within the new global film markets, New Zealand's rise to a level of international recognition has been swift. Since the early 1990s, New Zealand has produced such critical and commercial successes as the cult-horror *Braindead* (1992), the social dramas *Once Were Warriors* (1994) and *Heavenly Creatures* (1994), the family feel-good movies *Whale Rider* (2002) and *The World's Fastest Indian* (2005), and the comedy *Sione's Wedding* (2006). New Zealand's film industry has been a key component in the production of the multi-award winning *The Piano* (1993), *The Lord of the Rings* trilogy (2001–03), and *King Kong* (2005), and provided production facilities for *The Last Samurai* (2003), and *The Chronicles of Narnia: The Lion, the Witch and the Wardrobe* (2005).

This is not to say, however, that the footsteps created by New Zealand's contemporary film production can only be traced back to the early 1990s. In fact, a period of contemporary New Zealand cinema would be best viewed as commencing in the mid 1970s when there was the first evidence of a film renaissance. In the decade that followed, various New Zealand films gained notable overseas recognition. These films include the true crime drama *Beyond Reasonable Doubt* (1980), the anarchic road movie *Goodbye Pork Pie* (1980, the first New Zealand movie to receive nationwide release in the UK), the melodrama *Smash Palace* (1981), *Utu* (1983, New Zealand's own Western set during the nineteenth century Maori wars, which was widely praised by US critics), and *Vigil* (1984, the first New Zealand production selected to be screened in competition at the prestigious Cannes film festival). Moreover, New Zealand's contemporary cinema consists of more than the odd art house film, occasional genre successes, and a series of blockbusters and epic productions (predominantly financed from overseas). Since 1977, New Zealand has produced approximately 260 films, and many of these have had to seek exposure outside the overseas theatrical circuits and general widespread distribution, quite often appearing instead on foreign cable channels or as video rental releases. Despite the success of a series of films since the mid 1970s (particularly those made since the early 1990s), which have repeatedly focused attention on this nation, the full extent of New Zealand's film industry remains perhaps one of the best-kept secrets in world cinema.

1977

This collection takes as its starting point the year 1977 in its definition of a contemporary New Zealand cinema. The year was significant for the establishment of an Interim Film Commission, which in 1978 became the New Zealand Film Commission (NZFC), a government constituted and funded body with the responsibility for assisting the development of a local film industry. 1977 is also significant as marking the release of two films—*Wild Man* and *Sleeping Dogs*—which drew particular emphasis to the need for Government support for film production in New Zealand. The comedy *Wild Man* was directed by Geoff Murphy, and *Sleeping Dogs* (based on C.K. Stead's 1971 political novel *Smith's Dream*) was directed by Roger Donaldson; in the respective lead roles, the iconic Bruno Lawrence was the eponymous Wild Man, and Sam Neill played Smith. These movies were the feature film debuts for Murphy, Donaldson, Lawrence and Neill, four filmmakers who in their own ways continued to act as primary figures in the development of a contemporary New Zealand cinema.

Placing this period in context, only four years earlier New Zealand had been forced into a position where as a nation it needed to seek stronger cultural independence. New Zealand's cultural and political economy had been woven into an identity that was markedly British, but in 1973 after a decade of political negotiation the UK joined the European Union (then the European Economic Community—the EEC). Amongst the conditions that were set by the EEC on the UK's membership, the favoured trade terms between this mother nation and its former colony had to cease. This became a significant part of what James Belich has described as a 'gradual disconnection from Britain', in the post-war years.[1] It is no accident that a cultural renaissance followed in New Zealand, with Colin James viewing the 1980s as a period of 'adolescent independence'.[2]

In fact, a New Zealand Film Commission was being discussed in 1970, when the New Zealand Arts Council sponsored a symposium on 'The Role of Film and Television in Establishing a Nation's Identity'. That same year, the Australian Film Development Corporation (later the Australian Film Commission) was established and this was instrumental in creating a new wave of local film production. By the late 1960s, the film industry in Australia had reached a point of enervation, though Australian cinema, in comparison to that in New Zealand, has always had a much stronger movie heritage. For instance, before 1970, New Zealand had made just five feature films in the previous thirty years, with what existed of a commercial feature film industry consisting of resourceful independent filmmakers, namely John O'Shea and Rudall Hayward. Working with the model of the new Australian film industry, in the mid 1970s Jim Booth from New Zealand's department of Internal Affairs, wrote the document *Proposal to Establish a New Zealand Film Production Commission*, which became part of the foundations of the NZFC.

When New Zealand's film renaissance began in the mid 1970s an industry coalesced from four key areas of cultural production: the

National Film Unit (NFU), Pacific Films, The Acme Sausage Company/ Blerta group of artists, performers, and practitioners, and the Alternative Cinema group of filmmakers. The producer Aardvark Films should be added as a fifth element, though its contribution to feature film making is not as significant. The NFU, which produced documentaries, newsreels and Government promotional films, was established in 1941 following a recommendation from documentary filmmaker John Grierson, during his visit in 1940. Pacific Films, established in 1948 by Roger Mirams and Alun Falconer, became only New Zealand's second film production house (following the NFU). Compared to the NFU its output was more artistic, and it was associated with a diversity of productions, from the commercial features of John O'Shea—*Broken Barrier* (1952, co-directed with Mirams), *Runaway* (1964), and *Don't Let it Get You* (1966)—to documentaries, corporates or industry sponsored instructional films, sports items such as the coverage of rugby matches, cinemagazines or news compilation films with a local interest, television and cinema advertisements, and television programmes such as the seminal Barry Barclay directed six-part series *Tangata Whenua* (1974). Barclay made his feature debut in 1987 with *Ngati*, a production regarded as the first fiction feature by an indigenous filmmaker anywhere; two years earlier fellow Pacific Films director Gaylene Preston made her feature debut with *Mr Wrong*, one of New Zealand's earliest features directed solely by a woman. Alongside Paul Maunder (*Landfall*, 1975), John Laing (*Beyond Reasonable Doubt*, 1980), and Sam Pillsbury (*The Scarecrow*, 1982), who had worked predominantly at the NFU, these filmmakers became part of the core of directors who made their feature film debuts in the 1970s and 1980s.

The NFU and Pacific Films were based in Wellington. In contrast, the filmmakers cooperative Alternative Cinema which was established in 1972, was located in Auckland. It was led by Geoff Steven who directed the landmark experimental feature *Test Pictures: Eleven Vignettes From A Relationship* (1975). The more commercial small-town satire *Skin Deep* (1978) was Steven's second feature, and its origins were in his three-screen art gallery video presentation, 'Aspects of a Small Town'. The work of the Alternative Cinema collective, whose members included later feature filmmakers David Blyth and Gregor Nicholas was, in one way, closely connected to the display areas of city art galleries and community exhibition spaces, with artists exploring the visual and aural properties of film and video. One such artist was Leon Narbey, who had become known during the 1960s and 1970s for his small art films and experimental shorts, which often focused on the interactions between light and sound. Narbey, who later became one of New Zealand's most celebrated cinematographers, made his feature debut as director of photography on *Skin Deep*. Steven's film career in this period provides an interesting example of how the nature of the local film industry changed. In the brief three-year period between Steven's first and second features, the New Zealand government established a system of support for film production. This meant that whilst

Test Pictures: Eleven Vignettes From A Relationship revealed the director's resourcefulness in stretching a NZ$14,000 budget (NZ$7000 funded by the Queen Elizabeth II Arts Council), *Skin Deep* was the first production to have assistance from the Interim Film Commission and had a budget of NZ$180,000.

Also based in Auckland was Aardvark Films, who achieved prominence with *Sleeping Dogs* following work producing commercials, television programmes, and documentaries in the 1970s. Often in combination with Mune Productions (operated by Ian Mune, who had a lead role in *Sleeping Dogs* as well as co-writing the screenplay), Aardvark Films made important programmes such as the television series *Winners and Losers* (1975–76). Mune's work connected with Murphy's The Acme Sausage Company and Lawrence's Blerta (The Bruno Lawrence Electric Revelation and Travelling Apparition), film producers whose activities were entwined. Murphy and Lawrence had emerged from the Waimarama commune that Murphy had established in 1971 with Alun Bollinger and Martyn Sanderson, two figures who have been ever-present in the contemporary New Zealand film industry in their respective primary roles as director of photography and character actor.

Blerta was also loosely the name of a psychedelic bus, which transported the Lawrence troupe of performers (which included Murphy) and their families around New Zealand, and later Australia, between 1971 and 1975. The group presented a mixed media package of family entertainment, musical performance, anarchy, and absurdist and surreal comedy, with distinct counter-cultural statements. Like Aardvark Films/Mune Productions, The Acme Sausage Company and Blerta were commissioned to make the occasional television programme such as the Murphy directed children's comedy series of five six-minute episodes of *Percy the Policeman* (1974), and the series of six thirty-minute *Blerta* programmes (1976), from which the *Wild Man* episode was expanded into a feature film. But opportunities were limited. New Zealand television, which had first begun transmission in 1960, favoured cheaper overseas product, and a second channel, TV2, was not added until 1975. New Zealand television was also very conservative and the skits, zany sketches, and sudden musical performances in the *Blerta* series challenged traditional programming expectations. Moreover, the Keystonesque *Percy the Policeman* was considered to be so anarchic and subversive in its portrayal of the police that it was never actually broadcast. Such rebelliousness, however, found greater expression in film and became a notable theme in many of the movies of the New Zealand new wave.

The New Wave and After

Whilst the movies of Murphy or Lawrence dominate New Zealand's new wave (they worked respectively on seven and sixteen separate productions, including four films together between 1977 and 1986), the largely male local film industry seemed to share their general interest in male-centric, testosterone-fuelled action-dramas, of law-breaking, stunts and car chases.

The impact made by *Wild Man* and *Sleeping Dogs* cannot be ignored, neither can the influence of the Waimarama commune and the Blerta troupe, who were also associated with *Goodbye Pork Pie*, a movie which finally seemed to demonstrate that New Zealand films could have a local voice and still be successful.

Mainstream film audiences in New Zealand had been familiar, and seemingly content, with foreign films (mainly American and British) which depicted distant stories and accents. For John O'Shea, the post 1977 explosion in New Zealand filmmaking was not just a quest for local cultural expression but for a new local audience that was interested in experiencing its own stories on film. As he argues,

> [t]he 'explosion' of New Zealand films was more of an implosion—a bursting out within New Zealand of films searching for audiences at home, hoping to find a common awareness, a new consciousness of identity, a search to familiarise ourselves with our own image. Or as the Minister setting up the Film Commission said: 'We need to find our own heroes'.[3]

Goodbye Pork Pie with its defiant underdogs John (Tony Barry) and Gerry (Kelly Johnson) in their yellow Mini car challenging law and authority, gave New Zealand arguably its first recognisable local screen heroes, though it should be noted at the same time that the film has been criticised for its misogynism and sexist attitudes. It was supposedly the first New Zealand film 'to recover its costs from the domestic market alone', which would suggest it offered cultural value for a significant percentage of the New Zealand population.[4] The film certainly captured the imagination of New Zealanders as John and Gerry raced their Mini from Northland at the very top of New Zealand to Invercargill in the deep south, taking in a variety of cities, towns, communities and stretches of regional landscape en route. New Zealand's then Prime Minister Robert Muldoon attended the film's premiere and was even photographed wearing a promotional tie-in baseball cap. Yet the mistreatment of women and the total exclusion of the Maori raises questions about the film's celebration of local identity, as it presented culturally specific heroes that surely can only ever be a part of what O'Shea perceives as 'our own image'. *Goodbye Pork Pie*'s views on masculinity were far from being unique and in 1989 Roger Horrocks wrote that 'from a feminist point of view it is depressing to see that the New Zealand films most popular in their own country have been conspicuously old-fashioned in their treatment of women ... [these] films seem to offer an escape from the social problems of today into a rural dream when men were men'.[5]

New Zealand films during this renaissance were not only concerned with attracting a significant local audience, but also overseas exposure. This drive to the international mainstream can be observed in many developing national film industries and in New Zealand the action-dramas which were produced were an attempt to create commercial movies that spoke the language of the genre-driven high-energy narratives of the foreign markets. This led to less than successful films such as the *Mad Max*-inspired *Battletruck* (1982), the Western-styled *Wild Horses* (1983), and the slasher-style teenage horror-thriller *Bridge to Nowhere* (1986). New Zealand Government tax breaks (as in Australia) fuelled the new wave of film production by attracting foreign investment. A boom in filmmaking in New Zealand followed with many productions—such as the NZ$13 million *Raiders of the Lost Ark*-inspired pirate film *Savage Islands* (1983), starring Tommy Lee Jones—filmed and (co-)produced locally and receiving extensive overseas exposure. But these films, too, were largely action-focused and were criticised for creating an Americanised product that stifled local creativity and which appeared to be producers' projects built upon financial incentives. For instance, producers such as Antony I. Ginnane, John Barnett and David Hemmings, with the companies Hemdale and Endeavour, drew on available funding and made a number of Australian-New Zealand co-productions. This resulted in films such as *Race for the Yankee Zephyr* (1981), *Strange Behaviour* (1982), and *Mesmerized* (1984), transnational productions focused on maximising overseas commercial appeal through the importation of known American actors (such as George Peppard and Jodie Foster), and the application of genre conventions.

The producers of such features were exploiting a loophole in the system of tax breaks. As a consequence, the loophole was closed in 1982, though a decision was made to allow films that were already at a particular stage of production or planning to benefit under the old system if they managed to complete before September 1984. Subsequently, there was a rush of films and the release of twenty-five features in 1984–85. If the new wave or film renaissance began in 1977, then it effectively ended in 1986, with the release of the last of these tax break films.

Towards the end of this period the dominance of the male Pakeha (European) filmmaker was partly fragmenting and being decentred, with an increasing presence of women filmmakers (such as the directors Yvonne Mackay, Melanie Read, Preston, and the producers Bridget Ikin, Robin Laing and Robin Scholes) and Maori filmmakers (Barclay and Merata Mita) within the New Zealand film industry. But ultimately, this national cinema found it difficult to recover from the experience of the mid 1980s and with a lack of opportunities certain key directors left for careers in the American market. Donaldson left in the mid 1980s, and since his arrival in Hollywood he has directed films such as *No Way Out* (1987), *Cocktail* (1988), *Species* (1995) and *Dante's Peak* (1997). Murphy followed a few years later, with Hollywood keen to employ his skills at handling action narratives. His films in the US include *Young Guns II* (1990), *Freejack* (1992) and *Under Siege 2* (1995), but with his employment in Hollywood now more as a second unit director he returned to New Zealand in 2004 to direct the political thriller *Spooked*. Other New Zealand directors who relocated to America include Pillsbury (after directing *Starlight Hotel* in 1988), and

Vincent Ward (after directing *Map of the Human Heart* in 1993). Ward has since returned to New Zealand and Pillsbury and Donaldson were briefly part of the New Zealand film industry again when they made, respectively, *Crooked Earth* (2001) and *The World's Fastest Indian* (2005), by which time a new group of filmmakers had taken their place.

If New Zealand's new wave of filmmaking was 1977 to 1986, then it could be argued that this national cinema experienced a second, albeit smaller, renaissance between 1992 and 1995, when not only Peter Jackson (*Braindead* and *Heavenly Creatures*), Lee Tamahori (*Once Were Warriors*) and Jane Campion (*The Piano*) firmly established their international reputations, but directors such as Alison Maclean (*Crush*, 1992), and Peter Wells and Stewart Main (*Desperate Remedies*, 1993) emerged into the feature film industry with their striking psychological dramas, after having spent the 1980s making provocative short fiction films.

A possible third new wave can been detected amongst the films that have been emerging in the years post 2005, which have been marked by the impressive and stylish first and second time features of directors such as Glenn Standring (*Perfect Creature*, 2006), Chris Graham (*Sione's Wedding*), Toa Fraser (*No. 2*, 2006), Jonathan King (*Black Sheep*, 2006), Robert Sarkies (*Out of the Blue*, 2006), Taika Waititi (*Eagle Versus Shark*, 2007) and Peter Burger (*The Tattooist*, 2007). There is here a wave within a wave, with this cultural surge partly powered by the confidence on-screen of a young generation of Pacific island voices. The biggest producer of fiction films within Polynesia is New Zealand, though its output marks this as a small national cinema. However, New Zealand's cultural diversity and the fact that the country has several of the largest diasporas of Pacific island people has been reflected in a growing number of films—features and shorts—that are focused on Pacific cultures. In particular, the films *Sione's Wedding* and *No. 2*, the former by the highly successful Naked Samoans comedy group, the team behind the television series *bro'Town* (2004–), have brought to a post-Middle Earth New Zealand transnational films of Pacific culture which add refreshing stories of humour, warmth, life and community. This works against the view of New Zealand as a space of dark fantasy or the Gothic that has dominated screen production—as can be observed with the films *Perfect Creature*, *Black Sheep*, and *Out of the Blue*—and which suggests a cinema of unsettlement.

In 2005, Vincent Ward directed *River Queen*, his first New Zealand feature film in seventeen years, an epic drama set during the period of the nineteenth-century New Zealand wars, when the Europeans were faced with a conflict that challenged their settlement claims. Having seemingly returned to the New Zealand film industry, Ward has followed *River Queen* with the personal documentary *Rain of the Children* (2007), which revisits his earlier documentary *In Spring One Plants Alone* (1980). In comparison, amongst the filmmakers who emerged in the 1980s and 1990s, Jackson has stood out for his decision to remain throughout his career in New Zealand, insisting that Hollywood instead comes to him. For instance, of the second wave of filmmakers Maclean, like Tamahori, left for America soon after the release of a first feature, a path also followed by Christine Jeffs who, after her much celebrated feature debut *Rain* (2001), has made the American film *Sylvia* (2003). Tamahori, meanwhile, has made high impact action-dramas, perhaps most significantly the James Bond movie *Die Another Day* (2002).

Lindsay Shelton, the former Marketing Director of the NZFC, has said that 'a New Zealand filmmaker working in another country is not lost to the New Zealand industry because he or she will always be identified as the New Zealand film maker'.[6] This is perhaps true considering the manner in which New Zealanders embrace their cultural identity, and seemingly celebrate anything which denotes international achievement or recognition. Interestingly, one of the most commercially successful of New Zealand's overseas directors is Andrew Adamson, who has not made a New Zealand produced film. He left for Hollywood in his mid-twenties, where he later directed *Shrek* (2001) and *Shrek 2* (2004), as well as returning to New Zealand for Disney to direct *The Chronicles of Narnia: The Lion, the Witch and the Wardrobe*. But could Shelton's statement be extended to New Zealand actors, such as Cliff Curtis, Temuera Morrison, Rena Owen and Karl Urban, who have been performing with varying degrees of success in Hollywood films? For instance, since the mid 1990s and following their appearance in *Once Were Warriors*, actors Curtis and Morrison have featured in a range of Hollywood blockbusters and high exposure films, but frequently as figures representing ethnic minorities and foreign cultures other than their own identity as Maori. Such roles include a Mexican, Iraqi, Puerto Rican, a Lebanese, Pakistani and Colombian in respectively *Speed 2* (1997), *Three Kings* (1999), *Bringing Out the Dead* (1999), *The Insider* (1999), *Vertical Limit* (2000), *Blow* (2001) and *Collateral Damage* (2002). The submersion of a Maori or New Zealand identity beneath the cultural makeup of another nationality could question issues of 'recognition', but it also points to the ways in which issues become complicated in the definition of a contemporary national cinema.

New Zealand Cinema

Like many other contemporary film industries (and especially those with a global presence) New Zealand's cinema is transnational, extending outside its geographical boundaries. New Zealand's national cinema is not simply the local industry, but as with its films in foreign markets it includes the presence of New Zealand actors, directors and film practitioners overseas. It is also includes the presence of foreign actors and genres in New Zealand made movies, with additional consideration to be given to those foreign films employing New Zealand's film industry and production facilities. Furthermore, for a full understanding of New Zealand cinema there is a need to go beyond the fiction feature film and recognise other forms of screen culture, such as the short film, the documentary and experimental films, in which New Zealand has a strong heritage. In fact there is a need to move beyond the production industry altogether in considering the diversity of cinema forms in the country. For New Zealand's cinema industry, as with all others, clearly consists of the processes of film publicity, exhibition, film classification and regulation. New Zealand's cinema is also its cinema culture, its film societies, film festivals, fans, or forms of film appreciation, film journalism, the print media and film merchandise. Here, New Zealand's cinema is surely therefore more than just New Zealand films, but the cultural choices, the range of movies and movie related products— irrelevant of the country of origin—that are available to rent, buy and view in New Zealand.

For example, there have been relatively few New Zealand produced film journals and magazines. Two such publications were *Cinema, Stage and TV* and *Sequence*. The latter was produced as a membership benefit in support of the Wellington Film Society, and predominantly contained reviews and short articles on foreign art house films or classics of world cinema. In contrast, the former was a commercial film monthly begun in 1956 and which included small ads for film fans and pen pals, interviews with the stars of the day and adverts for the current releases. Both publications were produced solely for the New Zealand market with the content reflecting local interests, but this also reveals that cinema culture in New Zealand for mainstream theatrical releases and film society screenings was very much foreign. This is not to say that this culture was alien to New Zealand. On the contrary, New Zealand cinema is marked by an overseas culture whether it is American, English, French or Italian, with the covers of *Cinema, Stage and TV* over its first few years of production featuring film stars such as James Dean, Tab Hunter, Anne Heywood, Diana Dors and Sophia Loren.

The study of New Zealand cinema has focused almost solely on film made in New Zealand and then it has tended to lean towards the early period of the pioneers, and repeatedly from a historical perspective. New Zealand as a contemporary cinema, or a cinema post 1977, has attracted quite a number of studies but these have been mainly interested in certain high profile films or filmmakers since the early 1990s, with the work of Jane Campion (in particular *The Piano*), Peter Jackson (in particular *The Lord of the Rings*) and the movie *Once Were Warriors* attracting most critical attention. Within the same period, there are films such as *Scarfies* (1999) and *In My Father's Den* (2004), which performed impressively at the New Zealand box office, and *The Irrefutable Truth About Demons* (2000), *Snakeskin* (2001), *The Locals* (2003) and *Perfect Strangers* (2003), which have registered notable retail and rental sales of videos and DVDs in overseas markets. These productions demonstrate that in studying New Zealand cinema the value of an industry's mass consumption and critical significance cannot be defined just by patterns of international theatrical exhibition.

This collection works within these parameters and explores a range of issues, and a diversity of films that assist in defining New Zealand's contemporary cinema. The first section of the book, 'Industry and Commerce', opens with Gregory Waller's article on the NZFC which addresses questions of a national cinema through cultural policy and considers the emergence and sustainment of a government assisted feature film industry beginning with the initial discussions in the early 1970s. Working within the broad terms of a film culture Waller explores both the policies of the New Zealand government and the NZFC in establishing a local film industry, which can also compete internationally, and where national identity is closely connected yet is far from being a simple concept. The tax loophole of the early 1980s is a crucial part of this history. It is the focus of Nick Roddick's article which continues Waller's discussion by exploring the effects of a period of tax-driven film production from the perspective of the film industry. Roddick sees the closure of the tax loophole as a highly damaging act that, whilst seemingly unavoidable, altered forever the careers of many of New Zealand's key filmmakers.

As the last of the tax break films were being completed and the production of feature films was entering a period of enervation, New Zealand's short film industry was beginning to show significant growth with the NZFC establishing both the Short Film Fund and, in collaboration with Creative New Zealand, the Screen Innovation Production Fund in 1985. The short film has become a central element of film production within New Zealand with many filmmakers such as Maclean, Caro, Grant Lahood, Jeffs, Sarkies, Brad McGann and Standring first establishing their reputations on the festival circuits with highly innovative short fictions. Yet this aspect of the film industry is repeatedly neglected by critical studies of New Zealand's national cinema. Alex Cole-Baker's article on the short film here is like Roddick's contribution written from a position of inside knowledge of the industry. Baker has produced four short films and worked on many others and the issues that interest her the most are funding and distribution, which are both constant challenges to the maker of short films.

Similarly, Suzette Major has had experience working with the local cinema industry. Her article on the marketing of the New Zealand feature film connects back to Waller's with the recognition of a New Zealand film industry that has since the mid 1980s become increasingly driven by business thinking and concepts. This has created a tension between a creative industry and film as an art form and the commercial or economic factors that take control of a film's market value. Again, an overriding issue is the marketability of New Zealand movies internationally and therefore the extent to which the promotion of a film, and the image that it presents, is central to its success. Major moves through the different issues and stages in marketing a New Zealand film and the impact of such approaches on the industry concluding that the formula associated with the Hollywood marketing machine based on promoting a film's stars, awards or genre has been modified in New Zealand. Instead, many

New Zealand films are being marketed with a greater celebration of local cultural identity.

The final two articles in the first section move away from the NZFC and film production and focus on film-related institutions. A national office for a Film Censor in New Zealand began in 1916, and films screened locally have been subjected to particularly strict regulation. But as Chris Watson writes, whilst the regulation of the movies has shown signs of a more liberal approach since the 1980s, the growth of other media forms such as video and DVD have introduced new arenas for debate as to whether a film is deemed to be 'injurious to the public good'. And as Watson reveals in his study of the foreign films *Baise Moi* (2000) and *The Passion of the Christ* (2004) the pressure exerted by a local group such as The Society for Promotion of Community Standards has meant that there has been a history of decisions made by the Censor's office which have been challenged as both too weak and too harsh. In comparison, the New Zealand Film Archive (NZFA), the subject of an article by Sarah Davy and Diane Pivac, has only been in operation since 1981. In that time, as Davy and Pivac establish, the NZFA has evolved into a major institution with a progressive approach that seeks to move away from the kind of authorative mode of communication that has been conventionally employed by the heritage sector of museums, galleries and older archives, to one that is more socially inclusive and prepared to listen and involve the local community. The Archive has an important role as an entrusted guardian of the nation's heritage of film images and as part of its responsibilities for protecting and providing access to New Zealand's cinema history it works with community groups. This has involved, for instance, consultation and advice from the Maori community as to the best ways of storing and presenting film that is regarded as taonga (treasures) with immense historical, social and cultural value.

The second section of this book, 'Aesthetics and Form', focuses on issues specific to the style and nature of contemporary New Zealand film. Articles in this section remain concerned with the film industry and a national cinema, but move more towards the film text itself placing it within a cultural and social context. Ian Conrich's article considers a group of New Zealand films that focus on small town communities and it uses both social and cultural readings as well as studies of the American small town movie to develop an understanding of the themes and ideologies that the films contain. And whilst there are many similarities between the New Zealand and American forms, not least the community as a microcosm of the nation, the former shows its characters with a greater awareness for the reality of their situation, as opposed to the imaginary and ideal spaces of small town life depicted in the latter. One of the small town movies, *Magik and Rose* (1999), that forms a focus for Conrich's discussion is also a key text for Ann Hardy, in her article on a group of films that exhibit what she views as a neo-utopian sensibility. As with Conrich's study, Hardy is concerned with depictions of New Zealand society, and here she observes that in the years surrounding the millennium a group of youthful features engaged with the fantastic and the supernatural. Incorporating also elements of realism these films depict environments in which everyday life is disturbed by psychic forces or spiritual acts. Hardy argues that this group of films that present a utopianism, and Edenic environments combined with magic realism, Maori exoticism and popular concepts of spirituality could be precisely the type of productions that can have a local impact whilst also packaging New Zealand as an idyllic alternative to the world and appealing to international audiences.

Some fifteen to twenty-five years before these movies, in the first decade of the NZFC's operation, the industry had a predilection for adapting local works of fiction. This was to such an extent that, as Brian McDonnell observes in his article, as much as one quarter of the films made in the first ten years of the Commision were adaptations. For McDonnell, there is a pragmatic reason for this pattern with few experienced scriptwriters in a newly emerging industry. There was therefore greater stability, from a position of investment, in a film proposal that was based on a known and published book or play. At a national level New Zealand literature had established an audience long before New Zealand made movies, and it therefore became an essential component for film production during the film new wave. Through three case studies, McDonnell explores the relationship between these two mediums and the properties— economic, industrial and aesthetic—that functioned in the making of film adaptations in New Zealand. Equally important as a prevalent form in New Zealand's post 1977 cinema is the documentary film. In contrast to the fiction adaptation, there was in the non-fiction film a local voice that frequently politicised the nation and revealed it to be a site of resistance and confrontation. Such social issues are addressed in the final article in this section, in which Annie Goldson and Jo Smith examine the emergence of alternative documentary forms and the work of filmmakers such as Barclay, Mita, Goldson, Wells, Preston and Alister Barry who made protest films, films engaging with Maoridom and racial and sexual difference, and representing union struggles and challenges to government policies. These oppositions to nationalism are explored in contrast and in relation to the government non-fiction films of the NFU, made over the three decades prior to New Zealand's new wave.

Issues of ideology, nation and identity are continued in the final section of the book. In the first article, Stuart Murray focuses on 1980s film production and the years in which the emerging New Zealand film industry strived to establish an identity. Murray sees in the narratives of many of the films made during this period a precariousness and anxiety in the depictions of community. Such challenges and crises are, as Murray argues, also found in the society, politics and culture of the time when New Zealand experienced a series of nation defining events. He concludes that the unease through which the national imaginary was interrogated was replaced by a group of films in the 1990s that were more irreverent in their conceptions of the nation. These issues and films of the 1990s are picked up by Mark Williams in the article that follows, and he is especially drawn to the productions that appeared in the later part of the decade and in the years immediately after Sam Neill's and Judy Rymer's documentary on New Zealand film, *Cinema of Unease* (1995), which argued that post 1977 productions had been marked by a dark and psychological content. Williams sees within these films of the late 1990s a post-nationalism, which compared to its development in literature has been slow to emerge. These films have appeared during the Labour government of Helen Clark, which has been intent on promoting nationalism through the arts, yet Williams sees the new political imaginary of this era associated with a recirculation of images and a continuation of the nation through traditional myths of identity. For instance, New Zealand remains an apparent pastoral paradise in much of its cinema images. However, Williams, like Hardy, is encouraged by a group of youthful films produced either side of the millennium which have questioned the images of nationalism, have worked outside the defining myths, and are able to challenge its traditional images.

Murray and Williams see the incompleteness or fragility of New Zealand's nationalism, and the instability found in the film narratives, as a weakness in Pakeha identity. Politically, New Zealand is a bicultural nation—though there are increasing positions being made for the country's multiculturalism—and part of the Pakeha unease in this post-settler nation has been due to its unsettled relationship with the indigenous population. Michelle Keown's article in this section observes the change in film representations of the Maori from the objectification and stereotyping of the earlier years of New Zealand's film history to the 1970s and 1980s, when the cross-cultural love story was still a persistent screen fantasy. With the Maori renaissance that had begun in the early 1970s, however, images of the Maori underwent a transformation. In the 1970s many Maori voiced opposition to integrationist policies and protested at Maori inequality, with grievance directed towards land claims and ownership. Within these socio-political developments, film—both fiction and non-fiction—became an instrument for Maori filmmakers to control their own image and develop alternatives to the Pakeha produced dominant representations of Maori culture. Taking four films and three Maori filmmakers, Keown examines cultural identity and issues of nationalism, where self and community are preoccupations. But as she argues, whilst there have been other films made in New Zealand since 1977 that have been significant for their Maori involvement, Maori filmmakers in general have found a shortage of opportunities to make fiction features and have turned more to documentary, video and short film productions.

The Maori on screen have been marginalised by the dominant image of the Pakeha male which has become associated with the defining New Zealand films of the new wave. In Russell Campbell's article, Pakeha masculinity is adressed as a socio-historical construct of a post-settler nation, with New Zealand film displaying the Kiwi bloke and the contradictions that exist in the stereotypes: the frontier or pioneering male, hardened and itinerant, versus the settled or domesticated male with respectability and a plot of family land. New Zealand film of the new wave traded on traditional images of the Pakeha male, whilst also redefining the form on screen as society and culture of the 1970s and 1980s altered. This has resulted in another Pakeha male archetype in the 1990s, that of the bloke under siege, stripped of authority. Covering almost twenty-five years of contemporary New Zealand film, Campbell's article shows that whilst respresentations of the Pakeha male have changed under pressure from society, masculinity remains for this national cinema an area of central significance. Masculinity has frequently been defined in opposition to difference and here the book concludes with Angela Marie Smith's article which considers specific images of marginalisation in New Zealand's cinema of disability. Concentrating on *The End of the Golden Weather* (1991) and *Crush*, she sees these films as significant representations of the ways in which New Zealand imagines itself. For Smith, disability in New Zealand film and literature has become a metaphor for the damage to the land, and for isolation, alienation and abandonment. As the articles by Murray, Williams and Campbell establish, there is a discernible cultural unease in contemporary New Zealand cinema and this reflects historical tensions and issues of nation and formation. In Smith's article the continued return to narratives depicting physical and mental dysfunctionality shows the extent to which disability and colonisation are interconnected. With New Zealand's cinema continuing to evolve and seeking to establish both its local and international voice there are complex and myriad factors—economic, political, historical, social, cultural and aesthetic—that combine to establish a specific film culture and films with a unique identity. As this collection demonstrates, contemporary New Zealand cinema requires in its study a multi-directional approach.

Notes

1. James Belich, *Paradise Reforged: A History of the New Zealanders. From the 1880s to the Year 2000* (Auckland: Allen Lane, 2001), 439.
2. Colin James, *New Territory: The transformation of New Zealand 1984–92* (Wellington: Bridget Williams Books, 1992), 36.
3. John O'Shea, *Don't Let It Get You. Memories – Documents* (Victoria: Victoria University Press, 1999), 28.
4. Helen Martin and Sam Edwards, *New Zealand Film, 1912–1996* (Oxford: Oxford University Press, 1997), 76.
5. Roger Horrocks, 'Hollywood Strikes Back', in *Te Ao Marama/ Il mondo della luce – Il cinema della Nuova Zelanda*, ed. Jonathan Dennis and Sergio Toffeti (Torino: Le Nuove Muse, 1989), 112.
6. *Moving Pictures*, television documentary, UK broadcast, BBC2, 23 January 1993.

1
Industry and Commerce

The New Zealand Film Commission:
PROMOTING AN INDUSTRY,
FORGING A NATIONAL IDENTITY

Gregory A. Waller

I am prepared to fight for a film industry because I think it's something special. Even Iceland has a feature film industry! It's like a flagship for a country. It's telling people we exist (Vincent Ward, quoted in Louise Guerin, 'Feast before Famine', *Listener*, 2 August 1986, 14).[1]

The New Zealand cinema can be and has been defined in terms of actual films produced, acknowledged auteurs, festival screenings, historical overviews and analytical readings. I do not propose here to displace or somehow correct these sometimes contradictory ways of articulating a national cinema, but to traverse another discursive terrain in that area broadly termed 'film culture'.[2] I am interested in the role played by the government-constituted and funded New Zealand Film Commission (NZFC) and by matters of film-related cultural policy articulated in position papers, formal proposals, parliamentary debates and annual reports, and taken up, in turn, by local newspapers, general-interest magazines and trade publications. Thus the questions that govern my inquiry are: What arguments were offered in New Zealand in support of a government-assisted feature film industry during a period in which New Zealand moved toward an official commitment to biculturalism, reconfigured its relation to the United States, Great Britain and the South Pacific, and embraced free-market economics? How and why have concerns about national identity, cultural imperialism and the international marketplace figured in the creation, justification, fiscal decisions and policy-making of the NZFC?

Making the Case for a New Zealand Feature Film Industry
Commissioned by Parliament to 'encourage, foster, and promote the arts', the New Zealand Arts Council in 1970 sponsored a symposium on 'The Role of Film and Television in Establishing a Nation's Identity'.[3] The participants passed resolutions calling for the establishment of a National Screen Organisation responsible for financing, exporting and archiving New Zealand film and television; and urging the Arts Council to encourage educational work in 'the visual media', to survey the 'influence' of these media on New Zealand society, and to 'foster creative activity in films for

cinema and television'.[4] This unequivocal call for the government to support New Zealand film was based on the assumption that filmmaking was a creative, professional endeavour, an art worth fostering, as demonstrated by the European auteurs whose works graced the film society circuit.

Out of this meeting came the formally constituted Film Industry Working Party, which in October 1973 forwarded its Proposal for a National Screen Organisation that would be responsible for 'encouraging the capacity of screen production in New Zealand to realise production of significant cultural worth'.[5] 'Cultural' was synonymous here with 'screen art', which, in turn, was perfectly compatible with what the Working Party called the New Zealand 'screen industry'.[6] Thus the proposal argued that the best way to 'facilitate the work of every kind of screen artist' was to establish by statute an overseeing agency whose board of directors would include not only artists, but also representatives of the motion picture industry and experts in broadcasting and finance.[7]

Such an organisation figured prominently in the *Final Report* of the Film Industry Working Party, which in April 1975 called for the creation of an interim New Zealand Motion Picture Council, entrusted with the task of 'establishing a viable motion picture industry in this country'.[8] This planned industry would without question be driven by feature-film production since the Working Party reasoned that 'a country does not have a film industry until feature films are made on a reasonably regular basis'.[9] The other kind of motion picture specifically acknowledged was the 'experimental or personal' film, which the proposed New Zealand Motion Picture Council would also fund.[10]

The Working Party predicted that government support for film production would 'yield great social, artistic, and economic benefits', not least of all because 'motion pictures are the most potent communications force for social development and change'.[11] Driven by deep concern over a marketplace thoroughly dominated by foreign-made product, the Working Party invoked the principal of spectatorial 'right': 'New Zealanders have a right to see films and television programmes related to what is important to New Zealanders', for 'motion pictures made in New Zealand . . . can have a more intimate and immediate relevance to our lives'.[12] Indeed, the Working Party's self-styled 'main argument' for a viable, national (or indigenous—the terms are in this document interchangeable) film industry is that it will 'ensure that New Zealanders are not subjected to a constant diet of programmes from other cultures'.[13] An indigenous film industry thus looked to be a main line of defence against cultural imperialism. Once up and running, this industry will (inevitably?) produce films that, the report quite optimistically believed, 'reflect our way of life with truth and artistry showing New Zealand to New Zealanders and the world'.[14] Truth and art in this report are assumed to be unproblematic concepts (and goals), as are the co-joined notions of 'New Zealand', 'New Zealanders' and 'our way of life'. This at a time when the social dynamics of the country were being altered by a massive influx of Polynesian—as opposed to European—immigrants and a Maori 'cultural resurgence'.[15]

Arguments concerning state support for a film industry were broached in parliamentary debate during 1975, but it was not until October 1977 that Minister for the Arts Allen Highet created an Interim Film Commission, based quite closely on Jim Booth's *Proposal to Establish a New Zealand Film Production Commission*. (Booth would later serve as executive director of the New Zealand Film Commission [1983–88] before becoming an independent producer of films like Peter Jackson's *Meet the Feebles* [1990].) With the model of the then-expanding Australian film industry in mind, Booth insisted that any such film commission in New Zealand be run 'strictly on an investment basis with an eye very firmly on the market', meaning that the funding of 'art' or 'experimental' films remain the purview of the Arts Council.[16] Nevertheless, the Commission envisioned in this proposal would 'be concerned with a wide range of product', including short films, co-productions and tele-films, though its primary focus would be feature films.[17] The 'benefits' of a 'market oriented' film commission 'will be immense', Booth concludes, in terms of promoting, first, 'cinematograph expressions particular to New Zealand, to counter the largely unrelieved diet of films from foreign cultures'; and, second, exportable, income-generating product that will 'do much to announce the existence of New Zealand to the world at large' and so begin to counter the country's notorious 'antipodean cultural cringe'.[18] Neither of these goals has much to do with truthful representation or indigenous artistry.

One of the designated responsibilities of the Interim Film Commission was to advise the Minister for the Arts about legislation to create a permanent commission. In this capacity it prepared *Towards a New Zealand Motion Picture Production Policy* (February 1978) and *Design for the Motion Picture Production Industry* (May 1978), which offered decidedly different arguments. The first of these reports underscored the social utility of a thriving feature-film industry, which would allow filmmakers to 'capture visual images of the way we are and the way we feel and think . . . to expand our knowledge of ourselves'.[19] 'How else', the report asked, 'can we come to cherish a picture of our nation's past and a vision of its future?'[20] Motion pictures, in other words, are intimately bound up with, and are literally indispensable in leading citizens toward a national identity. Furthermore, the Interim Film Commission insisted that through its feature films New Zealand could come to 'greater awareness' of its 'role and responsibility as a populous and developing South Pacific nation'.[21] Such high-minded aspirations, repeated almost verbatim by Minister Highet when he introduced the New Zealand Film Commission Bill in Parliament and publicly announced the formation of the NZFC in 1978, may sound suitably vague and noncontroversial.[22] The political climate at the time would suggest otherwise. Labour's foreign policy in the 1970s had a decidedly 'Pacific orientation', including an active stand against French nuclear testing in the region. In response, the more conservative National Party, which came to power in 1975, sought, according to one historian, to 're-emphasize New Zealand's traditional links with the English-speaking and Western European world'.[23] In this context, touting the regional advantages of a New Zealand film industry could signify a commitment to multiculturalism, an acknowledgement of new economic and political priorities, or even a way of relegating regional concerns to the realm of the merely cultural.

The second of the Interim Film Commission's reports took a quite different approach, arguing that a well-managed film industry 'has considerable potential to give New Zealand the economic, morale and cultural benefits that are so needed in these difficult times'.[24] With rising unemployment, high inflation and increasing budget deficits, the times were indeed difficult and—the logic here ran—the need greater for a film industry whose prime benefits were not cultural but economic. Government support for a New Zealand feature film industry, this report concluded, 'is justified on economic reasons alone'.[25]

In their analysis of the Australian film industry, Dermody and Jacka identify 'two major framing discourses of Australian film': one emphasising matters of national identity, social concerns, local audiences and art; the other emphasising the business of entertainment, commercialism and the international market.[26] The official documents that pushed for and helped dictate the legislatively mandated role of the NZFC foreground similar concerns but without posing them in strictly oppositional terms. Broadly speaking, during the 1970s, arguments based on the state's responsibility to underwrite screen art gave way to explicitly economic rationales. The most constant refrain in this discourse, however, was that film—and, more precisely, a local feature film industry—significantly contributes to national identity.

A Journal of the Boom Years, 1978–1984
Through an Act of Parliament, the NZFC formally came into existence on 12 October 1978. It was designed very much along the lines laid out by the Interim Film Commission, and its Chair from 1978–85 was William Sheat, who had served as head of the Arts Council, the Film Industry Working Party and the Interim Film Commission.[27] In addition to the chair, the NZFC governing board was composed of a representative of the Secretary for Internal Affairs and five appointed members. The administrative staff included an executive director and a marketing director. What an industry commentator noted in 1985 seems to have been basically true for all of Sheat's term: the 'composition of the Film Commission is pakeha [European], professional, and predominantly male', with 'effective control' of decision making vested in the chair, deputy chair, and executive staff.[28] Taking over from Sheat as Chair in 1985 was David Gascoigne, a Wellington lawyer who had much the same background, having served as Deputy Chair of the NZFC since its inception, as well as President of the New Zealand Federation of Film Societies.[29]

The NZFC received funds from the Department of Internal Affairs to cover administrative costs and an annual grant from the Lottery Board (derived from gaming revenues).[30] Between 1979 and 1982, the Internal Affairs contribution grew from NZ$46,000 to NZ$194,000, while the Lottery Board funds went from NZ$640,000 to NZ$800,000. With this modest budget the commission was to carry out several charges: 'to encourage and also to participate and assist in the making, promotion, distribution, and exhibition of films'; to support archival and educational activities; and to 'encourage and promote cohesion within the New Zealand film industry'.[31] For all intents and purposes, 'film' had become synonymous with 'film industry'.[32] And any film given assistance by the NZFC was required by law to have 'significant New Zealand content', which could be determined by the 'subject' of the film, the shooting locations, site of technical facilities and the 'nationalities and places of residence' of investors, copyright holders or filmmakers (including producers, writers and actors).[33] These criteria drew upon quite different conceptualisations of the filmic text (as defined by narrative and thematic concerns, authorship, ownership, diegetic referent), making apparent the problems that can arise in attributing some sort of national identity to an individual feature film. The Act also insisted that the NZFC 'have due regard to the observance of standards that are generally acceptable in the community'.[34] This, too, could be taken as another way of defining a 'New Zealand film', with the nation here being conceived of as a 'community' with certain [moral] 'standards'.[35]

The NZFC's policy is articulated in, among other publications, the report it is required to present to the House of Representatives each year. The first such report (submitted in June 1979) is particularly detailed, since it also includes a history of how the NZFC came into being. According to this narrative of origins, the feature film industry was launched, in ideal democratic welfare state fashion, through the efforts of a few dedicated filmmakers, notably Geoff Murphy and Roger Donaldson, whose 'momentum' was then recognised and 'sustained' by a responsive government bureaucracy, which provided the funding for a 'central advisory body', the NZFC.[36] Politicians, audiences, and profit-minded producers do not figure in this account.

As laid out in its first few annual reports, the NZFC's goal was nothing less than forging an 'indigenous motion picture industry', which was described in terms often borrowed directly from Booth's policy statement and the Interim Film Commission's reports.[37] Thus, for example, there is very little talk of 'screen art' and 'creative expression', while there is a strongly stated commitment by the NZFC to promote 'cinematograph expressions particular to New Zealand', which would 'counter the largely unrelieved diet of films from foreign cultures', serve as a means of national self-understanding, and increase awareness of New Zealand's regional role.[38] Minister of the Arts Highet had used much the same argument before Parliament when he called for 'essentially New Zealand films of cultural value which interpret the New Zealand experience to New Zealanders'.[39]

The NZFC garnered positive press coverage in newspapers and magazines like the *National Business Review*, and it clearly had a substantive, immediate effect on the local industry.[40] During the 1980–81 fiscal year, for example, the NZFC invested in three productions and evaluated eighty applications for developmental assistance, awarding funds to twenty feature and six short film projects.[41] All told, between 1979 and 1982, eleven feature films were released that had been produced at least in part with NZFC funds. In its glossy 1981 publicity brochure, the NZFC could tout, among 'New Zealand's New Films', *Beyond Reasonable Doubt* (1980), *Goodbye Pork Pie* (1980), *The Scarecrow* (1982), and *Smash Palace* (1981).[42]

The most significant determinant on the New Zealand film industry during the early 1980s, however, was neither NZFC funding nor home talent. Rather, it was a tax shelter system that allowed substantial, immediate write-offs for investment in the production of New Zealand films. Existing policy even permitted investors to claim tax liability for monies contributed by the NZFC. The NZFC brought the situation to the attention of the Inland Revenue Department, whose extensive investigation of film investors would drag on through most of the decade, strongly discouraging any further private investment. Instead of modifying the tax system along the lines of the Australian model as the NZFC had suggested, the National government in its August 1982 budget closed the loophole, prohibiting so-called geared up investments.[43] Any project already initiated under the old system could retain its original tax status if a 'double-head fine cut' (that is, a version shot and edited to its final length, but not necessarily finished with post-production) was completed by the end of September 1984. The effect of these policy changes was to boost production dramatically in the short term, but only for projects initiated under the old system. As a result, twenty New Zealand features and six co-productions were released in 1984–85, more than in 1986–89 combined.

NZFC annual reports between 1980–83 trumpeted the growth of the industry, noting in particular overseas sales, which brought export earnings into the country while 'making New Zealand more readily identifiable and known in the world community'.[44] The NZFC also insisted that its success could be gauged in terms of public discourse, that is, what it referred to as the 'widespread and positive public discussion not only of the films themselves but also about the subjects and attitudes revealed on the screen, and how these can lead to a better understanding of the New Zealand character and way of life'.[45]

In retrospect, few commentators from within the industry found much to praise about the old tax incentive system.[46] Writing in the new trade magazine, *Onfilm*, Bruce Jesson argued that with the encouragement of overseas investment had come an increasing commercialisation of New Zealand film, a shift from 'director's projects' to 'producer's projects', and, worse, 'an Americanisation of the industry' that 'decapitates' its creativity.[47]

1. Al (Bruno Lawrence) takes a hostage in the powerful *Smash Palace*, part of the explosion of 'New Zealand's new films' in the early 1980s. Courtesy of the Ian Conrich collection of New Zealand cinema and visual culture.

By the mid 1980s, much of the discourse about the film industry came to operate within a pessimistic culture-versus-commerce scenario that had not been nearly as prominent in the 1970s. The NZFC's 1985 annual report, for example, began with the assertion that 'a film industry is about culture and money. It involves an endless tug of war between finance, investment and economic returns on the one hand and art, culture and national identity on the other'.[48]

Living with the 'Free Market'

By way of compensating for closing the tax loophole that had boosted film production, the National budget in 1982 allocated a NZ$1.75 million 'government grant' to the NZFC, setting a precedent for the rest of the decade. With government grants, Lottery Board funds, an Internal Affairs administration grant, and income from previous film investments, the NZFC had NZ$3.4 million to work with in 1983 and NZ$3.8 million in 1984 and 1985.[49] The commission may have aspired toward having a reduced 'investment role', but it was for all purposes the only game in town. After Labour's victory in the 1984 elections, the Minister for the Arts predicted new tax incentives to encourage investment in feature production and even identified film as the 'third dimension in our foreign policy'.[50] Though Labour's 1984 budget included no changes in tax policy, Prime Minister David Lange came out publicly in favour of a 'New Zealand feature film industry', which 'can make us think about what we are' and 'make statements about New Zealand overseas which are worth immeasurable amounts to us in focusing attention on New Zealand'.[51]

With substantial increases in Lottery Board funding after 1988, the NZFC's total annual budget rose from NZ$7.3 in 1986 to NZ$14.5

million in 1991, a period in which Labour, directed by Minister of Finance
Roger Douglas, instituted supply-side, 'market-liberal' economic policies
'aimed at dismantling the infrastructure of economic regulations and
restrictions that had been built up by successive governments over fifty
years'.[52] Labour's commitment to the NZFC came at a time when Air
New Zealand, Telecom and other former government-run public service
enterprises were sold off.

Perhaps more important, the watchwords of 'Rogernomics' were
efficiency, accountability, decentralisation and internationalisation.[53] The
NZFC's 1984 guidelines had begun to place increased emphasis on 'the
appropriateness of the [proposed] budget to both the project and the
potential market'.[54] Under the direction of Booth and Gascoigne, the
NZFC in 1986 formulated a revised statement of Role and Operation,
geared toward the production of 'first class films of international calibre'.[55]
(One frequently cited model of 'international' success in the late 1980s
was the Australian blockbuster, Crocodile Dundee [1986].) The principal
change was the introduction of Producer Oriented Development Schemes
(PODS), which allocated funds to established production houses for project
development. These were designed to 'reduce the centralising influence'
of the NZFC and to 'devolve both responsibility and accountability' to
'experienced producers'.[56] To the same end, the NZFC announced in 1989
a new 'Super PODS scheme . . . available to market-proven producers
who were 'develop[ing] feature film projects for the domestic market
with demonstrated sales potential overseas'.[57] The Commission's more
stringent 1989 guidelines insisted that each project demonstrate the
potential for: achieving theatrical distribution in at least three major
offshore markets; reaching a New Zealand box office take of $100,000;
and returning net earnings equal to at least fifty percent of costs.[58] At the
same time, the Commission continued to underscore the importance of
pre-sale agreements and began to put more emphasis on trained 'script
consultants' and to demand completion guarantees to help control cost
overruns.[59] Out of the NZFC's much-publicised attempt to 'revive' the
industry in 1989 by deciding to fund five feature productions, with either
direct investment or loans secured against presales to overseas markets,
came one of the commission's most acclaimed and biggest earning films
up to that date, Jane Campion's An Angel at My Table (1990), which was
originally designed as a television mini-series.[60]

The NZFC's public rhetoric and policy shifts of the mid and late 1980s
should be seen not only in terms of decentralisation, internationalism and
market-driven decision-making, but also in terms of what future Deputy
Chair of the NZFC Mike Nicolaidi called a veritable 'Kiwi cultural
revolution', with film and 'art generally . . . feeding on the nourishment of
a more vigorous, multicultural and competitive environment'.[61] Labour's
nuclear-free stance and increased responsiveness to Maori demands for
full biculturalism brought matters of national identity strongly to the
fore.[62] 'In the 1980s', writes historian Peter Simpson, 'cultural nationalism

remained a live issue for both advocates and detractors in every sphere of cultural expression'.[63]

Caught in the marketplace without a loophole to hold on to, the NZFC insisted that it was a 'buffer' protecting New Zealand from 'the power of the American film production and distribution machine'.[64] The NZFC also took pains, again, to spell out in its 1984–86 annual reports the 'principal reasons for Government support for the film industry': the 'cultural' role of film as 'a tool in the expression of the New Zealand cultural identity'; the 'identification of New Zealand overseas', especially to a 'discriminating and sophisticated world market'; and the in-country 'economic' benefits, including export income.[65] The NZFC, in its public pronouncements at least, did not explore the potential contradiction between film as tool of self-expression and as enticement to upscale overseas consumers. By 1987 it was evoking a somewhat more nuanced view of cultural nationalism, especially in a brochure entitled *Every Nation Needs Its Story-tellers*. References in past NZFC documents to New Zealand's Pacific identity gave way to a more exclusive focus on 'our culture, heritage and diversity'.[66]

In effect, prodded by Labour's economic and cultural agenda, the NZFC revised its working policies and reconceptualised its sense of the New Zealand film industry. The 1986 annual report introduced a new cinematic category into the NZFC discourse: 'New Zealand language films', that is, 'films of high quality made for New Zealand by New Zealanders, but without necessarily having international appeal' and thus dependent on government subsidy.[67] There is little suggestion by this date that the New Zealand language film might be marketable internationally precisely *because* of its 'indigenous' qualities.[68]

While no separate monies were specifically set aside for New Zealand language feature films, the NZFC had in 1985 formalised its commitment to non-feature and, perhaps, non-traditional filmmaking by establishing a Short Film Fund (SFF) intended to 'fill the major gap in the industry between purely commercial production and feature films' and to encourage 'new film-makers and new approaches to film-making'.[69] By 1991 the SFF received about 10 per cent of the total NZFC expenditure, which was invested in seventeen productions and twenty-four script development projects.[70] (In 2001, by way of contrast, 13.5 per cent of available NZFC funds were committed to short film and 'series' production.) Operating relatively independently of the NZFC proper, the SFF promoted what it termed 'quality' work in fiction, documentary and animation that was still designed for standard exhibition outlets, i.e., television and movie theatres.[71] Along with the Arts Council, the NZFC also committed modest funds to the Creative Development Fund, which supported more experimental film and media projects.

Thus, in accord with the pragmatics of free-market economics, the imperatives of cultural nationalism and the newfound insistence on the diversity of New Zealanders, the NZFC in the later 1980s formally and publicly redefined its sense of the New Zealand film industry to include:

commercially-minded feature films out to crack overseas markets, New Zealand language feature films, and domestically marketable short films of quality. In addition, it complemented its market-driven support of established production companies with a formally acknowledged commitment to Maori filmmakers, a commitment in keeping with the tenor of the times. Under Labour in the 1980s, there were, for example, 'moves to devolve greater responsibility for Maori issues to Maori organisations', as well as increasingly prominent Maori land claims.[72] As a result, cultural geographer Eric Pawson could point in 1992 to the 'vitality of Maoridom', since 'there is now much wider recognition of the validity of Maori cultural values'.[73]

In the late 1980s the NZFC played a part in this process by backing two 'particularly indigenous' feature films written and directed by Maori, Barry Barclay's *Ngati* (1987) and Merata Mita's *Mauri* (1988).[74] The 1991 annual report emphasised the 'diversity of New Zealand's film-makers and the range of audience tastes reflected by our cinema-goers', while the following year the NZFC prepared a new, 'expanded' Statement of Purpose: 'New Zealand films, and the New Zealand film industry, are reflective of the cultural diversity of the nation and in this spirit the Film Commission supports the aspirations of Maori filmmakers'.[75] This meant that Maori were supposed to be more fully included in the NZFC's decision-making processes and that Maori filmmaking would be treated as a separate cinematic category, presumably overlapping but not synonymous with the category of New Zealand language films.[76]

This commitment to Maori filmmaking continued despite the new National government's 1991 budget, which cut its grant to the NZFC by NZ$2.7 million, as part of a larger effort to deal with the budget deficit. Though the Lottery Board grant slightly increased, the overall effect was a 20 per cent reduction in funds for the NZFC.[77] Even with the cut, the short-term future, at least, looked bright. The summer of 1992 registered what *Variety* called a 'production boom', with three features fully funded by the NZFC, two co-productions, and a range of major television productions, including ABC's mini-series, *The Tommyknockers* (1993).[78]

In Search of Cultural and International Capital

Even before the awards started to roll in for Peter Jackson *Heavenly Creatures* (1994), recently appointed NZFC Chairperson Phillip Pryke had some justification for claiming that 'New Zealand has become the toast of the world's film community': *The Piano* ([1993]—a film not financed by the NZFC) was garnering international acclaim and awards; and *Once Were Warriors* (1994) was on its way to becoming the top box office film ever in New Zealand and would be profitably exhibited across the world, cracking even the US market.[79] The Commission would, however, find it difficult to keep up the momentum through the mid 1990s. By the end of 1996, a *Hollywood Reporter* survey of the New Zealand film industry saw only 'a production lull, static funding and a string of box office flops'.[80]

2. Trading on the success of *Once Were Warriors*, Communicado's release of *Broken English* sought to repeat an exportable style, seen here in a UK publicity postcard. Courtesy of the Ian Conrich collection of New Zealand cinema and visual culture.

Pryke, an investment banker who had earlier advised the government in its sale of Telecom, took over as Chairperson of the NZFC early in 1993. He vowed to further devolve control to the private sector and bring 'market-driven' operating principles even more to the fore, while still supporting what he called the occasional 'New Zealand icon' like *The End of the Golden Weather* (1991) or *Once Were Warriors*.[81] In February 1994, the former director of Film Queensland, Richard Stewart, was hired as the NZFC's new CEO. Stewart's immediate objective was to encourage greater private investment in the industry and to establish 'co-production and co-financing arrangements' with the Asia Pacific Region, meaning, in particular, Australia and Japan.[82] He announced in July 1994 that the commission would no longer handle the sales for larger budget feature films (as opposed to short films, low-budget first films, and what Stewart euphemistically called 'culturally relevant films'), a decision intended to force feature-film producers to secure more up-front investment in the form of 'sales advances'.[83] In its 1995 annual report the NZFC announced it would 'cease fully financing films', a short-lived but nonetheless significant policy shift, given that from 1979–94, the NZFC had fully financed thirty-eight feature films while co-financing only fifteen.[84]

From 1993–96, the National government's funding (which still consisted of a direct grant and a more substantial Lottery Board grant) for the NZFC remained roughly constant at around NZ$8.75 million. Yet with income from films and writebacks, the NZFC's total budget rose from NZ$10 million in 1994 to more than NZ$13 million by 1995 and 1996. While the NZFC certainly did help to develop and finance excellent films during this period (like, for instance, Gaylene Preston's feature-length documentary, *War Stories* [1995]), there was no release that approached the box office success of *Once Were Warriors*, not even *Broken English* (1996), another film from Communicado Productions (the producers of *Once Were Warriors*) that packaged contemporary racial politics and domestic urban melodrama in a slick, exportable style.

One new 1995 initiative (and yet another way to conceptualise the range of feature-film production) was a partnership with New Zealand television designed to generate 'ultra-low-budget feature films', each budgeted at around NZ$700,000.[85] Eventually this alliance was formalised as the ScreenVisioNZ Programme, also involving London-based Portman Entertainment. An even more narrowly circumscribed target was identified in 1998, with a not very successful NZFC funding initiative that encouraged 'feel-good/comedy script[s] . . . firmly rooted in New Zealand culture' showcasing 'engaging and sympathetic characters'.[86]

Government funding rose to NZ$9.8 million in 1997 (and then to NZ$10 million in 2000), but more significantly, the direction of the NZFC changed with the appointment of Alan Sorrell as Chairperson in April 1996. Richard Stewart abruptly left the NZFC in December 1996 and was replaced by new CEO Ruth Harley (an experienced television executive). Harley from the first undertook a strong lobbying effort for additional state funding.[87] After more than a decade of radical restructuring of the New Zealand economy, what arguments could be made in the late 1990s for increased government funding of the national film industry? The NZFC's annual reports for 1996 and 1997 somewhat defensively reiterate earlier claims, praising NZ films for 'displaying our country's natural assets' or for offering an alternative to the nation's still-troubling cultural 'colonisation' by the US: 'New Zealand films uniquely represent New Zealand culture . . . films fly the flag'.[88] Harley would eventually take a more sophisticated tack, promoting the idea that popular feature films create 'cultural capital' that benefits the entire nation now and in the future.[89] Thus the 2001–04 Strategic Plan (October 2001) asserts that the most important charge of the NZFC is to generate 'cultural capital', for

this is what makes us New Zealanders, establishes our uniqueness and our point of difference from other places and peoples . . . By working to ensure that each film reaches its optimal audience both within NZ and overseas, the Commission contributes to the constant renewal of New Zealand's stock of cultural film capital. No other agency has this mandate or capability to fulfill this function.[90]

In practical terms, the NZFC sought to create cultural capital by following a three-year strategic plan announced in 1998, calling for: a substantial increase in the number of films developed and released, a more accurate measurement of the 'New Zealand-ness' of these films, and a greater involvement of Maori filmmakers. Between 1999–2001, twenty-one feature films were produced with some NZFC investment. The most commercially successful of these was *What Becomes of the Broken Hearted?* (1999), the sequel to *Once Were Warriors*.

By the time it issued its next three-year strategic plan in October 2001, the NZFC could celebrate its achievements as a self-admittedly 'small player' in helping to develop a 'culture-based sustainable screen industry'.[91] Looking towards 2004, the NZFC reiterated its commitment to the production of 'distinctively New Zealand' feature films, to 'developing Maori story telling/tellers', to both 'cultural and financial returns' on investment, and to script and talent development.[92] In addition, the 2001–04 strategic plan underscored that the NZFC would actively participate in (and not simply react to) ongoing cultural policy debates by 'establishing a base for measuring cultural capital' and 'developing some specifications on what a sustainable industry might look like'.[93]

The direction of the NZFC from the late 1990s on was very much in keeping with the economic policies of the Labour government, which came to power in December 1999. Fulfilling a campaign promise, Labour Prime Minister (and also Minister for Arts, Culture and Heritage) Helen Clark announced in May 2000 a major government investment in arts, culture and heritage, comprised of an NZ$80 million initial expenditure with a NZ$20 million increase in each of the next three years. The most substantial new Labour film initiative was a one-time NZ$22 million grant to establish a Film Production Fund.[94] Very much modelled on the career of Peter Jackson (who had recently brought the filming of the *Lord of the Rings* trilogy to New Zealand), this fund was designed to work with, but remain independent of the NZFC. Unlike the NZFC, the Film Production Fund 'will not be constrained . . . by the need to balance commercial and cultural imperatives. It can focus purely on the commercial objectives'. Once again—as in earlier government investments in the New Zealand film industry—the emphasis was on feature-film production and the fostering of a national 'talent base'. The Film Production Fund was not, however, designed to nurture new talent as much as it was to serve as a means of advancing the careers of those New Zealand filmmakers who already had proven successful with what Clark called 'highly subsidised, low budget first films'. The ideal Film Production Fund film would be an 'intermediate scale' feature film, commercially profitable, attractive to overseas markets, and able, in turn, to convince 'international commercial investors' to finance subsequent productions.[95] The first production to secure Film Production Fund support was the internationally acclaimed adaptation of Witi Ihimaera's novel *Whale Rider* (2002), directed by Niki Caro.[96]

Both the Film Production Fund and the NZFC would yield, the new Prime Minister argued, a full measure of economic benefits: generating employment, boosting export earnings and contributing to the GNP. And, simultaneously, this sector had and would continue to provide a means for New Zealanders, in the words of a speech Clark gave in May 2000, to 'express our cultural identities' and to take 'pride in our diverse cultures'. Through 'vibrant arts and cultural activities' a strong and confident cultural identity can emerge'. The slippage here—between 'cultural' and 'cultures', between 'identities' and 'identity'—is revealing, and seems to suggest a move toward a multi- rather than bicultural New Zealand, though Clark still holds out the promise of a singular national/cultural identity, New Zealand's mark of distinction in the face of twenty-first century globalisation.[97] Or as she put it in a speech at The Film Unit: 'we are not a suburb of Los Angeles, London or Sydney. We can express our differences, our uniqueness, so positively through our creative people. Film . . . has a big role to play in that, and in promoting New Zealand's distinctive identity to a wider world'.[98] The New Zealand film industry would remain a key target of opportunity in subsequent Labour economic policy statements, like *Growing an Innovative New Zealand* (February 2002), which underscores the need to 'brand' New Zealand internationally 'as being technologically advanced, creative and successful'.[99] In the economic if not in the cultural realm, Peter Jackson had become the poster child and entrepreneurial seer of the New New Zealand.

There seems to me no question that the New Zealand Film Commission has since the late 1970s actively shaped, promoted, and on occasion kept alive the feature-film industry in New Zealand, not least of all by the commission's commitment to the production of short films. The fact that the NZFC has been to some degree responsible for *Smash Palace*, *Utu* (1982), *Vigil* (1984), *Ngati*, *An Angel at My Table*, *Braindead* (1992), *Once Were Warriors*, *Heavenly Creatures* and *War Stories* strikes me as a quite laudable achievement. Perhaps the commission—being a state-funded institution subject to party politics in an era of major economic and social change—is also to be commended because these well-received films do not follow one obvious cinematic blueprint and do not consistently create the same New Zealand.

But evaluating the NZFC as a state investment is not the primary point here. My focus has been on the history of this agency and of the discourse concerning film, cultural policy and national identity in New Zealand since the 1970s. This history involves the orchestration of bicultural voices, the reinvention or reclamation of tradition, and the presentation of a face or a consumable narrative to the world. Film serves, or is at least assumed to serve, a privileged role in the process of national identity, that is, in the making and remaking, in the marketing and understanding of New Zealand. Throughout the cultural policy discourse during this period, film itself also gets redefined and invested with multiple meanings: specifically in the NZFC's shifting categories (such as short, experimental, ultra-low-budget feature, Maori film, New Zealand language film, culturally relevant film, intermediate-scale film) and more broadly in the sense of film as, for instance, growth industry, investment opportunity, government-supported art, public service gesture or auteurist expression; as vehicle for national self-expression or self-examination, commodity for the international market, signifier of the nation, or postcard from the Antipodes. These ways of thinking about film and national identity, like the specific decisions and policies of the NZFC, are rooted in the political, social and cultural conditions in New Zealand.

Notes

1. This is a revised and updated version of 'The New Zealand Film Commission: promoting an industry, forging a national identity', *Historical Journal of Film, Radio and Television* 16, no. 2 (June 1996): 243–62. I would have been unable to undertake the original research for this project without the support of the Fulbright Scholars Awards programme and the advice, assistance and generosity of a great many people in New Zealand, including Laurie Cox of the New Zealand–United States Educational Foundation; Ruth Jeffery and Lindsay Shelton of the New Zealand Film Commission; William Sheat, former Chair of the New Zealand Film Commission; Diane Pivac of the New Zealand Film Archive; director Barry Barclay; producer Jim Booth; Russell Campbell of Victoria University; and my hosts in the Film and Television Studies programme at the University of Waikato, Sam Edwards and Geoff Lealand. David Newman graciously provided me with material from *Onfilm*. In producing this revised version, I have relied on material provided by Lindsay Shelton and editorial suggestions from Brenda Weber.
2. See, among many discussions of 'film culture', Susan Dermody and Elizabeth Jacka, *The Screening of Australia: Anatomy of a Film Industry* vol. 1 (Sydney: Currency Press, 1987), 23–27; Thomas Elsaesser, *New German Cinema: A History* (Basingstoke, Hampshire: Macmillan, 1989), 18–32, 36–48; and *Film Policy: International, National and Regional Perspectives*, ed. Albert Moran (New York: Routledge, 1996).
3. For background on government funding of the arts in New Zealand, see W.H. Oliver, 'The Awakening Imagination, 1940–1980', in *Oxford History of New Zealand* (Auckland: Oxford University Press, 1992), 541, 558–62.
4. *Report of Arts Conference '70*, resolutions 117, 118.
5. Film Industry Working Party, *Submission to Committee on Broadcasting* (October 1973), 3.
6. Ibid., 5.
7. Ibid., 4.
8. Film Industry Working Party, *Final Report* (April 1975), 23.
9. Ibid., 16.
10. Ibid., 13. The QEII Arts Council had established its own 'Creative Film

Fund' in 1973 and partially funded fourteen projects in 1974, principally documentaries and what it called 'educational films'.

11. Ibid., 5.
12. Ibid., 6, 5.
13. Ibid., 6.
14. Ibid., 23.
15. Graeme Dunsall, 'The Social Pattern', *Oxford History of New Zealand* (Auckland: Oxford University Press, 1992), 452.
16. J.L. Booth, *Proposal to Establish a New Zealand Film Production Commission* (July 1977), 6.
17. Ibid., 14.
18. Ibid., 1, 25.
19. Interim Film Commission, *Towards a New Zealand Motion Picture Production Policy* (February 1978), 8–9.
20. Ibid., 9.
21. Ibid., 8.
22. *New Zealand Parliamentary Debate* 420 (24 August 1978), 2864; *New Zealand Parliamentary Debate* 421 (28 September 1978), 3992–94.
23. Alan McRobie, 'The Politics of Volatility', *Oxford History of New Zealand* (Auckland: Oxford University Press, 1992), 394. See also Roderic Alley, 'New Zealand and the South Pacific', *New Zealand and the Pacific*, ed. Roderic Alley (Boulder, Colorado: Westview Press, 1984), 135–54; and Keith Barber, 'New Zealand Race Relations Policy, 1970–1988', *Sites* 18 (Winter 1989): 6–7.
24. Interim Film Commission, *Design for the Motion Picture Production Industry* (May 1978), 1.
25. Ibid., 9. See R.J. Stephens, *Public Policy and the New Zealand Feature Film Industry: An Economic Appraisal*, New Zealand Film Commission Research Paper (1984), for a critique of this type of 'economic' rationale.
26. Dermody and Jacka, *Screening of Australia*, 197–99.
27. See John O'Shea, 'Sheat–Anchor at the Helm', *Onfilm* 2, no. 6 (October 1985): 12–13.
28. Bruce Jesson, 'Commission with a New (Bank) Role', *Onfilm* 2, no. 5 (August 1985): 14.
29. *NZ Film* 26 (September 1985): 16; Sue May, 'Gascoigne: He Has Ways', *Onfilm* 2, no. 6 (October 1985): 14–19.
30. David B. Newman, 'The Independent New Zealand Motion Picture Industry: 1960–1985', M.A. thesis (Victoria University, 1987), 66.
31. *New Zealand Film Commission Act* (1978, no. 61), 8. This Act closely follows the model of the Australian Film Development Corporation Act (1970).
32. Ibid.
33. Ibid., 9.
34. Ibid., 10.
35. Ibid. In fact, the only serious debate in Parliament over the NZFC Act concerned this acknowledgment of 'community standards', which would, argued one Labour member, make for 'a sort of sanitised film commission, which supports the making of certain types of innocuous films only' (*New*

Zealand Parliamentary Debate 421 [28 September 1978], 3999).
36. *Annual Report of the New Zealand Film Commission* [hereafter *NZFC Annual Report*] (1979), 11. Murphy's own account of the 1970s has passionate, committed maverick filmmakers hemmed in on one side by the National Film Unit and on the other by the New Zealand Broadcasting Corporation, with its complete control over television programming. Against all odds, the independents manage to succeed ('The End of the Beginning', *Film in Aotearoa New Zealand*, ed. Jonathan Dennis and Jan Bieringa [Wellington: Victoria University Press, 1992], 130–35). See also Geoff Steven's documentary on these filmmakers, *Cowboys of Culture* (1991), and Geoff Chapple, 'New Zealand Films: A New Wave?' *Listener*, 17 April 1982, 15–16.
37. Ibid., 13. See also 'New Zealand Supplement', *Cinema Papers* (May–June 1980): 22.
38. *NZFC Annual Report* (1979), 12.
39. *New Zealand Parliamentary Debates* 421 (28 September 1978), 3992.
40. See, for example, Brenda Gillespie, 'Commission Adds Weight to Film Industry', *National Business Review*, 19 September 1979, 16; and 'New Zealand Commission Funds Assigned with More Selectivity', *Variety*, 5 May 1983, n.p. in New Zealand Film Commission clipping file, New Zealand Film Archive, Wellington (hereafter NZFA file).
41. *NZFC Annual Report* (1981), 7.
42. For an 'inside' view of the NZFC's activities during this period, see the interviews in 'New Zealand Supplement', *Cinema Papers* (May–June 1980): 21–31, 42.
43. See NZFC memorandum, 'Tax and Films: Analysis and Recommendation' (29 September 1982).
44. *NZFC Annual Report* (1981), 3. See also *NZFC Annual Report* (1982), 4; *New Zealand Parliamentary Debate* 447 (12 October 1982), 3930; and William Sheat, 'An Overview of the New Zealand Film Industry' (30 September 1980), a briefing prepared for the Minister in charge of the National Film Unit.
45. *NZFC Annual Report* (1980), 4. The NZFA file contains a good sampling of press coverage from this period.
46. For contrasting views, see Antony I. Ginnane, 'Pictures for Profit', *Onfilm* 1, no. 5 (August 1984): 18, 38; and Nicholas Reid, *A Decade of New Zealand Film: Sleeping Dogs to Came a Hot Friday* (Dunedin: John McIndoe, 1986), 13–14.
47. Bruce Jesson, 'Money Talks', *Onfilm* 1, no. 4 (June 1984): 19–20. The fear that co-productions operated as 'a kind of cultural colonisation' registered particularly strongly. See Gordon Campbell, 'Prisoners of the US dollar?' *Listener*, 24 April 1982, 23; David Tossman, 'Five Ways Forward', *Onfilm* 1, no. 1 (December 1983): 5–7; and Stephen Ballantyne, 'The New Zealand film industry—what future?' *New Zealand Art News* 2, no. 1 (April–May 1985): 2, 19.
48. *NZFC Annual Report* (1985), 3.
49. These figures come from the *NZFC's Annual Reports*. Note that Lottery Board

funds, by law, were intended to 'assist cultural development in New Zealand', and the Board's contributions to the NZFC were 'specifically oriented toward indigenous New Zealand films' (*Briefing Notes* 6 [May 1984]: 1–2).

50. Quoted in Pam Graham, 'Filmmakers face lean times', *Wellington Dominion*, 5 January 1985 (NZFA file).

51. Quoted in Rachel Lang, 'Going for broke . . . or breaks', *Onfilm* 2, no. 2 (March 1985): 28.

52. McRobie, 'The Politics of Volatility', 402–03.

53. Gary Hawke, 'Economic Trends and Economic Policy, 1938–1992', *Oxford History of New Zealand* (Auckland: Oxford University Press, 1992), 441.

54. *NZFC Annual Report* (1985), 4.

55. New Zealand Film Commission, *Role and Operation* (1986).

56. Ibid. On the generally dismal economic condition of the film industry during the late 1980s, see Leo Schulz, 'Making Money out of Movies', *Export Business*, (February 1987): 13–17; and Jonathan Dowling, 'Focussing on Movie Money', *New Zealand Financial Review* 7, no. 16 (November 1988): 32–35.

57. *NZFC Annual Report* (1990), 12. Awarded to what *Variety* called 'the industry's most seasoned producers' (Philip Wakefield, 'Record Hot Summer Heads for Islands', *Variety*, 5 October 1992, 52), Super PODS further institutionalised the shift from a director-oriented cinema to a production company-oriented cinema. See *Briefing Notes* 26 (July 1990): 1–2.

58. *NZFC Annual Report* (1989), 7.

59. Rachel Lang, 'Cash Flow Criteria', *Onfilm* 6, no. 6 (October 1989): 15–16. See also the 'Script Readers' Checklist' (a guide to 'good stories, well-told') in New Zealand Film Commission, *1988/89 Priorities*, 13–14.

60. For the issue of funding in the late 1980s, see Peter Calder, 'A kiss of life for our film-makers', *Christchurch Star*, 3 March 1989; Helen Smyth, 'Zilch represents the film industry', *Wellington Dominion*, 13 March 1989, 11; and Anne Byrnes, 'The NZ picture is looking good', *NBR Weekly Magazine*, 5 October 1990, 8–9.

61. Mike Nicolaidi, 'Unique Identity Shaping for New Zealand Nation Under Lange Leadership', *Variety*, 30 April 1986, 117.

62. Hawke, 'Economic Trends and Economic Policy', 447.

63. Peter Simpson, 'The Recognition of Difference', *Oxford History of New Zealand* (Auckland: Oxford University Press, 1992), 572. See Roger Horrocks, 'Moving Images in New Zealand', in *Headlands: Thinking Through New Zealand Art*, ed. Mary Barr (Sydney: Museum of Contemporary Art, 1992), 139.

64. *NZFC Annual Report* (1987), 2.

65. *NZFC Annual Report* (1985), 3; *NZFC Annual Report* (1984), 3.

66. New Zealand Film Commission, *Every Nation Needs Its Story-tellers* (1987), 1–2.

67. *NZFC Annual Report* (1986), 4. In its brochure entitled, *1988/89 Priorities*, the NZFC announced its commitment to 'make' one 'New Zealand Language' feature film each year, with the rest being, in its words, 'strong stories, well told

by writers skilled in the craft, with a universal theme from a New Zealand perspective', 2, 9.

68. Alan Williamson, 'Calculated risk—the Jim Booth philosophy', *Wellington Evening Post*, 13 May 1989, 8.

69. *NZFC Annual Report* (1986), 7; *NZFC Annual Report* (1987), 3.

70. *NZFC Annual Report* (1991), 19.

71. See Jesson, 'Commission with a New (Bank) Role', 14; Roger Horrocks, 'The Long View on Short Films', *Onfilm* 4, no. 1 (December 1986): 24–25; and Merril Cole, 'Screening for attention', *Arts Times* (October 1987): 5.

72. Barber argues that these moves were, however, a means of 'appropriating Maori organisations for the purpose of implementing government policies' ('New Zealand Race Relations Policy', 14–15).

73. Eric Pawson, 'Two New Zealands: Maori and European', *Inventing Places: Studies in Cultural Geography*, ed. Kay Anderson and Faye Gayle (Melbourne: Longman Cheshire Press, 1992), 30.

74. *NZFC Annual Report* (1988), 3.

75. *NZFC Annual Report* (1991), 5, 17; *NZFC Annual Report* (1992), 6.

76. See New Zealand Film Commission *Briefing Notes* 32 (October 1991): 5; Deborah Coddington, 'The New Zealand Picture Show: What is the Film Commission Up To?', *North & South* (April 1992): 102–03; Transcript of seminars at the New Zealand Film and Television Conference (1992), Supplement to *Onfilm* (December 1992): 9.

77. See, for example, in NZFA file: Mike Houlahan, 'Film industry savaged by cuts', *Wellington Evening Post*, 31 July 1991; Peter Calder, 'Angels and Turkeys', *New Zealand Herald*, 2 August 1991.

78. Wakefield, 'Record Hot Summer', 46.

79. NZFC Annual Report (1994), 4.

80. Phillip Wakefield, 'N.Z. Film Feels Squeeze as Poor Admits Take Toll', *Hollywood Reporter*, 31 December 1996.

81. Philip Wakefield, 'New chief takes aim at "welfare"', *Onfilm* 10, no. 4 (May 1993): 5.

82. NZFC Briefing Notes, *Onfilm* 11, no. 4 (May 1994): 13; Philip Wakefield, 'Cash in kitty blunts production slate', *Onfilm* 11, no. 4 (May 1994): 5.

83. 'Commish exits sales role', *Onfilm* 11, no. 6 (July 1994): 1; NZFC Briefing Notes, *Onfilm* 11, no. 6 (July 1994): 18.

84. *NZFC Annual Report* (1995): 13.

85. Ibid, 14.

86. *NZFC Annual Report* (1998), 9. See also 'N.Z. Film Rethinks Funding', *Hollywood Reporter*, 21 July 1998; and Peter Calder, 'Homegrown Pics Not Hits', *Variety*, 16 October 2000, 108.

87. Paul Smith, 'Industry Needs New Direction', *Variety*, 13 October 1997, 167; and Peter Calder, 'Commish Turns Org Around', *Variety*, 19 October 1998, 66.

88. *NZFC Annual Report* (1997), 7–8.

89. See Ruth Harley, 'Cultural Capital and the Knowledge Economy', speech delivered at the 1999 Public Service Senior Management Conference, at

<http://pssm.asc.govt.nz/previous/1999/papers/harley.asp> (accessed 15 May 2002). Harley borrows the concept of 'cultural capital' from New Zealand economist George F. Barker, director of the Centre for Law and Economics at Australian National University. The NZFC had commissioned Barker to write a monograph on this topic, which was published as *Cultural Capital and Policy* (Wellington: Australian National University, 2000).

90. New Zealand Film Commission, *2001–2004 Strategic Plan*, sec. 4.

91. Ibid., sec. 6.

92. Ibid.

93. Ibid. See also New Zealand Film Commission, *Statement of Objectives: Twelve Months to 30 June 2002* (23 August 2001).

94. For a critical editorial response to Clark's arts initiative see 'Music to the Ears of the Arts Lobby', *Wellington Evening Post*, 7 January 2000, 6.

95. For Clark's press release, see <http://www.executive.govt.nz/minister/clark/arts/pr.htm>; additional information was provided in the accompanying 'Questions and Answers' <http://www.executive.govt.nz/minister/clark/arts/qa.htm> (accessed 15 May 2002).

96. Phil Wakefield, 'N.Z. Prod'n Fund Closing in on Initial Projects', *Hollywood Reporter*, 10 May 2001.

97. Rt Hon Helen Clark, 'Building Cultural Identity' (18 May 2000) <http://www.executive.govt.nz/speech.cfm?speechralph=31070&SR=1>(accessed 15 May 2002).

98. Rt Hon Helen Clark, 'Speech at Opening of the Lower Hutt Film Unit' (7 February 2000) <http://www.executive.govt.nz/speech.cfm?speechralph=30450&SR=1> (accessed 15 May 2002).

99. *Growing an Innovative New Zealand* (February 2002) <http://www.executive.govt.nz/minister/clark/innovate/index.htm> (accessed 15 May 2002).

2

Boom and Bust:
Tax-driven Film Production in New Zealand in the 1980s

Nick Roddick

As proudly independent—not to say quirky—in its film culture as in its national character, New Zealand nevertheless experienced the same problems and challenges as other emerging film cultures when the money to be made out of tax breaks and tax-driven co-productions overtook creativity and the need for national self-expression as a motive for making films. It was, to use a phrase that will be familiar to any historian of the national industries that produce cinema (as opposed to any historian of national cinema cultures), a time when the deal was more important than the film.

The government-led tax breaks came in between the growth period of the 1970s and the market forces of the late 1980s. Modelled on the Australian 10B (later 10BA) scheme, the tax provision of the early 1980s permitted investors to write off 150 per cent of their investment in a New Zealand film. Because of the way tax law works, producers were able, by channelling money through intermediary companies, some of them offshore, to raise this write-off to around 200 per cent. At those levels, it became possible to produce low-budget films at very little risk to the producers, and with clear financial advantages to high-bracket tax payers, both individuals and corporations. Such financial backers would otherwise have had to pay substantial sums to the exchequer; this way, they stood the chance of recouping at least some of their investment, which could then be rolled over into another film investment without incurring any tax liability on the way. The only difference between the New Zealand scheme and the Australian one is that, because of differences in the former's corporate legal system, partnerships could be formed, providing a further barrier between the production itself and the tax man. With the paper-trail growing ever more confused and increasing amounts of tax money being diverted from revenue, government was bound sooner or later to revise the system. This became even more inevitable when large corporations entered the business of film finance, linking up with foreign producers and big-name projects. These, according to producer and director Larry Parr, included *Merry Christmas Mr Lawrence* (1984), a France/UK/New Zealand co-production, in whose financing the company Fletcher Challenge (primarily associated with construction work) was closely involved.[1] The film was shot mainly in New Zealand and on the New Zealand-administered island of Rarotonga (part of the Cook Islands), and was able (according to Parr) to gear the tax advantage up to 3.45:1—a level with which small-scale local producers could not compete and one designed to focus wonderfully the attention of the tax authorities. 'Everyone's making their money on the way in', said Geoff Murphy, who was New Zealand's leading director during the new wave. 'The investors . . . don't care whether the film's a success or not; the producers write themselves fat fees . . . the crews are paid great amounts as the film's made, [so] you could put it in the can and bury it and no one's going to be particularly upset. That's where I felt things were going'.[2]

Murphy was not alone. 'There are only so many good movies you could make, but there are lots of movies you could make if your sole motive was investment', commented Antony I. Ginnane. As a producer, Ginnane had been as ready as any at the time to develop competitive deal structures in both Australia and New Zealand. But, looking back twenty years later from the vantage-point of 2003, he nonetheless felt that the period dominated by the change in New Zealand tax legislation, in September 1984, was not the most memorable in terms of the quality of the films it engendered. Too many productions, he says, were 'motivated by greed'.[3]

The available evidence suggests both Murphy and Ginnane are right. There were, indeed, lots of movies made; few of them were good; a considerable amount of tax liability was offloaded by investors; some people—a few—even prospered. The main losers were the New Zealand exchequer; the country's international reputation, built up by a series of unique films; and, more damagingly, the careers of a number of the directors who had made them, and who then found themselves no longer able to work—or at any rate work in New Zealand. It was perhaps ironic that, the year the system changed, New Zealand had had its first film selected for competition in Cannes: Vincent Ward's *Vigil* (1984). What looked, to outside observers, like the flowering of a new national cinema was even then beginning to wilt.

The only people to profit from this period of transition—the moment at which, perhaps, New Zealand films ceased to be identified internationally as such (that is, ceased to be regarded as representatives of a new and promising cinematic culture, and became, instead, a series of individual films which happened to have been made in New Zealand)—were the lawyers and accountants who cluster around a film industry when it becomes, however briefly, a promising financial product. And product—the term film sellers use to describe their wares—was what it was briefly about, and not films. For a short period in the mid-1980s, New Zealand films joined kiwi fruit and venison as a product out of which a quick profit could be made. Any critical judgement of the success (or failure) of the films that came out in 1985 needs to take into account the unreal, hothouse atmosphere in which they were created—and, perhaps, recognise that the period was a major turning-point for New Zealand films. The country's cinema would never be quite the same again.

There is, however, little or no point in treating this as morally 'wrong', or in applying any overall value judgement to what happened. The balance between the art form (film) and the infrastructure necessary to create it (industry) is one of the endlessly fascinating features of the history of cinema. It is, moreover, a balance which is always shifting, not just from decade to decade or year to year, but often from day to day. Film, after all, is the only fully fledged art form to have emerged since capitalism became the dominant economic mode throughout much of the world, and its history and development as an art form have remained inextricably linked with the financial resources needed to sustain the industry that creates it. Indeed, changing financial structures have probably influenced cinema as much as technological changes like the development of widescreen lenses or three-strip Technicolor.

The Hollywood studio system, as I have argued elsewhere, was an industrial model whose raw material was art, but whose end-product was intended to be profit.[4] Even in Europe, where government subsidy for decades created a risk-free playground in which (certain favoured) filmmakers could create their artworks, the emphasis has now decisively shifted over to a mindset which can best be summed up by the term 'market forces'. Where once 'creativity' was the key word, now it is 'sustainability'.

But I am not concerned here with the first decade of the twenty-first century in Europe: I am concerned with a short period in the penultimate decade of the twentieth century in a country whose film industry was just coming out of a remarkable period of creative growth. That period of creative growth had, moreover (and, one might add, atypically), created an infrastructure which both looked as though it could sustain the growth in film production and, more importantly, required that growth to be continual if it were to sustain itself. It was a heady mixture, combining optimism, opportunity and ambition (or, if you will, greed), and it chimed remarkably with the temper of the times. This was also, it should be noted, a period which saw the rise of Reaganomics in the United States, the beginnings of Thatcherist monetarism in the UK—and, of course, the rise and fall of 'Rogernomics', the local equivalent of such global processes, in New Zealand.

Roger Douglas was appointed New Zealand's Finance Minister in 1984 and thus cannot be held directly responsible for what happened in the film industry. Indeed, it was the previous National government, headed by Robert Muldoon, which set up and then cancelled the tax breaks. But by the time they were scrapped, an economic climate in which subsidies were being reduced and trade barriers lowered created an atmosphere ideal for the fiscal follies which were enveloping the New Zealand film industry. It would have been surprising if a nascent film industry which embodied many of the hopes of Roger Douglas's economic theories—the desire to be self-sufficient and at the same time become a significant player in the early stages of the post-post-capitalist global economy—did not briefly go off the rails. And go off the rails the New Zealand film industry certainly did in 1984, as one set of tax legislation gave way to another.

It did so, moreover, in a way which may be different in detail but is identical in its broad outlines to similar derailments which were happening or had already happened in Australia, and would happen over the next twenty years in virtually every country in Europe. Much as individual filmmakers eventually reach a point where they have to stop using their (or their family's) credit cards to make a film and approach their chosen vocation like any other profession, so emerging film industries like New Zealand's are forced to set themselves up as 'proper' businesses, with cashflow projections, amortisation write-offs and sales targets. Virtually the only unique (or perhaps it was merely a distinguishing) feature of the New Zealand film industry's experience in the mid 1980s was that, at precisely the moment that it reached this stage, it found itself faced with a government that approved of such moves to competitive funding. One of the key aims of all transitional monetarist-tinged aid policies is to provide incentives which will help over-protected industries stand on their own feet. Money is available to prime the pump, but not to power the ongoing operation. In the film industry, however, rarely if ever does the pump get primed. Nor did it in New Zealand.

This article is not concerned with the artistic merits or demerits of the films made during this period—films ranging from *Battletruck* (1982) and *Savage Islands* (1983) to *Constance* (1984), *Pallet on the Floor* (1984) and *Other Halves* (1984)—but with the economic climate in which they were made. Much of the evidence here is drawn from a series of interviews I conducted in New Zealand and with Kiwi filmmakers in Cannes over a three-year period between 1983 and 1985, both before and after the change in tax legislation. My contention is that what happened in that brief period influenced filmmaking in New Zealand for a decade or more, both by making it much harder for emerging auteurs like Vincent Ward to work in their home country, and by creating a climate in which the 'creatives'—writers and directors—were constantly encouraged to second-guess the market as well as (and often instead of) focusing on plot, character, theme and other artistic ideas.

To a degree, of course, this is true of anyone setting out to make a film. But it was a heavy burden for a film industry so recently emerged from its artisanal stage to bear. It was, to borrow the title from another branch of New Zealand performance culture, the 'end of the golden weather', and it did much to create a 'them and us' atmosphere which the nascent New Zealand film industry had so far avoided, with filmmakers like Ward, Jane Campion and Melanie Read representing the 'us' faction, and Chris Kirkham, an executive with Fletcher Challenge, symbolising 'them'.

3. A Japanese promotional flyer for the action film *Battletruck* (1982), an example of the commercially-driven, internationally circulated films benefiting from the tax legislation of the period. Courtesy of the Ian Conrich collection of New Zealand cinema and visual culture.

Fletcher Challenge, one of New Zealand's largest business corporations, set up a division precisely to take advantage of what it saw first and foremost as a profit generating opportunity. It came in on the coat-tails of the original tax scheme, and sought ways to build a successful business model that would bring together the film crews, locations and low costs of New Zealand with what were, in 1985, vast sums of voracious international capital whose managers were happy to sail so close to the legal wind that that fine New Zealand word 'rort' can justifiably be invoked.[5] There was also, on the part of 'them', a breathtaking arrogance of the sort one often finds when businessmen from other sectors enter the film industry, see how chaotically things appear to be done, and believe they can do it better. For Fletcher Challenge's Chris Kirkham, speaking in March 1984, New Zealand film was 'amateurish [and] not marketable, because [the filmmakers are] not experienced enough—which means that they're not of sufficient quality . . . I mean, Roger Donaldson just had a lucky break with *Smash Palace*'. Kirkham did, however, concede of that film's director that 'maybe the guy had something at the start'.[6] Donaldson's 'something' has, of course, taken him on to a successful Hollywood career; Kirkham's brief paddle in the waters of film, by contrast, does not immediately make one think of 'marketability', let alone 'quality'.

There is, however, one factor which complicated the situation in New Zealand in a way which it did not—or did less—elsewhere: television. Broadly speaking, television, once the enemy of the seventh art, has established a working relationship with the movies in most parts of the world, and it has done so in two ways: co-production (that is, by putting up a proportion of the budget of a feature film, usually in return for broadcast rights); or acquisition (that is, by paying reasonable amounts to acquire the finished film after its theatrical run). In the years between 1975 and 1985, with very few exceptions, Television New Zealand (TVNZ), then the only local broadcaster, did neither. 'We're denied access to it, and we're paid poorly for it', commented John Maynard, who produced the early films of Vincent Ward and Jane Campion.[7]

There were reasons for this. At its foundation in the early 1960s, TVNZ had set up its own production unit, and this unit was exclusively responsible for making television drama. There had been no independent producers when TVNZ began; fifteen years later, there were many, but the production unit's exclusivity remained. This created an industry imbalance. 'One of the problems in this country is that there is no structure. There are commercials being made at the bottom, and there are small documentaries made', said producer and, at the time, energetic lobbyist John Barnett. 'Then there's a gap and there are features. In any other country, the bulk of the work is television. That doesn't happen here'.[8]

'There's not much a new filmmaker can do when he or she comes out of film school or wants to get a break', commented the late Jim Booth, subsequently a producer but at the time executive director of the New

Zealand Film Commission. 'There's not much . . . in the middle, because television is a closed, in-house shop. Basically, you've got to make a feature'.[9] This anomalous situation, in which filmmakers viewed almost any idea as having feature potential, would change with the arrival of a third television channel in 1985, and producers like Barnett and Maynard were among those quick to take advantage of the new opportunities, the latter developing *Seven Tales for Television* as a training ground for young writers and directors. But, in the years leading up to the period which is the subject of this article, 'there were silly and very arbitrary barriers . . . Fierce partisan lines were drawn between independent filmmakers and institutionalised and very safe career film and television producers and directors'.[10] It was, perhaps, another of those them-and-us situations which seem to be part of the New Zealand national psyche. But it did skew the production climate in a particular way, and it accounted for much of the anger that was to erupt during the changes to tax and other legislation in the mid 1980s.

Television had another marked influence on the growth of the New Zealand film industry, however: its healthy appetite for home-made commercials. Barnett's comments about commercials being 'at the bottom' is misleading: almost all the directors who established themselves in the late 1970s and early 1980s had previously worked in advertising, where standards were exceptionally high, thanks largely to the fact that commercials shown on TVNZ had to be locally produced. Almost as importantly, this high level of demand for top quality commercials built up an exceptionally strong crew base—including cinematographers such as Michael Seresin, Alun Bollinger and Stuart Dryburgh—and a growing number of facilities houses which not only ensured a disproportionately high quality-level of equipment supply and post-production facilities: they also proved a training ground for future producers, notably Don Reynolds, a former sound recordist who set up Associated Sounds in 1975 and soon became an active producer.

At all events, by the early 1980s, there was pressure building from a number of directions. There was a solid base of highly professional crew members trained on commercials but keen to make the occasional foray into the more 'grown-up' (if less well-paid) world of features; there were directors eager to put their own skills to work on stories rather than product promotion; and there was a perceptible if less easily demonstrable appetite for 'our own stories' told at a more sophisticated level than was being catered for by TVNZ's soap operas. To this was suddenly added a pot of money created as if by magic by tax provisions and seized upon by accountants who saw in film exactly the kind of industry suited to tax-shelter money. And why was this so? Because, as has already been suggested, film sits astride the watershed between culture and commerce, providing the alibi of the former and the cash thirst of the latter. Filmmaking also provides more ways of blurring the money trail than most businesses. But, as money eased its way ever more firmly into the driving seat, the cultural elements were quickly and effectively shouldered aside. The New Zealand new wave films had, if they were to justify their increased budgets (and occasional imported stars), to hold their own on the international market for independently produced films, which was going through one of its short-lived growth periods in the mid 1980s. And this required a particular kind of film.

'I think', said producer Rob Whitehouse in early 1984, 'it is more or less impossible to make what have commonly been called indigenous films in New Zealand any more'.[11] In terms of the dynamics of a commercial cinema, Whitehouse tried as hard as anyone to make a different kind of 'indigenous' movie, in such varying guises as *Savage Islands*, *Battletruck* and *The Scarecrow* (1982). But he was soon forced to recognise that the future lay in what have since become the two mainstays of the New Zealand industry: foreign television and the country's seemingly infinite supply of stunning locations. Whitehouse's next project after being interviewed in 1984 was an early attempt to raise money for the television miniseries *Rhodes*, produced by the UK's Zenith (an arm of what was then Central Television), which ended up having no New Zealand participation and was finally made in 1996.

The real problem with the New Zealand tax incentive scheme came less from its operation than from its demise, or rather from the fact that this demise was telegraphed so long in advance. When the Muldoon government announced the end of the scheme, they gave it a protracted playing out period, with the end of September 1984 set as its deadline. For tax lawyers and accountants, this was a little like announcing a firearms amnesty, but with the tacit implication that it was acceptable to use the guns freely until the actual end date. Inevitably, there was a whole lot of shooting going on. And many of the films which went into production before the deadline, as Whitehouse put it, 'weren't any bloody good, [which is] the reason why they hadn't got made before. They were sitting there on the shelf, so everybody got them down, dusted them off and leapt into production'.[12]

The government, Barnett claimed, had been warned this would happen, and happen it did. 'It's been fuelled in an absolutely abnormal manner by the tax situation', he said. 'People have only just realised what's slipping away, and they're doing their best to milk the situation'.[13] The figures prove him right. In the period leading up to the September 1984 deadline, eleven features had recently gone into production. Between October 1984 and May 1985, only one film successfully did so: the somewhat aptly titled *Bridge to Nowhere* (1986).

To make matters worse (or better, depending how the situation is regarded), not only did the government shut down the tax breaks: it also insisted that any film that would be eligible to benefit from its replacement—a not very attractive 100 per cent write-off of production money in the year in which it was spent ('something', as John Maynard tartly remarked, 'that any potato-grower can do'[14])—would need to be certified as a New Zealand movie, with the responsibility for certification falling on the New Zealand Film Commission.

The film industry was almost unanimously opposed to certification, although many producers privately recognised that something of the kind was necessary, if only to protect local filmmakers from the invasion of 'international' (in other words US) producers evidently favoured by Fletcher Challenge, who would have scant interest in local subject matter or performers. This became even more necessary when Fletcher Challenge announced a production deal with a US company called RKO Pictures, which sounded more impressive than it was. RKO had been a Hollywood studio until the mid-1950s, but was now little more than a shell company, which had made minor investments in such second-string movies as *The Best Little Whorehouse in Texas* (1982) and *D.C. Cab* (1983). However, the plan—to spend NZ$30 million on a number of commercial movies over a three-year period—came to nothing, providing proof, if it were needed, that even the sharpest financial minds could no longer put together a tax deal that made sense to foreign investors.

But part of the opposition to certification came from a recognition that a number of the key New Zealand films of the first wave had relied heavily on non-local talent. Donaldson was Australian, as was the female lead in *Smash Palace* (1982). *Beyond Reasonable Doubt* (1980) had an English writer, an English co-producer and an English lead, plus an Australian second lead. Hollywood veteran John Carradine had been brought in to star in *Scarecrow*, whose director, Sam Pillsbury, was also American. And yet those three are as recognisably 'New Zealand' as classic new wave movies such as *Middle Age Spread* (1979), *Goodbye Pork Pie* (1980) or *Utu* (1983).

So how crucial a turning point in the history of New Zealand film was that period in the mid 1980s when the government decided, like governments all over the world periodically do, that tax incentives designed to encourage local film production were being abused and exploited, resulting in an unacceptable diversion of tax revenue? How important are such considerations in the broader history of New Zealand film? Does it matter to anyone other than the film's producer, John Maynard, or its director, Vincent Ward, that *The Navigator: A Mediaeval Odyssey* (1988), proved impossible to finance in the prevailing financial climate (scheduled to be made in the winter of 1986, it was not finally shot until the following year)?

The answer is, in the very long term, probably not. Setbacks caused by the collapse of a financing plan, like those brought about by a month of unexpected rain or a more than usually temperamental star, are part and parcel of the business of filmmaking. But what the events of 1984 and 1985 did mean for the New Zealand film industry was that a sense of shared identity, even an artisanal approach to the making of films—true of

4. Temuera Morrison (left) and Lawrence Makoare in *Crooked Earth*, the film Sam Pillsbury directed on his return to New Zealand in 2001. Courtesy of the New Zealand Film Commission.

such undertakings as *Goodbye Pork Pie* and *Smash Palace*—were consigned to history.

The process whereby a nascent film culture comes to grips with the realities of industrial film production is usually a gradual one. In New Zealand, this happened, if not overnight, then over a distinctly short and bruising period of time. That this had an impact on New Zealand directors and on what they saw as the options available to them is also certain. Because film is such a collaborative industry and because, in the village-like atmosphere that prevailed in the New Zealand film industry in the mid 1980s, everyone knew how plans to fund everyone else's film were progressing, directors were inevitably drawn into the process of financing and were as affected as anyone by the change in the tax system.

There were, by and large, three phases to this change: the lead-up, when budgets remained low and films, though difficult to fund, could generally be got up and running; the transitional period, when money suddenly became available and almost any completed script had a chance of going into production; and the aftermath, when funding was tighter than it had been in the lead-up, but expectations (and therefore, budgets) were considerably higher. The short-term effect is that a number of careers ground to a halt. Ward, as has already been noted, saw *The Navigator* postponed; once it was completed, he left New Zealand feature production for almost twenty years, emerging only for the painful experience of *River Queen* (2005), three years in funding, from which he was for a period removed by the producers after relations with star Samantha Morton became irreparable.

But Ward was not the only one. Roger Donaldson had already left for Hollywood (and only returned in 2005 to make *The World's Fastest Indian*). Geoff Murphy made only one further New Zealand movie after *The Quiet Earth* (1985) before also boarding a plane for Los Angeles, where he has had rather less success than Donaldson but at least continues to make movies (returning to New Zealand in 2004 to direct *Spooked*). Sam Pillsbury, working with producer Larry Parr, managed one further film in his adopted country—*Starlight Hotel* (1987)—before working mainly for US television (although he did manage to return to make *Crooked Earth* in 2001); John Reid did not direct a feature between *Leave All Fair* (1985) and the ill-fated international co-production *The Last Tattoo* in 1994; and Geoff Steven made no films after the ambitious *Strata* (1983). In terms of the sudden termination of many flourishing careers, it is hard to think of a comparable example in recent cinema history.

So was the government right to have changed the rules? It depends where you stand. Fiscally, it probably had no choice: the New Zealand economy of the time could ill afford to relinquish tax revenue on the scale that it was doing. But, looking once again to the longer term, the question is harder to answer. Certainly the local film industry, with or without tax breaks, would have been unlikely ever to have provided the boost to tourism and international profile that came a decade-and-a-half later with *The Lord of the Rings* trilogy (2001–03). But the management of national resources of talent could certainly have been better handled. As Ginnane commented, sitting with me in a café in Cannes nearly two decades after the period about which we had just been talking, 'if you genuinely want to help the film industry in your jurisdiction, you have to turn half a blind eye'.[15]

Notes

1. Larry Parr, interview with author, March 1984.
2. Geoff Murphy, interview with author, May 1983.
3. Anthony I. Ginnane, interview with author, May 2003.
4. Nick Roddick, *A New Deal in Entertainment: Warner Brothers in the 1930s*, (London: British Film Institute, 1983).
5. For an engaging and unashamedly polemical account of the many 'rort' (meaning a trick or a scheme) occurring around this time, see Antony Molloy, *Thirty Pieces of Silver* (Auckland: Howling at the Moon, 1988).
6. Chris Kirkham, interview with author, March 1984.
7. John Maynard, interview with author, March 1984
8. John Barnett, interview with author, March 1984.

9.   Jim Booth, interview with author, March 1984.
10. Tom Finlayson, interview with author, March 1984.
11. Rob Whitehouse, interview with author, March 1984.
12. Ibid.
13. Barnett, interview with author, March 1984.
14. Maynard, interview with author, March 1984.
15. Ginnane, interview with author, May 2003.

3

The Short Film:

Issues of Funding and Distribution

Alex Cole-Baker

A fascinating and powerful range of New Zealand short films are made every year: fantasies, comedies, film noir and more, the impetus for which are just as much a mystery as with any film. But how are they made and where are they seen? What money is there available, and what impact do the different sources of funding have on a film? And indeed, as a specific form that is potentially economically non-viable, why do people even bother making short films? With budgets ranging from non-existent to minimal, somehow the producers and directors succeed to make them possible. As a producer of four short films, and having worked on many others, I will consider some of these issues in this discussion.

Officially, a film may be called short if it is under 60 minutes, i.e., not feature length (or 'too-long films' as in the view of New Zealand writer/ director, and short film supporter, Peter Wells).[1] However, for the purpose of this article, I will be adopting the more common view that short films are those of less than 30 minutes duration. This view is one shaped by both the marketplace, which dictates that short films under 12 minutes are more saleable than those of longer duration (a change from even ten years ago when 15 minutes seemed the upper limit), and festivals, where a 15-minute limit on duration is the norm, (and sometimes even 10 minutes, as marked in particular by the Berlin Film Festival's aggressive restrictions up until 2003).

Nowadays, most discussion of film tends to focus on features. But in the beginning, *all* films were short: starting out with the wonders of filmmakers such as the Lumière Brothers, Georges Méliès and R.W. Paul, whose early films were all no more than a few minutes. Short films today can be narrative dramas, experimental, animation or documentary. By their nature, they tend to be more allegorical, symbolic or iconical than feature films. The leaps and bounds an audience member is required to take when watching can be quite large simply due to the fact that there is less time in which to tell a story. Whenever I need to do a test screening for a short film I am producing, I always have to consider this: are the people who are about to watch literate in short film? If not, the viewers often cannot make the necessary connections in plot and themes. In the same way, music videos have a 'language' of their own, and it seems that my ability to read them declines as I get older, as they are ever changing to the vibrancy of new youth culture. For New Zealand shorts, the old duality of Greek drama—comedy and tragedy—neatly describes the majority 'where the emphasis is on the dark and the quirky'.[2] On the dark side, just looking at the cover of a marketed compilation video tape of New Zealand shorts reveals the subjects of murder, drowning, insanity, divorce and suicide.[3]

A number of characters recur in New Zealand shorts: the sporting hero (*Bradman* [1993], *Lovelock* [1992]); melancholic women (*La Vie en Rose* [1994], *I'm So Lonesome I Could Cry* [1994], *Bitch* [1995]); determined women (*Sci-Fi Betty* [1999], *A Game With No Rules* [1994]); the harassed husband (*Making Money* [1994], *Camping With Camus* [2000]); troublesome kids (*Dirty Creature* [1995], *Watermark* [2001], *Junk* [2001]); and blokes being blokes (*Beautiful* [2001], *Accidents* [1999]). The use of archetypes is a useful device when dealing with this limited timeframe, as audiences already have a good basis for understanding the characters and how they work.

As with characters, the landscape too has become archetypal and is one of the New Zealand film industry's greatest assets. It is promised as 'the world in one place' and offers a diversity of location possibilities: from deserts and rich rain forests, to snow-topped mountain ranges and glacial lakes.[4] Yet, although productions filmed in New Zealand can be made to appear as if set almost anywhere in the world, local filmmakers often draw on their own visions of the landscape: blues and greens abound. The comedy of this predictable view of the landscape is illustrated in the short, *Beautiful*. Two typical Kiwi blokes go fishing for the day in their little boat on a beautiful lake. The sun sparkles on the rich blue waters, reflecting the rolling hills surrounding them. But the serenity of the situation is broken when one starts to tell the other of his recent experimentation with bisexuality. This goes down like a lead balloon and the juxtaposition of the beautiful environment and the awkward conversation creates a highly humorous situation.

But what do these 'little' films cost and where does the money come from? And, more importantly, how do they manage on such tight budgets?

Funding

There are currently four main divisions of funding, and each gives support for a specific type of film. The divisions are:

1) *New Zealand Film Commission (NZFC) Short Film Fund (SFF)*:
   The highest level of funding available; narrative dramas ('mini features'), average budget NZ$70,000, equity financing.

2) *Screen Innovation Production Fund (SIPF)*:
   A partnership between Creative New Zealand (CNZ) and the NZFC. Less narrative focus than the SFF, films often experimental in style: 'innovation within or between moving-image genres'.[5]

Budgets under NZ$15,000 for emerging filmmakers, up to NZ$35,000 for filmmakers of note.

3) *Student Work*:
Made at the numerous tertiary institutions—can be anything in style or genre but often low in production value due to limited experience and resources. Often a technical lesson and suffering from 'overlength'.

4) *Self Funded*:
Work that is often highly political and/or personal and cannot break through the other funding schemes. However, this area also includes those who do not want to enter into the systems of the funding circles or have had no luck and are determined to make films regardless. Usually low in budget as returns are minimal and private investors few.

Of these four divisions the SFF and the SIPF are the two main funding bodies for short films in New Zealand. The NZFC, a wholly government owned entity, has funded short film since 1985. Peter Wells argues that 'the New Film Group in Auckland dragged that [the funding of short films] out of the Film Commission. It was when a speed wobble had developed in the feature film industry and the Film Commission was groping round [sic] in the dark a bit about future directions'.[6]

Interestingly, the main focus of the SFF in the mid 1980s was initially television documentaries, which were then proving popular.[7] The establishment of New Zealand On Air in 1989, a separate funding agency for television and radio, meant it was able to take over this aspect and leave the SFF to the production of fiction. There have been a number of changes over the years to this fund, most notably in the administering of funds, the size of budgets and the eligibility of applicants. In the early days of the SFF, a panel met several times a year to make funding decisions. This panel consisted of a combination of industry members (often filmmakers with features in development) and NZFC Board members, with NZFC staff also holding power to make recommendations on projects.[8] Applicants were often critical of the ability of the Board and staff (as mostly non-filmmakers) to select projects and manage the process, accusing them of being inaccessible, singular in their vision and overly commercial in their tastes. In the lead up to an official review of the SFF, the NZFC felt change was required, and that there was 'the need for filmmakers to have greater experience when embarking on a first feature than that offered by one or two theatrical shorts . . . with the objective of increasing the opportunities for filmmakers to tell longer form stories'.[9] However, this was not the outcome achieved, and for some, opportunities became fewer rather than greater.

It was in August 1997 that the SFF was reviewed by the Board (with feedback from industry members) and devolved: administration of the fund would now be handled outside of the NZFC. Several proposals were put forward at that time, including funding the production of films of varying lengths, such as five films of up to 24 minutes and three films of up to 12 minutes per year, but these were dismissed in favour of an annual slate of nine short films of around 12 minutes in length each. Tenders were then called for and three outside groups were contracted to select and executive produce the projects. These consortiums to date have consisted of combinations of two or three writers, producers and/or directors. The contract is held for one year but may be renewed for a maximum of a second year, as has been the case for a number of groups, like Frame Up Films and Swad/Saunders, to encourage an ongoing change in perspectives.

The consortiums now hold one funding round per year and though generally funding three projects, both MAP Film Productions in 1997, and Frame Up Films in 2000, for example, funded four projects each. A consortium receives about 140 applications, so competition is fierce. But it seems most likely that the consortiums receive the same projects, despite the best efforts of each to let applicants know what kind of projects they are looking for. In 1998, MAP Film Productions announced they were 'looking for strong, character based stories which in some way reflect contemporary New Zealand'; in 1999, Frame Up Films announced they were 'looking for cinematic sensibility; that is comprehensive narrative underpinned by subtext and metaphor and an awareness of the language of cinema'; and in 2001, Swad/Saunders Consortium announced '[o]ur primary aim is to harness the potential of talent fresh to film, who tackle strong and edgy narrative concepts'. Being in the industry long enough to know the people involved also gives a good basis for guessing what kind of projects are going to appeal to which consortium. And this really is about personal taste: one consortium can be concerned with the avant-garde and the surreal, and another, more intellectual and literary in its sensibilities, which fits with the NZFC's 'desire for a variety of approaches and styles' when assessing the short film tenders.[10] But, in talking to other applicants and having been one myself, in the end financial considerations dictate and with only nine films funded per year, there is the need to apply to *everyone* and hope to be funded by the most appropriate group; after all, they are going to have significant involvement in the film.

In the early to mid 1990s, NZFC short films had an average budget of around NZ$95,000. Each was shot on 35mm negative and completed to a 35mm print. In the August 1997 review, it was proposed that the average budget for a film (up to 12 minutes in length) be raised to NZ$100,000. However, with the devolved funds now covering nine films, the average budget is only NZ$70,000, and this is changing the face of New Zealand short filmmaking. The early to mid 1990s also saw the emergence of the so called 'bonsai epics': short films funded to about NZ$120,000, for filmmakers with a solid track record who would be allowed to make a film of 'epic' proportions. One such film was *Hinekaro Goes On a Picnic and Blows Up Another Obelisk* (1995), and on which I was Associate Producer

5. The 'bonsai epic': With a large budget, the production of *Hinekaro* was unprecedented for a New Zealand short film. Courtesy of Alex Cole-Baker.

(with Caterina De Nave as Producer). Written and directed by Christine Parker and based on a Keri Hulme short story, *Hinekaro* was an eight day 35mm shoot, had a crew of thirty and a cast of three including the already internationally established actress Rena Owen (who played Beth Heke in *Once Were Warriors* [1993]) as the voice of Hinekaro. Moreover, the short used part of the early effects of Peter Jackson's Weta facilities, containing ground-breaking visuals with a plate of food that morphed into a face and spat, and a beetle that came to life from within a book and scuttled off the page.[11] The likes of this had never been seen before in a New Zealand short film.

At present, each consortium receives NZ$250,000 to produce a minimum of three projects. About NZ$10,000 goes on processing costs (including phone bills and flights) and the consortium itself takes a NZ$30,000 fee for the task of selecting, developing and overseeing the production of the projects, leaving a remainder of NZ$210,000 for the three films. Consortiums have tended to split this three-ways into a budget of NZ$70,000 per film, not wanting to become involved in the business of rationalising budgets. This has been problematic, as some films are effectively 'overfunded' and others 'underfunded', but this is now slowly changing and projects of varying budgets are being considered, as well as producers being asked to rework their budgets as each consortium juggles their funds. But NZ$70,000 is still the average budget, if not the maximum, and is quite a change from the NZ$95,000 of the early 1990s. The question arises: where does that shortfall come from? The answer is that it is mainly taken from crew labour fees.

The 1997 review also gave rise to the Short Film Post Production Fund (SFPPF), providing completion finance, and finance for delivery requirements, on condition that films are showcased *in competition* at a significant international film festival.[12] Financial assistance of up to NZ$20,000 is provided and is not limited to films that have been previously funded by the NZFC but is also available to those funded by other sources. Depending on which is the case, funds are either considered as further equity or a grant. Technically, this means that a film could receive NZ$70,000 from a consortium, complete to tape, and then apply for finishing funds for print delivery on acceptance to Cannes, Melbourne, Edinburgh (or any other qualifying film festival), giving a total budget of NZ$90,000. But this tends not to be the case, as most consortiums require their applicants to complete to a 35mm print—a self-dictated requirement and not one placed on them by the NZFC. Notably, in 1999, Frame Up Films required a minimum completion to a 16mm answerprint, yet in 2000 the requirement changed to 35mm—for the same money. Occasionally, a film like *Trespass* (2002), which I produced, has needed to finish on 16mm due to unforeseen circumstances, usually reshoots or budget blow-outs, and may not originally be budgeted as such. Only in recent funding rounds, has there emerged the possibility that a project could be officially funded to NZ$70,000, or even NZ$85,000, to tape only.[13] Perhaps change is on its way. Again.

In one sense, finishing to tape is a sensible option: most short films will only have a life on tape, primarily used for television sales, unless they are accepted to one of the main festivals. Some smaller festivals will screen films on tape, again making the costs of a print unwarranted. I believe it is a good option to spend what money there is on production and wait and see what the reaction to it is before deciding on the final delivery format. However, this does little to encourage or appreciate the work of the many technicians who make significant sacrifices (usually financial) for the making of a short film: what happens to the quality of the lighting or Dolby Digital sound mix if a production only finishes on tape?

In addition, there have been extreme changes in the eligibility of applicants for funding. Prior to the introduction of consortium led funding, the SFF was very much a fund for experienced filmmakers only; those with clear futures in the making of features. Filmmakers were expected to have made one, if not two, films prior to applying for this level of funding— and self-funded films generally did not count. Developing future feature filmmakers is still key, but now first-time directors are able to access budgets of NZ$70,000—inconceivable in the past—*and* shoot on 35mm, a format once considered a privilege for the experienced only. Noticeably, some of these first-timers are expert in other areas of the industry, but somehow it seems that less experienced filmmakers are gaining access to more funds than before, and experienced filmmakers accessing less than before—hardly the original aim of the 1997 SFF review.

The SIPF has been in operation since 1996 following the review of the Creative Film and Video Fund (CFVF). The name change recognised the impact of new technologies on the way that moving images are conceived and constructed.[14] A 2001 SIPF document stated that:

The purpose of the Fund is to provide grants to emerging or experienced moving-image makers for innovative moving-image productions. The Fund will give priority to innovative art projects and production proposals in the following categories:

- projects by emerging video and filmmakers of promise that emphasise innovation within or between moving-image genres;
- projects by experimental or fine art film and video-makers;
- projects exploring digital technologies which give priority to the moving image;
- exceptional, innovative, non-commercial projects by established film and video makers.[15]

The original CFVF was established in 1985 as a partnership between the QE2 (Queen Elizabeth II) Arts Council and the NZFC. The SIPF continues to be a partnership with the NZFC but is run by Creative New Zealand (as the QE2 Arts Council has been renamed), another publicly funded body, whose scope covers all areas of arts in New Zealand. Early on, Television New Zealand, and later, New Zealand On Air, were also partners of the CFVF.

The SIPF has two funding rounds per year, attracting 70 to 90 proposals each time. On average, 33 projects are funded annually, so competition is tough but less so than with the SFF. Emerging filmmakers, those without a substantial body of work to date, are expected to submit budgets of under NZ$15,000. Experienced filmmakers can access budgets of about NZ$30–35,000. These are often artists working in the areas of experimental and non-commercial projects, not catered for by the SFF, as emerging filmmakers making narrative drama tend to seek NZFC money at some point in the process. Filmmakers applying to this fund are encouraged to make very small and manageable films, and to utilise the easy access of new technologies, such as shooting on digital formats. The SFPPF remains a possibility for those making drama.

The first film I produced, *La Vie en Rose* (1994), written and directed by Anna Reeves, was made for NZ$4,600. Having been unsuccessful with a previous film application, we were eager to make something and not wait for another funding round. A shorter script was written than the one for the first application and our first NZ$1,500 came from a grant from the Lion Foundation (established by Lion Nathan Breweries) via a couple of

6. The resourceful *La Vie en Rose*, made on a small budget and the recipient of several awards. Courtesy of Alex Cole-Baker.

local pubs with gambling machines, required by law to 'return something to the community'. Although this usually meant handling applications for local soccer teams or kindergartens, luckily for us the thought of artistic input into the community was of interest to them. On completion of an edit, the balance came from a Post Production grant from the (then) CFVF. Winning a number of local awards for Best Drama and Best Experimental short film, the NZFC later agreed to handle the film as Sales Agents.

The third and fourth funding divisions to consider here are student work and self-funded projects. In New Zealand, nearly 2000 film production students graduate from tertiary education every year, an astonishing amount for an industry that only holds around 8000 permanent positions. Not all are trainee directors, but those that are still create a large number of projects every year. Often, student works are classroom exercises or term projects required for grading. Projects are usually shot on tape, as lab costs for film are generally prohibitive to the institutions. These films most differ to other projects in that students are often able to utilise the equipment for extended periods of time, with no effect on their budgets. This, combined with new skills, often creates projects that are far longer than they should be.

Self-funded projects are fewer and far between, and are generally low in cost as the struggling artist stereotype tends to be one based on reality. A film with no official backing also finds it difficult to enlist the help of others, as it is assumed that there is good reason funding bodies have declined to be involved in such a project. More often they are made entirely by that one person or require a particularly charismatic director to succeed, one who can gather the assistance of 'comrades in arms': fellow ex-film-school friends or perhaps those of a similar political stance. But without the shackles of funders, a self-funded project can also benefit from being exactly what it wants to be; the more money received, the more input everyone else wants to have.

One such film I produced is called *Iosua* (1995), written and directed by Phillip Skelton. A sweet tale of a young boy's imagination as he plays with his goat and chicken, *Iosua* was self-funded by the director for about NZ$2,000. Skelton, for valid reasons of experimentation, wanted to make the film entirely silent—annoyed at the often invasive and leading (or misleading) presence of music scores. He wanted to see if a tale could be told by visuals alone, without the audience being told when and how to feel. The experiment was successful but made the film ultimately unmarketable and it was not picked up for distribution by the NZFC. In retrospect, I am not surprised; at each screening I attended, I had to make an announcement that it *was* a silent film—something I learnt after the first screening when people started yelling at the projectionist.

The *Iosua* project is probably about the greatest contrast to *Hinekaro* that I have experienced. But money is not everything: with only ten crew, no lights and one child actor (plus a goat and some chickens), we located to the coast for two days, stayed in a small nearby hut with bunk beds, and ate barbequed food (not chicken) under the stars each night. *Hinekaro*, by comparison, gained the reputation of being one of the most difficult shoots around for some time.

It seems astonishing then that a film could even be made for NZ$15,000, let alone NZ$2,000, when other films struggle at NZ$70,000. There are the obvious differences of scale; a 12-minute 35mm film will certainly cost more than a 3-minute video, but there are other factors at play when working out how much a film will cost. And nowhere more so than in short filmmaking is it true that budgeting is not an exact science. All short films require discounts and simply could not be made if full commercial rates applied. Therefore, the ability to bargain and secure favours plays a large part in determining the size of a budget. Filmmakers who also make commercials have great bargaining power, often able to play-off the payment of another job with the work on a short. A number of key companies support short filmmakers with permanent standard discounts. The SIPF support documentation 'Information for Applicants: June 2001– February 2002' provides excellent discount information for new filmmakers who have no contacts, on items such as film stock, lab processing and casting studios. Discounts on other equipment, like camera hire, tend to be negotiated case by case and often rely on personal contacts. But the biggest discounts seem to be on labour: it is the crew and the cast who, by waiving or heavily reducing their fees, subsidise short films the most.

In a strange way, one of the easiest films I produced was one where I had no money for crew, and little for anything else. It created a blanket value for all involved: no one was worth more, and more importantly, no one was worth less. For films with slightly more than 'no money' it becomes tricky: yes, you have enough to pay everyone NZ$50 each but to those who earn anywhere between NZ$400 and NZ$1,000 a day, will this offer seem offensive? Often, in this case, I find it is better to pool what little money there is and spend it on good catering and an appreciative amount of beer and pizza for the end of the day.

Those crew who are willing to work on short films for such meagre rates mainly do so for one or more of a number of reasons: benevolence—skilled and experienced crew who realise that emerging filmmakers need their help; those requiring a creative break—short films offer a change from the monotony of more commercial projects; and finally, and most commonly, those looking for a career step up—perhaps they are a Props Buyer on a bigger production and this gives them the opportunity to be an Art Director. What is often created on the set of a short film is a family-like environment, established by a group of people wishing to see through the success of a project.

There are, of course, those in the industry who do not discount for short films. The phrase 'we are not a charity' is often a response to such requests. And with the continuous reduction of budgets such as the now 'NZ$70,000 SFF short', and increase in number of films being made (due in the most part to digital technology), it is understandable that some people have begun to refuse to help, some in an effort to effect change in the funding provided.

Exposure

Where then do these short films go when they are finished? If they are awful and self-funded, they can remain in a cardboard box underneath the filmmaker's bed. However, most films have other people behind them who will want every effort made to have the film exhibited. The film's watchability obviously plays a large part in whether it is seen, but so too does its format and length. The three main areas where short films are shown are festivals, television and the theatrical circuit.

With festivals, there is a hierarchy, with Cannes as the most prestigious, requiring a 35mm print and a World Premiere. Competition is extreme and the prestige of acceptance even more so, often termed a 'career launcher'. Some festivals will play video, others will not. And films usually need to have been made within a certain timeframe—which is often within the last eighteen months. Festivals bring attention to both the short and the filmmaker. Information is usually published in a festival guide and, so, unlike television, audiences (and buyers) have a permanent record of who and what they saw. Moreover, many festivals have competition sections and there is nothing like winning an award to boost a filmmaker's marketability.

The most favoured form of exhibition following the festival circuit (particularly to keep premiere options open) is television. Unlike New Zealand, where there is very regimented television scheduling (practically everything starts on the hour or half-hour), many other countries have less structured and even advertising-free channels, with many shorts shown on cable. In these instances, short films are used as fillers in between other programmes, often to bring the schedule back to a half-hour start for the next main feature. New Zealand television has a growing tradition of showing short films, often packaged in a half or one-hour format with a presenter, like *Kiwi Shorts* and *Short Cuts*.[16] And internationally, television is where the money is. Often sold by the minute, the current average price is about US$100 per minute, with those under 10 minutes selling better than any others.[17] *La Vie en Rose*, which lasts 7 minutes, has been relatively successful. It has earned over four times its original budget to date. The most commercial shorts, like Alison Maclean's *Kitchen Sink* (1989), have grossed just over NZ$90,000 worldwide from mostly television and video sales.

Theatrical releases, those shown on a cinema screen before a feature, are very prestigious particularly as this is now rare in modern exhibition markets. In this environment, where the screening length of a programme is important to maximise schedules, one 15-minute short could lose a cinema in total at least an hour a day for no additional revenue. In a slightly different theatrical release style, a series of short films toured cinemas around New Zealand from 1995–98, titled *Five for Five*, as in 5 films for 5 dollars.[18] But a number of other avenues are opening up for short films. The Internet is a fast growing medium for exhibition, and there are now a number of sites on which New Zealand short films, can be viewed such as www.nzshortfilm.com and www.youtube.com. Tertiary institutions also establish screenings for industry people, to showcase student talent. The Moving Image Centre, which receives major funding from CNZ, organises a number of workshops and screenings every year, including *Short Fuse*, a monthly screening of around six to ten films, which it has been doing since 1995.[19] Women In Film and Television (WIFT) often screen a number of shorts by women filmmakers, following workshops that are also held several times a year. In addition, video compilations of New Zealand shorts have been released at times.[20]

As well as being one of the few governments in the world that funds short films, via the NZFC, New Zealand's is certainly the only one which is involved in their marketing. If the NZFC fund a short it becomes the Sales Agent, but occasionally it will pick up films from other sources. As the Sales Agent, the Commission enters short films in festivals, makes television sales, puts on showcases at festivals (such as Clermont-Ferrand), and takes them to markets like Cannes, AFM and MIFED where it also has a feature film presence.[21] As well as taking an investor position on this return (often at 70 per cent), they take a Distribution Fee of between 15 and 25 per cent to cover costs involved such as market attendance and general publicity, which cannot be allocated to a specific film.

Short films are clearly not made for money but rather talent development, but are they successful at this? Director/writer Grant Lahood made three wonderful short films in the late 1980s and early 1990s: *Snail's Pace* (1989), *The Singing Trophy* (1993), and then *Lemming Aid* (1994). The latter two were in competition at Cannes, where the first won a Technical Award: Special Mention and the second, the Jury Prize. However, when Lahood embarked on his first feature, *Chicken* (1996), it had a disastrous reception, so much so that it looked like no one would ever touch his work again. Luckily this was not the case and he was given the chance to direct the feature *Kombi Nation* (2003), which had a better reception. In Lahood's case, perhaps it would be fair to say that quirky short film humour does not extend to an hour and a half. There is no certainty that people who tell wonderful 10-minute stories might know how to fill a 90-minute feature. The two mediums *are* quite different in their workings. More often, unlike Lahood's early successes, the creative freedom inherent in the short film process does not equal market success, but, importantly, makers of short films must be allowed to make a number of mistakes if this process is to be used as talent development. Notably the NZFC does not talk about marketability in terms of short films, as the returns on short films are relatively small and few make all their money back.

The making of so many innovative short films in New Zealand has made for an exciting creative environment. With government assistance, we are a very lucky industry and, despite the struggles we perceive, we hold our own on the world stage, no matter whether our films are seen in cinemas, at festivals or on television. Many a career is launched from such penny-poor roots, whether through the self-funding of a film or through receiving full equity investment. And it is this over-riding success of the film and the filmmaker that takes centre focus, rather than any monetary return.

Notes

1. Peter Wells, 'Glamour on the Slopes: Or: the Films We Wanted to Live', *Film In Aotearoa New Zealand*, ed. Jonathan Dennis and Jan Bieringa (Wellington: Victoria University Press, 1992), 179.
2. Norelle Scott, quoted in Deborah Shepard, *Reframing Women: a history of New Zealand film* (Auckland: HarperCollins, 2000), 201.
3. *Short Takes, Dark Tales*, 'A selection of nine Short & Shady New Zealand Films', Endeavour/Roadshow, 1995.
4. See Ian Conrich's article 'The Space Between: Screen Representations of The New Zealand Small Town', in this collection, 103–08.
5. Screen Innovation Production Fund, *Information for Applicants: June 2001– February 2002*, 1.

6. Wells, 'Glamour on the Slopes', 180.
7. Sandy Gildea, information sheet *NZFC Short Films: A Brief History*, 2002, 1.
8. The final committee in 1997 included John Barnett as Chair, and Riwia Brown and Costa Botes as industry practitioners.
9. New Zealand Film Commission, *Short Film Fund Discussion Paper, July 1997*, 1.
10. New Zealand Film Commission, *Annual Report 1999–2000*, November 2000, 14.
11. WETA (WingNut Effects & Technological Allusions Ltd) was the facility responsible for the Oscar-winning effects for *The Lord of the Rings* trilogy.
12. New Zealand Film Commission, *Short Film Post Production Fund* guidelines, October 2001, 1.
13. As funding is government money, budgets are made public.
14. *Screen Innovation Production Fund, An Extended Introduction*, June 2001, 1.
15. Screen Innovation Production Fund, *Information for Applicants: June 2001–February 2002*, 1.
16. *Kiwi Shorts* ran in 1989 followed by *Kiwi Shorts II* in 1990. *Short Cuts* works on a similar format to *Kiwi Shorts* and in 2003 was on its third season.
17. This may be for a single screening or a licence to screen a number of times over a specified period of time.
18. Instigated by Kathleen Drumm of the NZFC, then Marketing Manager for short film.
19. Contactable at <www.mic.org.nz>.
20. For instance, *Short Takes, Dark Tales*, and *Short Takes, Comedy*, both Endeavour/ Roadshow, 1995.
21. AFM is the American Film Market, held in Santa Monica and traditionally late February each year, though in 2004 it has moved to a new date of November; MIFED is Milan's Mercato Internazionale del Film e del Documentario, which occurs in late October. Cannes occurs in May.

4

The Role of Marketing
in the New Zealand Feature Film

Suzette Major

Lights, camera, action . . . marketing. To some, the fourth term here may seem out of place. Filmmaking tends to concern an artistic vision. But it is also very much a business and, like most industries, marketing plays an integral role in its success. This essay explores the role of marketing in the New Zealand film industry. Drawing on examples of marketing strategies employed for New Zealand films, it shows how the industry has developed the business of marketing practices over the last two decades. The process of film marketing is considered, including the roles of those involved in the promotion process. The aim of such processes is to attract an audience, and to showcase New Zealand films internationally.

Since the mid 1980s, business thinking has become ingrained in the New Zealand film industry. This shift parallels the right-wing mentality that has become embedded in the New Zealand political scene, and which was felt throughout all local and national industries. Such thinking is reflected in the now common usage of terms such as user pays, market-driven, and deregulation. In 2000, the Labour led New Zealand government commissioned a report exploring cultural enterprises and creative industries in New Zealand, entitled *Heart of the Nation*.[1] While the report drew some criticism, it provides evidence of the change in how the arts sector, including the New Zealand film industry, frames itself. To refer to filmmaking as a 'creative industry' is to see this artistic pursuit through business eyes. By way of contrast, the notion of film as an art form, governed by humanistic, aesthetic or narrative objectives, exists in tension to this idea of film as an economic generator.

As part of this shift towards business thinking, expectations are now placed on New Zealand filmmakers to understand the concept of marketing. At present, if a local filmmaker is seeking funding from the largest funding body, the New Zealand Film Commission (NZFC), evidence of marketing thinking needs to be displayed. A filmmaker is asked to outline his or her target market, and to produce evidence of negotiations with international distributors. For many, speaking such marketing language proves a challenge. In 1996, research conducted on the role of marketing in the New Zealand film industry showed some apprehension towards this aspect of production.[2] Film directors, in particular, raised questions as to the potentially negative impact of business mentality on the filmmaking process. But that study was conducted in the year after the release of New Zealand's then highest grossing film, *Once Were Warriors* (1994), and as word filtered through the industry about the marketing behind this film, questions arose as to how to learn from its example, and how to apply such tactics successfully to other New Zealand films. Since then marketing thinking has developed. While there is still much to learn, strategies used in movies such as *Scarfies* (1999) and *Rain* (2001) are contemporary examples of effective film marketing.

So what exactly is film marketing? In simple terms, film marketing is any activity that helps find, reach and maximise a film's audience. In reality, it is a complex set of strategies, operated by a variety of players including unit publicists, sales agents, producers, distributors and exhibitors, which attracts a member of the public into the theatre. But film marketing is not limited to the general public, and does not only occur at the post-production end of the film. From the moment a filmic idea is put to paper, the process of film marketing begins. This analysis here outlines the process underlying the promotion of film, and uses examples of the marketing strategies behind New Zealand productions to demonstrate how film marketing comes to life.

Multiple Target Markets

Throughout a film's development, there are three main groups that must be targeted. First, the film idea is marketed to financiers in the endeavour to secure investment. The clichéd scenario of a film producer selling an idea, in dramatic and sensational style, while 'doing lunch', is not far from the truth. At this early stage, the marketability of the film (in terms of potential box-office takings) is speculated upon. Marketable features most commonly considered include the storyline, genre ingredients, previous experience of the key personnel (e.g., director, producer) and popularity of stars. Such formulaic decisions occur as commonly in New Zealand as they do in Hollywood. A difference between these industries, however, is that many Hollywood films are financed by one of the major studios, which have large and highly informed marketing and distribution departments who hold a comprehensive knowledge of market trends and international distribution arms. In New Zealand few opportunities exist for a film to be financed and distributed by a single entity. As such, mechanisms have developed to expedite the process of raising finance. One such device is the use of a sales agent. The NZFC often plays the role of sales agent for those films in which it has invested. Its responsibility is to sell, and ideally pre-sell, the film to international markets. This is a way New Zealand films, with limited money available domestically, can be made. The entire process of marketing to a sales agent, who in turn markets the film idea to international buyers, is often referred to as 'film project marketing'.[3]

On the second tier of targeted marketing is the film distributor. Film distribution companies such as Essential Films, and Columbia TriStar NZ, take responsibility for marketing the film within pre-negotiated territories.

They define the film's target audience, and then create and sustain that audience's awareness of the film. As explained by John Durie, Annika Pham and Neil Watson, 'just as a sales agent must find the best way of positioning a film for the international buyers in the industry, so a distributor must find the best way of positioning a film for its potential audience'.[4] Marketing hooks vary from country to country, and New Zealand has its own specific elements that appeal to New Zealand audiences.

The final tier of marketing for a film involves the public at large, or more specifically the target audience. Once a film is marketed to, and accepted by, financiers, and then distributors, it is the public who ultimately measures its success by way of box-office takings. This stage of film marketing embodies the more visible aspects of promotion such as film posters, trailers and merchandising. The focus of the analysis that follows is on this final stage of film marketing—the strategies employed by distributors to market the film to the public. These include the timing and release strategy, the prints and advertising (P&A) budget, publicity and promotional tactics.

Timing and Release Strategy

There are two main factors to consider in developing the timing and release strategy for a film: the date of release and the release pattern. The release date is crucial in that films have a limited shelf life. If a film is released against tough competition, and subsequently does not attract a large audience in the opening weekend, it may be pushed to ancillary markets (such as DVD/Video). The time of the year (e.g., holiday periods) and key dates in the film calendar (e.g., awards ceremonies, festivals) are also considered. Such factors can be used to the film's advantage, as in the case of *Once Were Warriors*, which was released within a week of its screening at Cannes. The publicists involved in marketing the film attended Cannes, and hyped *Once Were Warriors* to the festival crowd, which in turn generated interest back in New Zealand. As explained by Rachel Stace, a publicist for *Once Were Warriors*, 'I would send back press releases [from Cannes] ... saying things like 'tickets are selling fast' ... it was great because it was just in the news here [New Zealand] all the time, everyone rushing to go and see it, plus the momentum just kept going because I was feeding all this stuff back'.[5]

Scarfies also took advantage of Cannes, and was strategically released after its screening at the festival. As explained by co-scriptwriter Duncan Sarkies, 'Robert [Duncan's brother, the film's director] said to me that the reason we were going to Cannes was so that New Zealand people would like it ... There is that kind of "we like it to have done well over there first and then we can like it; we don't have to have a cultural cringe about it"'.[6] For *Scarfies*, the release date of 5 August 1999 was also selected for the lack of film competition. The only other film to release in New Zealand on that date was Stanley Kubrick's *Eyes Wide Shut* (1999). *Scarfies* had five weeks clear playing time before a number of Hollywood blockbusters entered the market in anticipation for the September school holidays. Six weeks after

7. Publicity card in support of the marketing of *Once Were Warriors* at the Cannes Film Festival. Courtesy of the New Zealand Film Commission.

the initial release date, Essential Films, *Scarfies'* distributor, gave a further marketing push, to take advantage of the building word-of-mouth.

Along with the release date, film distributors also need to decide on the pattern of release. The release pattern involves determining the number of film prints and the locations at which they will play. In general, one of two strategies is usually employed. Either a film is released widely (known in the industry as a 'splash') to attract high audience numbers quickly, or, as is the case for many New Zealand films, a platform release strategy is used. Platform release is where a limited number of prints are shown over a period of time, and a film aims to build on word-of-mouth as a way of sustaining box-office takings. *Scarfies* employed a platform release, first showing in the main urban centres and, one month later, moving to smaller theatres throughout the country. The film's premiere was held in Dunedin on 10 July 1999, as part of the overall marketing strategy of focusing on the local scarfies culture.[7] From here, the platform release allowed word-of-mouth to develop and kept the film in theatres for more than six months. *Scarfies* eventually grossed NZ\$1,250,669 at the New Zealand box-office.[8]

The importance of word-of-mouth alluded to here is a crucial factor in the marketing strategies for New Zealand films. The experiences of those in the industry suggest that New Zealand audiences often look to others when deciding on which film to see. This audience behavioural characteristic was consciously played on in the advertising and publicity campaign behind *Once Were Warriors*, as will be discussed below.

Advertising Campaigns

The essential ingredients for an effective film advertising campaign include test screenings, film posters, trailers and press advertising (via TV, radio, websites and print media). Test screenings are an area that cause particular unease. What right do test audiences have in determining the storyline of a film? Filmmakers hold up examples such as *Fatal Attraction* (1987), in which the ending of the film was significantly altered following the test screenings, as evidence of the potential to jeopardise artistic and narrative integrity. But such cases are few, and in New Zealand now, most films are subject to test screening research prior to release.

The purpose of test screenings is not only to evaluate the narrative impact of the film, but also to confirm target audiences, test trailers and advertising material, and identify what is likely to succeed. In relation to *Scarfies*, the test screenings impacted on the overall market positioning of the film.[9] Originally, advertising flyers promoted an image of happy, student life with the five 'scarfies', or students, standing outside their run-down home. This influenced the test audience's expectations and resulted in negative feedback from people who anticipated a 'brighter' film. The findings led to a change in focus towards the edgier, thriller element of *Scarfies*.

At the heart of advertising decisions is the target market of the film. For example, the target markets of *What Becomes of the Broken Hearted?* (1999) were two-tiered. First, this sequel to *Once Were Warriors* was targeted at young males, interested in the film's action elements (such as the gang scenes). The second, and significantly different target market, was women who had seen the original movie, and were particularly moved by its storyline, but felt uneasy about viewing such violent scenes again. There were two television advertisements cut for *What Becomes of the Broken Hearted?* The first, targeted at young males included footage from the gang scenes, with fast-paced music and a voiceover which spoke of action and excitement. The second trailer, with a background of soft violin music, focused on the redemption of the previously violent Jake Heke (Temuera Morrison) and on scenes surrounding his regret for his violent actions.

The impact of the target audience on marketing decisions is also seen in the placement of advertising. Posters and leaflets for *Scarfies* for example were displayed and left in record stores, universities, schools, bottle stores, cafés and on the set of *Shortland Street* (a popular primetime television soap in New Zealand)—all areas frequented by or visible to the primary target audience of students and 18–24 year olds. The backs of buses were also used in this advertising campaign, while a website provided an avenue for reviews, poster images and information regarding events (such as the premiere and road tour). Such advertising strategies are implemented to help build hype towards a film, prior to (and during) its release. Hype and interest are also generated through publicity and promotional tactics, such as merchandising, press screenings, and star interviews.

Publicity and Promotional Tactics

A particular feature of marketing a New Zealand film is the need to secure local media support. As explained by the marketing manager of Columbia TriStar NZ, distribution companies aim to cultivate a relationship with the media so that 'they have the will to help make the film a success'.[10] The media coverage of *Once Were Warriors* was an example of such a relationship. In the weeks building up to the movie's release, publicity stunts were organised as a way to foster media interest in the film. Guests invited to private screenings included members of the media and key personalities within New Zealand (such as cricketer Martin Crowe and broadcaster Paul Holmes). These 'opinion leaders' were drawn into the overall publicity campaign, as explained by Rachel Stace, '[the private screenings were designed] to get word-of-mouth going . . . we asked them [the "opinion leaders"] afterwards what they thought of it, and we could use their comments'.[11]

Stimulating word-of-mouth via the media was also part of the publicity campaign behind *Scarfies*. In this case, a 'star road tour' was organised in the weeks leading up to the film's release. The tour included key members of the cast and production crew, who 'dropped in' to local radio stations and newspapers in the main communities throughout New Zealand. The

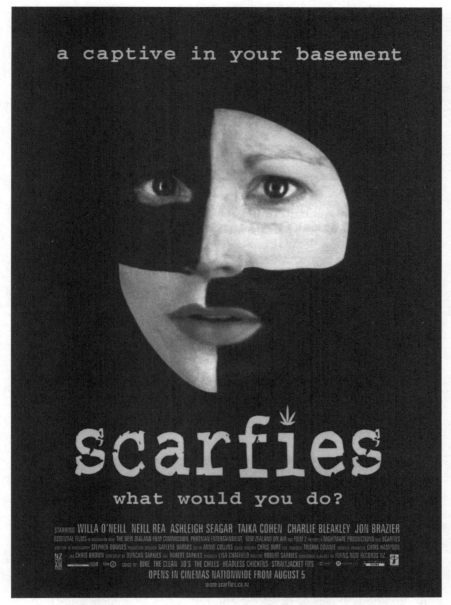

8. Promotional flyer for *Scarfies* for its New Zealand release. Courtesy of the Ian Conrich collection of New Zealand cinema and visual culture.

concentration of much of the local population into distinct urban areas worked in their favour, as each city, and a number of towns, from Dunedin to Auckland had the opportunity to meet the local stars.

In terms of promotional tactics, film marketeers look for opportunities to stretch the movie experience by offering tangible products such as caps, T-shirts and sweaters. Such merchandise is often part of competitions, held in conjunction with the media (e.g., give-aways via radio stations and the popular press). For *Scarfies* a particularly successful promotional tool was the soundtrack. This CD, featuring local artists under the Dunedin-based Flying Nun record label, was released on 8 July 1999 with a cover design featuring the same image as the film poster. Radio stations gave away the soundtrack CD as part of competitions.

Marketing New Zealand films

The above examples point to specific issues inherent to marketing a New Zealand film to New Zealand audiences. The size and nature of the industry impacts on the design of marketing campaigns. For example, marketing budgets for New Zealand films tend to be small relative to large overseas productions. With limited capital comes the need to develop clever strategies, which can be inexpensive. As such, publicity—which can be free—often constitutes a significant part of the overall marketing strategy. The 'star road tour' for example, organised as part of the marketing behind *Scarfies*, was inexpensive, yet effective. The term 'grassroots marketing' is often used to describe this process, with distribution companies needing to 'get back to basics', not spending extraordinary amounts on building hype towards the film, but finding other ways to arouse interest and stimulate word-of-mouth. The Internet is another inexpensive, yet effective, marketing medium. The website for *Scarfies* for example was launched one month prior to the film's release, with information that helped build hype towards the film. The site included details on the making of the movie, the city of Dunedin, definitions of the language used in the film, merchandise and the soundtrack. The website was continually updated during the film's theatrical release.

Internationally small film industries, such as New Zealand, find buyers primarily through film festivals and markets. A contingent from New Zealand attends the important markets such as Sundance (January), the Berlin Film Festival (February), the American Film Market (February/March), Cannes (May), and MIFED[12] (October/November). With films at various stages of development, the NZFC is dependent on these markets, not just for sales push, but also for creating interest among the press and public.

Once a film is bought by one of often several international distributors, that company takes primary responsibility for marketing the film to specified overseas territories. Materials used within the local market (New Zealand) can form the basis for overseas marketing campaigns; however, the translation process is not always successful. For example, the term 'scarfies' is New Zealand slang, and difficulties arose in finding an equivalent title in foreign languages. This caused a particular uproar in Poland. The title of the film changed to *Zapach Trawki, Smak Wolnosic* or *The Smell of Grass, the Taste of Freedom*, the grass in question being marijuana and the freedom what selling it brings. The Catholic Church in Poland complained about the association of marijuana and freedom. To add to the storm, the film posters depicted three sinister-looking people wearing Ku Klux Klan-type hoods, with the central figure brandishing a plastic envelope filled with green marijuana-like material. The Polish Society of Advertisers further condemned the marketing campaign, taking exception to what they saw as a deliberate and deplorable attempt to draw attention to the film.

In the same way that local distributors design marketing strategies with the New Zealand audience in mind, overseas distributors must also find the angle to suit their respective market. The campaign behind *Once Were Warriors* in Japan, for example, was based around Beth Heke (Rena Owen)—the leading female character—rather than her husband Jake. This shift in focus was to attract Japanese women, whom the local distributor felt would be more interested in viewing the film. In 2002, Essential Films launched *Rain* in the Australian market, and again needed to consider local audience characteristics. In general, Australian audiences do not value New Zealand films, so the distribution company attempted to market the film as an international production—through such techniques as a high profile gala-type launch—rather than highlighting its New Zealand details.

Part of the challenge in distributing New Zealand films overseas is that international markets are largely unfamiliar with New Zealand— New Zealand humour, New Zealand characteristics and New Zealand storylines can appear distinctly foreign. The saturation of American culture, through all forms of the media, but in particular television and film, means audiences throughout the world understand America and its way of life much better than a small country supposedly on the edge of the world.

In sum, over the past two decades, the New Zealand film industry has increasingly accepted and developed marketing practices. For many, it may feel like the wave of marketing thinking has swept over the industry. But, rather than drowning in the complexities of marketing, the New Zealand film industry seems to have learnt to surf the wave, with increasingly sophisticated marketing strategies, that have been successful in promoting productions. Marketing though does not provide all the answers. The success of a film still hinges primarily on the film itself. If New Zealand attempted to wholly follow Hollywood's marketing cues, to the point of shaping scripts based on market demand, then the essence of local creative vision would be lost. Rather than adopting Hollywood's marketing formula, and promoting New Zealand films to an audience based solely on stars, awards and genre, New Zealand has been brave enough to celebrate its own unique culture.

Notes

1. Heart of the Nation Strategic Working Group, *The Heart of the Nation: A Cultural Strategy for Aotearoa New Zealand*, prepared for the Prime Minister and Minster of Arts, Culture and Heritage (New Zealand, 2000).

2. Suzette Major, *Directing the Viewer: The Marketing Concept and the New Zealand Film Industry*, unpublished Masters thesis (University of Waikato, 1996).

3. See Michael Weise, *Film and Video Marketing* (Stoneham, Massachusetts: Michael Weise Productions, 1989); Major, *Directing the Viewer*.

4. John Durie, Annika Pham and Neil Watson, *Marketing and Selling Your Film Around the World* (Los Angeles: Silman-James Press, 2000), 85.

5. Rachel Stace, transcript for interview conducted 23 March 1996, 3.

6. Tania Burkhart, Kasey Butler and Kelly Dunseath, '*Scarfies*: A Case Study of Film Distribution and Promotion within New Zealand', unpublished report, prepared for Suzette Major, 18 October 1999, 8.

7. Scarfies is an ethos unique to New Zealand, and refers to the local University of Otago students wearing blue and yellow scarves.

8. New Zealand Film Commission *Annual Report*, for the year ended 30 June 2000.

9. *Scarfies* focused on the lives of five university students that move into a run-down flat. Unbeknown to the flatmates, the basement houses a thriving crop of marijuana, which the students sell and then enjoy a good life spending the proceeds. But the students face a series of dilemmas when the house owner, and drugs cultivator, is released from prison and returns to find his crop missing.

10. Christine Massey, public lecture, University of Waikato, 2001.

11. Stace, transcript for interview conducted 23 March 1996, 2.

12. MIFED is Milan's Mercato Internazionale del Film e del Documentario. In 2004 AFM switched to a November market, in direct competition with MIFED.

5

New Zealand Film Censorship

Chris Watson

Historically, New Zealand was often one of the last to receive new film titles. This enabled the country's censors to take into account international treatment—and predominantly the decisions of the British Board of Film Censors (BBFC)—regarding controversial films such as *Intolerance* (1916) and *All Quiet on the Western Front* (1930) or, later, the furore that greeted *Last Tango in Paris* (1973) and *Monty Python's the Life of Brian* (1979). However, this is not to say that New Zealand's history of film censorship and classification is without its unique and distinctive characteristics and decisions. A national office for a Film Censor in New Zealand was established in 1916, following the Cinematograph Film Censorship Act, in August 1916, and just three years after the establishment of the BBFC. The first Chief Film Censor was a Mr W. Jolliffe, who acted in office alone. But the office soon grew and can be seen to have had a significant effect on the local cinema industry.[1] This is most apparent when considering contemporary New Zealand cinema—the focus of this article—a period which has become marked by a series of debates as to what constitutes 'the public good', and by protracted legal considerations of a challenging new cinema of which the French film *Baise Moi* (2000) became a central case.

New Zealand's contemporary cinema is distinguished by the establishment of the New Zealand Film Commission (NZFC) in 1978, a government supported body founded to help advance the development of local film production. In the 30 years preceding the NZFC there were just two Chief Film Censors; as in the UK, such a senior post was often held for a long period of time. The first notable Chief Film Censor of the post-war period (and New Zealand's fourth since 1916) was Gordon Mirams, in office from 1949 until 1958. Mirams was a liberal[2] who like his counterpart at the BBFC, Arthur Watkins, argued for tolerance of 'art film' and passed many of the European classics that came before him including *Bitter Rice* (1948), *La Ronde* (1950) and *La Strada* (1954), whilst he took note of the popular concerns of the times and rejected titles destined for a mainstream or juvenile audience. Adolescents preferred representations that portrayed youngsters as rebels engaged in behaviour that often offended adults. Certain titles became the causes célèbres of the genre: *The Wild One* (1954); *Rebel Without a Cause* (1955) and *Rock Around the Clock* (1956). Mirams banned *The Wild One* and, after appeal, reluctantly gave *Rebel without a Cause* an R16 certificate (restricted to 16 years and over), which it still carries to this day.

Doug McIntosh was the Chief Censor who followed Mirams. A stricter censor, he kept the job from 1960 until his death in 1976. His most infamous decision related to the film *Ulysses* (1967). Concerned by the single use of the word 'fuck' and Molly Bloom's description of fellatio in her extended soliloquy, but acknowledging that the scenario was based on a famous novel, McIntosh decided to pass the film uncut but decreed that it should be screened to audiences segregated by gender. In major cities, this meant that one cinema would admit a male audience and another would be available for females. In smaller towns separation was achieved by seating the women upstairs and the men below or, as at the University of Otago, by dividing the audience by means of a rope down the centre of the auditorium. McIntosh made his decision under the provisions of a restrictive Cinematographic Films Act which had been passed in 1961 as part of the reaction to the moral panic engendered by the 1954 Mazengarb Report on morality and youth.[3] The key clause of 1961 Act stated:

> the approval of the censor shall not be given with respect to any film or to any part of a film which, in his opinion, depicts any matter that is contrary to public order of decency, or the exhibition of which would, for any other reason be undesirable in the public interest.[4]

Within this instruction the key words are 'in his [sic] opinion'. Thus, enormous power was given to the censor to make subjective decisions. These were driven by the fear that the new and frank portrayal of matters sexual, of drug taking and profane language, and graphic violence, which became apparent in the cinema of the 1960s, would bring about some form of imitative behaviour on the part of impressionable adults as well as by unruly young people.

McIntosh frequently chose to cut films rather than issue them with specified restrictions which he had power to do under the Act and which had been favoured by his more liberal predecessor, Mirams. However, refusing even a restricted certificate to films like *Last Tango in Paris* (1972) finally resulted in a public reaction against the practice of censorship.[5] The protests led to the introduction of the Cinematograph Films Act 1976. The Act decreed that a film was to be cut or banned only if it was 'injurious to the public good' which effectively removed the discretionary clause allowing the censor to rule on the basis of 'his opinion'. It thus became possible for McIntosh's deputy, Bernie Tunnicliffe, who subsequently took over as Chief Film Censor in 1977, to release *Last Tango in Paris* in August of that year, with an R20 certificate (restricted to those aged twenty and above).

Tunnicliffe also felt able to pass for exhibition a surrealist feature film made by David Blyth, a 21-year-old New Zealand director. Blyth's debut feature, *Angel Mine* (1978), was a 'maze of popular culture ... whose title referred to a drug'.[6] It included full-frontal male nudity and dream-like parodies of television commercials and suburban life in newly

'New Zealand's own erotic fantasy,
that's far too close to home!'
ANGEL MINE
a film by David Blyth
Starring:
Derek Ward – Jennifer Redford
Myra De Groot, Mike Wilson

9. Top page of New Zealand
pressbook for *Angel Mine*, with
censor's warning. Courtesy of the
New Zealand Film Commission.

developed Pakuranga, Auckland. The recently formed New Zealand Film
Commission had supported this film despite having been shown some
sequences indicating its likely content. Particularly noteworthy was the
opening, which showed a lavatory bowl, set on a deserted beach, on which
was seated a naked woman being slowly dressed, in reverse strip-tease, by
a sailor who had emerged from the sea. Censors have never found it as
easy to ban or cut New Zealand originated material as that from overseas,
and in this case a bemused Tunnicliffe gave *Angel Mine* an R18 certificate
with the rider 'Contains Punk Cult Material'. The Society for Promotion
of Community Standards (SCPS), under the chairmanship of Patricia
Bartlett, was outraged that public money from the Queen Elizabeth II
Arts Council should have been 'squandered' on such a project, and from
then on took a keen interest in the field of censorship. [7] She and the
Society made regular submissions whenever controversial material was
about to be considered.[8]

Organised objections to a more liberal interpretation of the 1976 Act
did not restrain the increasing tolerance expressed by public opinion.
Allan Highet, who was the National Party's Minister of Internal Affairs
from 1976 until 1983, commissioned a public opinion poll on censorship
which demonstrated that the general populace was actually very liberal in
its approach preferring classification to censorship.[9] As a result, Highet
promoted a new Bill that repeated the 1976 demand that material be cut

or banned only if it was 'likely to be injurious to the public good' and, in the new Films Act 1983 which he guided through Parliament, there was a subtle alteration to the first of the clauses that were designed to help him to decide this. In Section 13 (2), the new Films Act 1983 specified that 'in determining whether the exhibition of any film is likely to be injurious to the public good, the Chief Censor shall consider . . . the dominant effect of the film as a whole'.[10]

Arthur Everard the Chief Film Censor from 1984 until 1990, working under this new Act decided to rely on 'expert' advice regarding the effect or impact of a film before it would be cut or banned. With it proving extremely difficult to determine a film's effect he began to pass, for public viewing, films with explicit, hard-core sexual content. He did this on the basis that authorities such as Edward I. Donnerstein and Varda Burstyn had asserted that no harm would come from watching adult couples engaged in non-violent consensual sex.[11] Thus, in 1986, *Deep Throat* (1972), which had caused such controversy when it was first screened in America, was finally cleared for exhibition in New Zealand. Not that it was actually screened in a cinema. There were only two main cinema chains in the country and neither wished to screen hard-core pornographic films. Only Auckland's Classic cinema attempted to organise screenings.[12] In the end the city council, which owned the lease for the building, made even this impossible.

The situation was complicated by a new development. In the 1980s, video recorders became common. The growth in home entertainment systems led to the establishment of video libraries and the release of an extensive back-catalogue of movies. The requirements for a video censorship regime emerged a little later in New Zealand than in some other countries because, for a while, video players were subject to heavy taxation and could only be afforded by a minority. However, when tariffs were reduced and the ownership of video recorders spread there was a concern to regulate the content of pre-recorded tapes.[13] At first customs officers intercepted what they regarded as pornographic videos and pursued prosecutions through local courts. Unfortunately, the courts varied in their decisions and some rulings were challenged and lost on appeal. As a result, tapes could be passed in one jurisdiction but banned in another. For example, one of a series of video magazines containing relatively soft-core pornography entitled *Electric Blue* was seized by customs agents in Auckland and in Christchurch in 1984. The District Court ordered the Customs Department to release it in Auckland but upheld the seizure in Christchurch.

Importers began to send tapes to the film censor in order to obtain an advance opinion on whether a production was likely to be 'injurious to the public good'. With Everard of the opinion that the depiction of consensual sex had not been proven to be injurious, the way was clear for hard-core pornographic films to be imported, sold and openly offered for rental in New Zealand. By 1987, such tapes were to be seen on the shelves of video stores labelled with a fluorescent vermilion sticker: 'R18 EXPLICIT SEXUAL CONTENT MAY OFFEND'.

In reaction against this new found permissiveness a strong lobby group, known as Women Against Pornography, took particular exception to the videos being publicly available and worked with other interest groups to tighten controls. In particular, the feminist organisation found itself able to work alongside the SPCS, a conservative, Christian grouping. Together they lobbied for a second censorship office to be established to handle video recordings which, preferably, would be led by a woman. This happened, to a limited extent, when the Video Recordings Authority was established at the end of 1987. Pornographic tapes could still be passed for viewing but the decision was based around the term 'indecent' rather than 'injurious' and the decision makers were largely women under the leadership of ex-film censor Ainslie Witaszek. Thus a few of the more extreme acts of fetishism that Everard had passed, including bondage and urinophilia (urination in sex play), were generally forbidden by the video censors but were passed if the company submitted the tapes as being for use in specific cinemas. Individuals who then asked to rent such tapes were required to sign a declaration that they were planned for controlled public exhibition even though none were ever screened to the general public.

By the late 1980s, with three different censorship bodies in operation under three different acts of parliament, results were confusing. The three bodies were the Indecent Publications Tribunal which worked under the Indecent Publications Act 1963 and dealt with print publications, the Film Censor's Office, which was governed by the Films Act 1983, and the Video Recordings Authority, set up by the Video Recordings Act of 1987, which handled most of the video tapes destined for the home rental and sell-thru market. The film censor was the most liberal, followed by the video censor, but the Indecent Publications Tribunal was, by now, the most conservative. The irony of this was not lost on the public, for videotape images might be passed whilst banned in print form elsewhere. In particular, depictions of simulated group sex and images of actual sexual penetration were forbidden by the Indecent Publications Tribunal but appeared in the publicity slicks on videotape covers.

The coalition of feminists and fundamentalist Christians believed that Everard had 'opened the flood-gates to pornography' and planned to remove him as censor as soon as possible. The Society for the Promotion of Community Standards was not only angered by the passing of pornography, it also did not like the violent films belonging to the 'splatter' genre that were being certificated. Peter Jackson, later to direct the *Lord of the Rings* trilogy, was responsible for two of them.

Bad Taste (1988), Jackson's first feature film, combined slapstick and gore—and along with his later film *Braindead* (1992) has been defined as 'splatstick'. The censor gave *Bad Taste* an R16 certificate. The poster, which featured an alien with his middle finger raised in defiance, was censored in the UK by the London Underground which required the

10. Uncensored poster for the UK release of *Bad Taste*. Courtesy of the Ian Conrich collection of New Zealand cinema and visual culture.

removal of the offending digit. In between these two films Peter Jackson released *Meet the Feebles* (1990) which was a satirical interpretation of Jim Henson's *The Muppets*. This adult puppet movie featured characters such as Heidi the Hippo, a sexually promiscuous singer with a weight problem, and Trevor, a pot-smoking rat. Bartlett, who had tried to persuade the Indecent Publications Tribunal to ban sexually explicit comics which parodied characters favoured by children, was outraged that a movie could show Muppet characters in perverse situations and that the censors were prepared to give it an R16 rating.

An amendment to the 1983 Films Act limited the tenure of the censors to three years (with a possible renewal of no more than a second term of three years). It was argued that a censor would become desensitised over time whereupon he, or she, should be replaced. Ironically, it had never been thought that previous censors had become desensitised. Between 1916 and 1990, New Zealand had seven censors who had served for an average of ten years and seven months. However, the amendment was enough to ensure that Everard and his deputy, Anthony Hill, who had both been in office for six years were forced to stand down. In due course New Zealand's first female Chief Film Censor was appointed. Jane Wrightson held office from 1990 to 1993 and continued to work under the same Films Act as before but she no longer chose to rule on video tapes, all of which were sent to the female Video Censor. Thus, theatrically screened pornography was not a concern because few cinemas chose to exhibit any but its availability on video was still a continuing issue. It was from this situation that the Morris Report originated in 1987. Joanne Morris, a law lecturer, was invited by the Labour government to chair the Committee of Enquiry into Pornography. Working with Hilary Haines, from the Mental Health Foundation, and Jack Shallcrass, an Education Lecturer from Victoria University in Wellington, they produced a document that presented 202 recommendations for action. The main point was that a single body for censorship should be established to cover films, videos, print media and digital media such as computer games. Sweeping changes were recommended in the report but the eventual bill that went before parliament contained many new proposals that came from the perspective of the Minister of Justice and the Minister of Women's Affairs as well as that of Graeme Lee, the fundamentalist Christian Minister of Internal Affairs. By 1993 the resultant Films, Videos and Publications Act had been passed and the position of Chief Censor, covering all these areas, was advertised. An Australian, Kathryn Paterson, was appointed to the position and Lois Hutchinson, the previous Video Censor, was appointed to the post of Deputy Chief Censor of Film and Literature.

The act under which the office now operates still includes the test that should something be 'injurious to the public good' it should be prohibited but goes on to say that this can be a matter for the 'expert opinion' of the censor. In addition, for the first time, the Act lists specific behaviours which shall be deemed 'objectionable' and therefore proscribed. These include:

a) The exploitation of children or young persons, or both, for sexual purposes; or

b) The use of violence or coercion to compel any person to participate in, or submit to sexual conduct; or

c) Sexual conduct with or upon the body of a dead person; or

d) The use of urine or excrement in association with degrading or dehumanising conduct or sexual conduct; or

e) Bestiality; or,

f) Acts of torture or the infliction of extreme violence or extreme cruelty.[14]

Liberals saw this as a compromise of the 1983 Films Act in that it provided a 'shopping list' of behaviours which had to be banned. However, conservatives saw it as providing a much needed restraint on the ability of the censor to act according to his or her personal interpretation of what might be 'injurious'. The first signs of a problem were to be detected when magazines in which advertisements for videos or phone lines dealing with 'water sports' were listed. These fell under the automatic ban on 'the use of urine' which could result in the whole magazine being proscribed. Though at the same time the notorious art film *Salo: 120 Days of Sodom* (1975) was finally passed for exhibition, in a travelling film festival in 1997, despite containing examples of some of the prohibited acts. Paterson felt that the film did not 'support or condone' such behaviours and could, therefore, be passed.[15]

As in Britain, New Zealand does not have a written constitution. There is no equivalent of the American First Amendment which is used to defend free speech and which has proved a bulwark against forms of censorship. However, New Zealand does have a Bill of Rights, passed in 1990, which supports the right to information and which could be used to oppose censorship.

In America a perceived breach of constitutional rights can be challenged in the Supreme Court. New Zealand opened its own Supreme Court in mid 2004. Until this court was established a conflict with the Bill of Rights could be used as a defence at a lower court hearing and if challenged or ignored taken to the Appeal Court for a second hearing. However, the final recourse which had been to the Privy Council, in London, and will now be to the Supreme Court, in Wellington. Until 2004 the Privy Council acted as the equivalent of the American Supreme Court for those ex-dependencies and colonies which still wished to use that system.[16] When the Bill of Rights was promulgated it was the wish of Geoffrey Palmer, who was the instigator, that it should be the ultimate test against which all other laws would have to comply. However, the then Prime Minister, Wallace (Bill) Rowling, did not agree so its provisions are required to be taken into account by other Acts but they do not override them.[17] Thus, the film censor adds a justification along the following lines when declaring a publication (film, video, magazine etc) to be 'objectionable' and therefore banned:

> Considerations under the Films, Videos and Publications Classification Act 1993 have been weighed against the rights and freedoms outlined in s14 of the New Zealand Bill of Rights Act 1990 . . . in this instance the injury that the availability of the publication may cause to the public good is considered to outweigh the rights of the individual to have access to the material.[18]

Paterson was appointed Chief Censor in October 1993, and took up her post in April 1994. In interview in 1998, she thought it possible that if a decision to ban a film was taken through the court system as far as it could go, the final court throughout her term, the Privy Council, might decide that the Bill of Right's provision that 'information' should be available to all could negate the system of censorship. She doubted that any anti-censorship lobby could find a source of funding to undertake such a legally expensive course of action.[19] However, the pro-censorship lobby does have access to wealthy supporters and has undertaken a series of legal challenges that could eventually result in a definitive ruling as to whether or not the Bill of Rights has supremacy. In August 2001, Chief Censor Bill Hastings (who had replaced Patterson in 1999) and his classification office restricted the French film *Baise Moi* (with scenes of sexual violence) to 'study in a tertiary media or film studies course or as part of a film festival organised by an incorporated film society, and in both cases to persons aged 18 years and over'.[20] On the basis of this ruling an annual alternative film festival known as 'Beck's Incredible Film Festival' programmed the movie as a centrepiece for its 2002 screenings. The SPCS objected to this and asked that the film be sent to the Board of Review, which is the first stage in challenging the censor's rulings provided by the 1993 Films, Videos and Publications Classification Act. To its surprise the Board of Review judged that the Chief Censor had been too hard on the film and awarded it a less restrictive R18 certificate which meant that it could be shown to anyone over eighteen, and would also be available on video on the same basis. But the SPCS then took the case to the High Court and, on 11 April 2002, Justice Hammond granted an injunction forbidding the screening of *Baise Moi*, ruling that an 'arguable case' existed that the Board of Review had committed an error of law in allowing this film to be shown to just anyone over eighteen.[21] This injunction forced the cancellation of the *Baise Moi* screenings set for the Incredible Film Festival, resulting in a considerable loss for the organisers.[22]

The pro-censorship lobbyists did not have things all their own way. Two months later the New Zealand Council for Civil Liberties was given permission to intervene in the case because of the Bill of Rights' freedom of expression issues that it raised. Anthony Shaw submitted that: 'freedom of expression extended to information and ideas that offended, shocked or disturbed. Without broadmindedness and tolerance there was no democratic society'. Eventually, Justice Hammond ordered that the film be referred back to the Review Board for its classification to be reconsidered. The judge said that for many people censorship of free expression was in itself an evil, but that New Zealand's laws provided for it. He rejected the SPCS's arguments that the Board of Review had simply 'got it wrong', but agreed that it had raised an important legal question in respect of the film's classification for other mediums, such as video and television:

> Its position is that the board did not appreciate it was opening the lid of Pandora's box somewhat, by a simplistic, across the board, R18 classification . . . It follows from what I have said that the board did err, in law, in this instance in failing to have regard to the impact of the various formats in which this film might be presented.[23]

The suggestion that the censors should differentiate between media is a departure from the 1993 Films, Videos and Publications Classification Act's effort to be all encompassing in an attempt to remove the anomalies that had built up under three separate bodies. However, the censor does have the right to add a restrictive rider to the age classification and had done so in the case of *Baise Moi*. It was the Board of Review that removed the restriction to allow a blanket approval for its dissemination to all those over 18 without restricting its distribution solely to the cinema.[24]

In early September 2002 the Film and Literature Board of Review met again to reconsider the R18 classification given to *Baise Moi*. It is now classified R18 on film, which means it is available for general cinematic release. On video and DVD however, it is restricted to theatrical exhibition or exhibition as part of a tertiary media or film studies course, and in all cases to persons who have attained the age of 18 years. This means it will not be available for sale or hire in video shops.[25]

The SPCS, taking this decision as a precedent asked, without success, the Film and Literature Board of Review to reconsider Chief Censor Bill Hastings' R18 classification for *Kill Bill* (2003), in an attempt to obtain further restrictions placed on the DVD and video released in April 2004.[26] It is ironic, in view of the Society's abhorrence of the violence in *Kill Bill*, that it argued that the censor's ruling for the cinema screening and the release on DVD/video of Mel Gibson's *The Passion of the Christ* (2004) as a red sticker (a mandatory classification) 'Restricted to those 15 and over' was, in fact, too harsh.[27] Reviewers had universally commented on the extent and brutality of the violence suffered by Christ in this film.[28] David Lane, of the SPCS, asked the Board of Review to reduce the classification so that it could be seen by children as young as thirteen. The call to lower the rating was supported by other groups, normally conservative on matters of censorship, including the Catholic Communications Office and Vision Network NZ which represents 350 evangelical Christian churches and organisations.

It is possible that in the future such pressure groups might be in a position to raise the funds necessary to send a case to the new Supreme Court in Wellington, if, in their view, the Board of Review is too generous in the certification of a particular film. Should that happen a definitive and final ruling could be made that would affect the whole future of media censorship in New Zealand in the way that Kathryn Paterson anticipated in 1998.

Notes

1. For an extended discussion of New Zealand's film and video censorship and classification see Chris Watson and Roy Shuker, *In the Public Good? Censorship in New Zealand* (Palmerston North: Dunmore Press, 2000); and Chris Watson and Roy Shuker, 'New Zealand', *Censorship: A World Encyclopedia*, vol. 3, ed. Derek Jones (London and Chicago: Fitzroy Dearborn, 2001), 1704–11.
2. Mirams came to the job from a background as a writer, film critic and founder of the Wellington Film Society.
3. *The Report of the Special Committee on Moral Delinquency in Children and Adolescents* (known as the *Mazengarb Report* after its chairman Oswald Mazengarb) was distributed to every household in New Zealand in receipt of the family benefit (a government payment made to all parents).

4. *Cinematographic Films Act 1961* (Wellington: Department of Internal Affairs), 59, 1502.
5. Such reaction was aided by New Zealand's Federation of Film Societies which co-ordinated the campaign to get the Swedish film *Jag är nyfiken—en film i gult* (*I Am Curious: Yellow*, 1967) released, at least for its own members, many years after it had screened in Europe.
6. Roger Horrocks, 'Alternatives: Experimental Film Making in New Zealand', *Film In Aotearoa New Zealand*, ed. Jonathan Dennis and Jan Bieringa (Wellington: Victoria University Press, 1992), 69.
7. See Helen Martin and Sam Edwards, *New Zealand Film 1912–1996* (Auckland: Oxford University Press, 1997), 67.
8. Such submissions include one to the Indecent Publications Tribunal regarding an appeal by a bookshop proprietor specialising in comics, who had had a number of adult comics seized in 1990. Another submission was to the High Court in protest of the passing of two videos, *Inches* (1985) and *Pretty as You Feel* (1986), in 1987. The Society's cause was successful in the case of the comic ban but it failed to have the video rulings rescinded even though the judge sent them back to Arthur Everard, the Chief Film Censor for reconsideration.
9. Lewis Holden, *The General Public's Attitudes to Film Censorship in New Zealand*, Study Series no. 3 (Wellington: Research Unit, Department of Internal Affairs, June 1983).
10. *Films Act 1983* (Wellington: Department of Internal Affairs).
11. See, for instance, Edward I. Donnerstein, Daniel Linz, and Steven Penrod, *The Question of Pornography: Research Findings and Policy Implications* (New York: Free Press/Macmillan, 1987) and Varda Burstyn, 'Beyond Despair: Positive Strategies', *Women Against Censorship*, ed. Varda Burstyn (Vancouver: Douglas E. McIntyre, 1985).
12. The Classic, which was on Auckland's Queen Street, was run by an independent exhibitor. However, he was unable to access mainstream films, which were contracted first to the two exhibition chains, which owned all the other local picture houses. In desperation, he turned to erotic movies in order to keep his business afloat.
13. Allanah Ryan noted the strange nature of the alliance between feminists for whom a key issue was 'the woman's right to choose' and the fundamentalist Christians who were generally totally opposed to abortion and would have preferred women to stay in the home. On the matter of censorship the two groups found common agreement—that it 'demeaned womankind' and that 'Everard should go'. 'Policing Pornography', *Broadsheet* (May 1988): 38–81.
14. *The Films, Videos and Publications Classification Act 1993* (Wellington: Department of Internal Affairs) 94, 10.
15. Kathryn Paterson, interview with author, August 1988, held at the Classification Office, Wellington.
16. The New Zealand Government decided to cut ties to the Privy Council and to set up its own Supreme Court in July 2004.
17. Lady Glen Rowling, widow of the ex Prime Minister, interview with author,

in Nelson, March 2002.

18. Decision #64, 28 May 1998 OFLC Ref: 9601553.

19. Kathryn Paterson, interview with author, August 1988.

20. The Classification Office had consulted Rape Crisis, Women's Refuge, Stop (a group that deals with male sex offenders), and a university lecturer, Harriet Margolis, before making this decision. Margolis, of Victoria University in Wellington, stated that 'I think the film is structured such that, read in its entirety, *Baise Moi* is a serious piece of social critique'. (Office of Film and Literature Classification, *Notice of Decision*, 20 August 2001, 14).

21. This was not the only injunction granted. The SPCS also asked for and got *Visitor Q* (2001) and *Bully* (2001) pulled from the Incredible Film Festival and referred back to the Film and Literature Board of Review for reconsideration. They were not successful with two similar attempts to stop the Cannes award winning *La Pianiste* (*The Piano Teacher*, 2001) and *Y tu mamá también* (2001) being shown at the prestigious New Zealand International Film Festival.

22. See Gordon Campbell, 'Cut it Out: The Legal ping-pong regarding screenings of French film *Baise-Moi*', *Listener*, 25 May 2002, 26.

23. *The Dominion Post*, 24 July 2002, A13.

24. The 1993 Act does not cover broadcasting. However, broadcasters are expected to respect the classification given to films for the cinema. The matter is somewhat complex and not fully worked through. The Classification Office's website gives details of its interpretation as at September 2002 <www.censorship.govt.nz/news05.html>.

25. For details of this ruling go to <www.censorship.govt.nz/news05.html> and enter 'Baise Moi' as the search term.

26. *The Dominion Post*, 24 January 2004, A7.

27. In New Zealand, films released with the red mandatory sticker cannot be shown in any circumstances to an individual below the specified age, even if a parent or guardian is present or the film is viewed privately. As the Censor's website advises: 'Few people realise that this law [the Film, Videos, and Publications Classification Act, 1993] also applies to parents and guardians who let children watch restricted videos and DVDs, and play restricted computer games, in their own homes. Parents who let their children watch restricted videos in their home commit an offence. The Act specifically says that it is no excuse that the parent, or cinema operator, or shop manager, did not know that it was a restricted publication. This makes sense because of the bright red labels affixed to publications that clearly state what the restriction is . . . For this reason, parents who show their children, or allow their children to watch, restricted videos and DVDs, or who allow their children to play restricted computer games, commit an offence, and do their children, and society, a disservice'. See <http://www.censorship.govt.nz/news17.html>.

28. For example, Raybon Kan wrote in the *Sunday Star Times* 'You think the *Rocky* films are violent? The exploding head in *Pulp Fiction? The Silence of the Lambs? Hannibal?* The cop having his ear cut off in *Reservoir Dogs?* Forget about it. They are the pastel drawings of Dr Seuss compared to *The Passion of the Christ*. 29 February 2004, A11.

6

'With a Strong Sense of Place':
The New Zealand Film Archive/Nga Kaitiaki O Nga Taonga Whitiahua

Sarah Davy and Diane Pivac

I don't think I had a vision for what I wanted so much as a vision of what I didn't want: to be still stuck in the 19th century. We could be new, more involved with our constituents and with a strong sense of place.[1] (Jonathan Dennis, Founding Director, New Zealand Film Archive [1997])

Founded in 1981, the New Zealand Film Archive/Nga Kaitiaki O Nga Taonga Whitiahua (NZFA) had a comparatively late start. In one sense, this timing was tragic, since it was too late to prevent the loss of many elements of New Zealand's cinematic heritage. Organisationally, though, as founding director Jonathan Dennis discovered, the youth of the archive was a strength.[2] It had the advantage of drawing on a wealth of support and experience from the world's film archiving community in Europe and America, established almost 50 years earlier.[3] This ensured the NZFA upheld the fundamental principles of film archiving, as developed though the International Federation of Film Archives (FIAF): balancing the preservation and access requirements of its collection to ensure its survival. In other respects, the Archive was free to make its own way. Dennis's experience of large, formal northern hemisphere film archives fostered a conviction that simply replicating their often monolithic, passive, collection-centric ethos was not an option. A new, more energetic, creative, people-oriented perspective was required in order for the film archive to become personally relevant to the people of New Zealand.[4]

The ambition of the film archive to become an actively integral part of the cultural landscape and lives of the community it serves is an objective which has only relatively recently begun to challenge the heritage sector at large as museums, archives and galleries world-wide grapple with the practical application of the concept of social inclusion and responsibility. This can be described as the notion of the way collections can be developed and utiliszed through partnership with stakeholders 'to represent diversity and envision inclusion' potentially benefiting and empowering individuals, communities and wider society.[5] Key to this process is a shift from the conventional mode of communication employed by heritage organisations: from a single voice of authority delivering a monologue

11. The early days of the NZFA: Jonathan Davis, founding director, in the Archive's cramped offices at Courtenay Place, Wellington, 1981–82. Courtesy of NZFA.

into active listeners in conversation with their constituencies, in what Constance Perin has termed 'the communicative circle'.[6]

In this light, this article explores the unique organisational character of the NZFA and its relationships with stakeholders (including depositors, Iwi [tribes], filmmakers, audiences and fellow organisations). Its independent status and progressive access strategies will be examined, along with the proactive way it works to meet its responsibilities to the films in its care (reflected in the Archive's adoption of the principles of the Treaty of Waitangi/Te Tiriti O Waitangi in its Constitution and operations, and the Maori component of its title—Nga Kaitiaki O Nga Taonga Whitiahua: the guardians of treasured images of light).

The groundwork for the NZFA was laid from the late 1950s and into the 1960s through the work of Walter Harris, Supervisor of the National Film Library (NFL), and his successor, Ray Hayes. Film archival activity was first carried out during this period, thanks to their efforts in locating, researching, identifying and copying New Zealand film material. This embryonic work did not, however, have the institutional support to be sustained. After a considerable hiatus, a renewed push to formally establish a New Zealand Film Archive occurred in the late 1970s, with the formation of a group drawn from representatives of the National Film Unit (NFU), National Archives, the Federation of Film Societies (FFS) and TVNZ. Impetus was provided by the revival of the New Zealand film industry, Australia's Edmonson Report and the establishment of the New Zealand Film Commission (NZFC) in 1978.[7] As Dennis noted:

With the quickening and revitalisation of film-making in the 1970s came the possibility (though pretty low on the list) of establishing a film archive. Not a new idea, and not my idea—one that had more or less lain dormant for a decade or two. But an archive for whom and of what, no one quite knew.[8]

From 1978 Dennis, with his colleague Clive Sowry, began examining and organising the NFL's nitrate holdings, part of which would form the initial core of the NZFA's film collection. The work exposed the excitement and tragedy of identifying the nation's lost cinematic heritage and generated a sense of urgency for the task ahead. 'Where is the Film Archive?' repeatedly read Dennis's impatient postcards home while on a subsequent study tour of major European and North American archives in 1979–80. After further consultative work by a group representing the NZFC, NFU, National Archives and the Education Department (representing the NFL), the NZFA was incorporated as an independent Charitable Trust on 9 March 1981. Three weeks later, Dennis was appointed Director.

[The Archive] had very little to distinguish it as particular to the South Pacific region, with two main cultural constituencies (the indigenous Maori, and the *Pakeha* or European) near the end of the twentieth century. But it did begin with great freedom: few had any real idea of what a film archive was actually supposed to be, assuming benevolently that it would largely mean someone discreetly pottering away in a vault somewhere. This allowed the Archive, for a few years at least, to discover, define and present its own mission, and for some unexpected possibilities to emerge.[9]

In any case, the NZFA's collections were unlike those of most other national film archives, with their primary emphasis on preserving feature films. The sporadic nature of New Zealand feature film production until the 1970s meant that the NZFA has more in common with the world's regional film archives, with a strong commitment to personal, local, small-gauge filmmaking. Dennis recognised that the NZFA could only function effectively as a 'national' institution if it actively operated at a regional level.[10] This was reflected in its unwavering commitment to a principle of accessibility. 'There is a real feeling, I think', he said in 1987, 'that the Film Archive of New Zealand is an institution without walls'.[11] Despite limitations of space and resources, outreach screenings were prioritised. Distance and geographical isolation were no barrier. Even before the Archive formally had a film collection, Dennis and Sowry would travel with a slide show, and in 1983 the Travelling Film Show began, taking film programmes to a diverse range of venues and communities throughout New Zealand and the South Pacific.

The NZFA also differed from its counterparts in its constitutional establishment. Its status as an independent Charitable Trust is rare in the film archiving world. The trust is overseen by a Board of Trustees which now represents 'film, archival, Maori and community interests'.[12] Since 1999, Trustees have been elected by a Convocation, an electoral college of up to 30 people established to ensure appropriate representation on the Board (which must be 50 per cent Maori and 50 per cent Pakeha [European]). The NZFA's independent status ensured its work would not be hamstrung or undermined by political tension over agendas, policies or the allocation of resources that is so often a feature of archives established within umbrella institutions, such as libraries, museums, universities or film institutes. Initially, though, this lack of organisational protection made the Archive vulnerable.

However, like many passionate film archivists before him, Dennis was a persuasive and tireless publicist for the cause.[13] His mission was to convince New Zealanders that fragile moving image artefacts were integral to their cultural heritage and as valid and important an archival resource as books and documents.[14] With the support of David Fowler, Director of the NFU and the first chairman of the Archive Board of Trustees, he successfully led the fledgling Archive into a calculated long-running series of highly publicised media dramas to procure funding, emphasising its cinematic rescue mission in the face of poverty and neglect.[15]

The Archive's organisational growth and consolidation from these extremely tenuous beginnings is reflected in its occupation of an ever-expanding series of premises in central Wellington. For the first sixteen months, with a staff of one full-time and two part-time workers, it shared tiny offices with the FFS and the Film Festival in Courtenay Place.[16] In 1982, the Archive moved to the top floor of a building in Wakefield Street. Twenty times larger, it opened with a library and a Cinema Museum, enabling a regular exhibition programme. The first of these was an exhibition of New Zealand-born film artist Len Lye's filmmaking ephemera. Forced out to make way for hotel redevelopment in 1985, the Archive relocated to makeshift premises above a car repair business in Tory Street (illuminated by Lye's handwriting of 'the Film Archive' in turquoise neon). The NZFA did not own a permanent home until 1993, when archive staff working in seven different Wellington locations were brought together in the John Chambers building on the corner of Cable Street and Jervois Quay (along with the safety film collection).[17] For the first time, the Archive had a concrete sense of place, organisationally and physically. The building was acquired with assistance from the Bank of New Zealand (BNZ), and this relationship was consolidated through a long-term successful sponsorship arrangement with the Archive. In preparation for the move a major retrospective cataloguing, conservation and accessioning project entitled RECCAP was undertaken, which resulted in the Archive's entire collection being entered onto its own database, enabling full collection management and increasing access. From 1995 the building incorporated an exhibition space, The Film Centre. A NZFA office in Auckland opened in 1999. 2003 saw the Wellington Archive relocate to even larger premises, Te Anakura Whitiahua, in Taranaki Street. Home to the Archive's thirty-

12. The NZFA's neon sign, copied from the handwriting of artist and filmmaker, Len Lye. Courtesy of NZFA.

two Wellington staff and its collections, it incorporates a new kind of facility known as a mediaplex, comprising a selection of various types of on-screen access to the collections.[18]

The challenge for any film archive is to balance access requirements of the collection with those of its preservation. The Archive's first film repairer began work in 1981, and the development of its film preservation programme through the 1980s was assisted by Harold Brown, a pioneering UK expert on film identification and repair, who trained the staff in the painstaking and exacting methods he had developed for this work. Addressing the preservation and access needs of its collection was relatively straightforward, but for the NZFA in the mid 1980s there was a third key requirement for which there were no international authorities or precedents to guide or consult: the establishment of bicultural archival policies. Within New Zealand, the NZFA was not alone in facing this challenge. The 1986 Te Maori exhibition was a major catalyst for change in the way museums and archives had traditionally managed collections of taonga Maori (Maori cultural treasures).[19] Te Maori illuminated issues of cultural safety, public accountability and new perspectives on ownership and authority:

> Te Maori was a journey of rediscovery, where the powerful processes of contextualisation and traditions within museums were subverted. For many Maori it said *no turning back*. The message was clear. For museums to be legitimate in the eyes of the Maori people they had to break with Western traditions of so-called sound museological practice and make Maori's [sic] the players in the script which informs, educates and communicates, not only to the museum profession but to the world at large.[20]

Subsequently, in order to begin to redress the balance of power, a new wave of Maori archive and museum professionals were recruited at organisations such as the Museum of New Zealand (now Te Papa Tongarewa). It was a time of change and vulnerability for heritage institutions and particularly for some of their Pakeha staff as many questioned their own agenda, began to address the challenges presented by Maori protocol, language and perspectives on ownership and control, and were often made acutely aware of their shortcomings in relation to the cultural safety of collections.[21] As Dennis wrote:

> Whatever skills and qualifications I had in archiving, they had not necessarily prepared me well for dealing with living images. Initially this involved learning to regard these images not merely as ethnographic documents, but as living objects with their own *wairua* (spiritual energy) and *mana* (authority, prestige, power). Ultimately it meant deciding how to let go— firstly of other people's documented cultures.[22]

Meeting the needs of collections of taonga Maori meant that Pakeha like Dennis had to relinquish control so that more culturally appropriate structures and policies could be developed by, for and with Maori. From 1987 the Maori advisory body Te Manu Aute worked with the Archive to find an approach and develop an appropriate policy for archiving moving images.[23] This led to the establishment of a kaupapa (constitution) in 1988, based on the principles of partnership, protection and access expressed within the Treaty of Waitangi/Te Tiriti O Waitangi. Also at this time, the Archive appointed a Maori to its Board of Trustees, recruited its first Maori collection manager and, alongside many New Zealand cultural organisations at this time, in line with 1987 government policy making Maori an official language, adopted a Maori name: Nga Kaitiaki O Nga Taonga Whitiahua. The Archive had been supported by a kaumatua (elder), Mrs Witarina Harris since 1982.[24]

The means of working through an evolving bicultural process in a practical way initially arose out of the Archive's film preservation programme. Its first major preservation project was *He Pito Whakaatu A Te Maori*, four films of Maori life shot by James McDonald for the Dominion Museum (*Te Hui Aroha Ki Turanga/Gisborne Hui Aroha* [1919], *He Pito Whakaatu I Te Hui I Rotorua/Scenes at the Rotorua Hui* [1920], *He Pito Whakaatu I Te Noho A Te Maori I Te Awa O Whanganui/Scenes of Maori Life on the Whanganui River* [1921], and *He Pito Whakaatu I Te Noho A Te Maori I Te Tairawhiti/ Scenes of Maori Life on the East Coast* [1923]). The five-year preservation process of these films, completed in March 1986, provided the groundwork for a new type of consultative working process through access to the material. The films were given a social and cultural context by the relevant Iwi, who assisted with identification and the creation of bilingual intertitles.[25] They were then returned for screening for the first time in the areas where they had been filmed. As Merata Mita observes of this process:

These showings demonstrate a process of retrieving and restoring history, heritage, pride, consciousness and Maori identity . . . It is not uncommon for archival screenings to be complemented by an appreciative living soundtrack of laughter, exclamations of recognition, crying, calling out and greetings . . . Because what the audience sees are resurrections taking place, a past life lives again, wisdom is shared and something from the heart and spirit responds to that short but inspiring on-screen journey from darkness to light. This was acknowledged by the Archive and the remaining descendants as a way of returning images from a time past, back to the tribes and areas from which they were taken. No other film archive in the world has gone to such lengths to engage in dialogue or ensure that material with indigenous content is seen by those whose ancestors and lifestyle are in the subject matter.[26]

Mita worked with the Archive on a groundbreaking project *Mana Waka* (1990). This remarkable film was originally commissioned by Princess Te Puea Herangi in the 1930s as a record of the construction of three great waka taua (war canoes) on Turangawaewae marae (meeting place); a project commemorating the hundredth anniversary of the signing of the Treaty of Waitangi in 1940. Mita writes

What was surprising was the decision to film it, because film was still regarded with a great deal of suspicion and was not an accessible means of recording for the Maori . . . It was a decision made ahead of its time, especially given the tapu nature of canoe building and there were mixed feelings from many people over the public exposition on film of these last sacred rites.[27]

R.G.H. Manley duly filmed the event, but for financial and other reasons, the film was not completed at the time. Remarkably, the mute unedited original nitrate material survived, so that 50 years later the Archive was able to make a preservation copy. The challenge then arose as to how to make the material into an accessible form. To support the work in a way that would enable the resolution of differences between the diverse groups involved, a then unorthodox process of 'consult, cut and show' was developed where Mita and editor Annie Collins edited the film on the marae in consultation with Iwi representatives.[28] The film has been described by John O'Shea as 'the saga of the transition of forest giant to giant canoe, compiled . . . into a celebratory documentary feature, embellished with sound'.[29]

Central to the operation of the Film Archive is the concept of guardianship/kaitiaki of the collection. The Archive's role as kaitiaki extends over the whole collection, and the same promises of care are made to all. The NZFA has been established as a pataka tuturu, or storehouse, where the copyright of the material is maintained and the physical ownership of the original film artefact remains with the depositor. The Archive requires permission from the relevant depositors before releasing material, even though it is not a legal requirement. This process generates and maintains trust, goodwill, and an awareness of the work of the archive.

The Archive's guardianship of all the moving image material in its care not only embodies a safe-keeping role on a physical level, but also a metaphysical one. The work of conservation of the moving image as defined by Paolo Cherchi Usai, 'involves all the activities necessary to prevent or minimise the process of physical degradation of the archival artifact'.[30] At the NZFA, this is extended to encompass the artefact's social and spiritual context and value, with the associated acknowledgement that an interested individual or group may also have an active concern with its welfare and safe-keeping.[31] For example, as part of the protective principle of mana tuturu (Maori spiritual guardianship), an on-going relationship is maintained with whanau (family), hapu (sub-tribe) and Iwi (tribe) representatives who visit and are visited by the Archive to acknowledge, reinforce and maintain kaitiaki/guardianship of their Taonga Whitiahua (moving image treasures) held there.[32]

This process is consolidated through the the unique marae-based outreach screenings project Te Hokinga Mai O Nga Taonga Whitiahua (Te Hokinga Mai), established in partnership with National Services of Te Papa in 1996. Through the process of reacquainting Iwi Maori with the holdings of the archive that feature their people, events and geography, the NZFA has invited Iwi to identify people who can give cultural guidance about the care of the collection and appropriate clearances for the reuse of their taonga (treasured images). From this process of consultation and dialogue, the Archive's partnership with the Iwi has been formalised and acknowledged in a *Memorandum of Understanding*, which incorporates Iwi-specific supporting documents detailing 'the agreed methodology for access to taonga housed at the Film Archive'.[33] As well as ensuring the Archive can more confidently carry out its work, this process also serves as a basis for the formation of archival policies safeguarding the integrity of the collections.

The physical archival functions of acquisition, preservation and access of New Zealand's moving image heritage are informed and supplemented in this way through on-going dialogue with the people who have entrusted the Archive as an accessible place of cultural safety and source of present, past and future creativity:

> Fundamentally, engaging with the ideas around social inclusion requires us to recognise that the *cultural* is inextricably linked with the *social*, and more particularly, that collecting, documenting, conserving and interpreting are simply the means to an end. They are functions through which the [archive] . . . can pursue its goals—social goals which must centre around the benefit to individuals, communities and society.[34]

Recognising this, Frank Stark, the Archive's fourth Chief Executive (from 1993), devised an innovative three-part interlocking organisational model for the Archive, called 'Collect, Protect, Project', which simplified the arcane terminology of the traditional film archiving functions of acquisition (collect), preservation (protect) and access (project).[35] Stark has described it as 'a virtuous triangle, which consciously mimics the virtuous circle of environmental recycling and underpins the structure of the Archive and the collegial groups of staff within it'.[36] The way this re-definition of the work of a film archive provides a basis for communication between its different functions highlights the symbiotic relationship of the components of the film archival process, too often compartmentalised (both in theory and practice) into three separate and isolated units that lack an ongoing dialogue with each other. The new terminology also works to increase the external visibility, accessibility and understanding of the Archive's work and so formed the key concept behind the design and structure of the Archive's website.[37]

Within this new framework, Stark has sought to creatively and financially strengthen the Archive's position into the twenty-first century, developing and implementing a variety of funding, access and collection development strategies. Until 1992 it was solely dependent on Government grants, which have now been widened to include contractual relationships with a range of organisations in the corporate and public sectors. By 2002, as Stark notes, 'the Archive's annual budget had increased from $1.1 million to $2.4 million, and the proportion coming directly from Government had declined to less than 40%'.[38]

From 1996 a nationwide public network of public video access sites was gradually set up within museums and art galleries across the country, in Auckland, Whangarei, Christchurch, Dunedin, New Plymouth, Hamilton and Palmerston North, to enable free regional access to selected parts of the collection.[39] In 1997 the Archive was contracted by New Zealand on Air (NZOA) to be the national archive for television. The National Television Collection was established, and by 2003 contained more than 5,000 hours of television for free viewing and research.[40] New audiences were reached and exhibition strategies for moving images tested through the Archive's Film Centre which celebrated the familiar (such as Movie Monsters [1996], an exhibition of models from Peter Jackson's Weta Workshops) alongside more challenging exhibits.[41]

ReWorked (1999) and the SoundTracks series (from 2001) revised perceptions of the creative possibilities of archival footage[42] through Archive collaborations with guest artists and musicians respectively to reinterpret films from the collection.[43] PALeo Neo (1999) was conceived as an acquisition, exhibition and documentation project of New Zealand video art from the 1970s to the 1990s. Not only did it develop and define the Archive's video art collection (and its relationship with video artists), but in the process it also acted as a catalyst for the Archive's first engagement with video preservation. This reflected a wider cultural shift in emphasis from film to video: since 1999 the Film Archive has accessioned more videotapes than film elements into the collection.

The comprehensive Last Film Search was the result of the Archive's long-term partnership with the BNZ. Launched in 1992, its aim was to locate and preserve at-risk New Zealand film of social and historical importance. Initially aiming for films on vulnerable nitrate stock, its remit soon extended to safety and small-gauge films, reflecting the reality of New Zealand's film production history (as well as a growing awareness in the film archival community that the deterioration caused by vinegar syndrome and colour fading made safety stock as much, if not more, at risk).[44] Each of the thirteen regional searches began with a free public screening of treasures from the Archive's collection, with locally relevant films. Archive staff then set up in local BNZ branches to answer enquiries and assess film collections, also visiting those unable to come in. Within a year of each search a return screening was held to show the best of the films collected. The success of this seven year project was not only that it acquired over 7,000 new films for the Archive's collection, but that with its local and personal approach it also travelled deep into New Zealand's hinterland, reaching audiences hitherto unknown to the Archive, raising its profile and generating goodwill through extensive community networking, successful PR and a supportive sponsor. This work was consolidated in the subsequent (2000) project The Travelling Film Show, a national touring celebration of the films collected during the Last Film Search. Together, the two projects travelled thousands of miles and screened hundreds of New Zealand films to people in venues as diverse as tents, town halls and schools.

As Jane Paul and Diane Pivac note, the Last Film Search was nationally unprecedented in its scope and breadth, which 'meant the Film Archive had to adapt many new processes very quickly to keep up with acquisition, accessioning, preservation and depositor and project requirements'.[45] Procedural flexibility was key here in order to meet the needs of people offering material: for example, films could be lent to the Archive for duplication instead of being deposited, and there was also an option for video copies to be made for the depositor by the Archive. Through the subsequent 2001 Reeltime project ('our history on screen, on tape and online'), the Archive's partnership with the BNZ moved into increasing access to the Archive's collections on the internet through an enhanced website with an online catalogue, and in the development of the 2003 OnTape initiative. This is a free national video resource for secondary schools of film and video extracts linked with topic areas in the New Zealand curriculum. OnTape has successfully extended the accessibility of the Archive's education work through screenings for schools, begun in 1997, which were only previously available for those in the Wellington region.

The Archive has continued to develop initiatives in partnership with fellow heritage institutions, such as the National Library, Auckland Museum and Te Papa, curating screening programmes and working with museums to source and provide footage to support their exhibitions. With

Archives New Zealand, the primary repository under the Archives Act (1957), the NZFA works to preserve the collections of the NFU, the government's principal film producer from 1941–90. The NZFC also has a responsibility for film archiving under its founding 1978 Act of Parliament alongside its role to invest in the development, production, sale and promotion of New Zealand feature films. The NZFA and the NZFC, which shared premises in the Film Centre between 1993 and 2003, work closely. As well as providing funding for the Archive, the NZFC has deposited much of their collections of documentation and film elements with the Archive for preservation.

Because of its dedicated engagement with new media, the NZFA now holds one of the largest directly accessible collections in the film archiving world, and this is reflected within the mediaplex, its new screen-based access initiative. According to Stark, 'the word mediaplex was essentially invented to echo multiplex while invoking flexibility and multiplicity'. Audiences are offered a choice of routes into the collection through engagement on several levels: from a café 'departure lounge' with pre-programmed screens, through internet access to the Archive's website, reference library viewing, regular cinema and exhibition programming to fully assisted film research. This makes the NZFA one of the few film archives with a national remit able to offer such a diverse and thorough selection of access options. These access strategies have ensured continual growth in the numbers of New Zealanders who have directly experienced the work of the Archive, through schools, touring programmes, street screens, video access sites and the website. These have increased from virtually nil in 1993 to around 250,000 annually in 2003.[46]

For the NZFA, realising its ambitious founding objective to connect with New Zealanders in active, creative and meaningful ways continues to be an ongoing process. Its experience shows that tenacity coupled with genuine openness and commitment to change are among the qualities required to engage with the challenges of maintaining ongoing dialogue with a diverse range of stakeholders without compromising the long-term preservation of the collection. The process of active listening inherent within the 'communicative circle' allows the Archive to identify and develop the different ways in which the community contributes to, utilises and experiences the moving image material in its care. Many of the resulting innovative access strategies and productive partnerships extend nationally. In this way, as an 'archive without walls', it engages huge numbers of New Zealanders in its work of collecting, protecting and projecting their moving image heritage, fostering a strong personal, local and national sense of place in the process.

We would like to thank the following for their support and assistance in writing this article: Frank Stark, Lawrence Wharerau, Bronwyn Taylor, Virginia Callanan, Susan Abasa, Ken and Sue Davy, Fraser Hooper.

Notes

1. Jonathan Dennis, email to Sarah Davy, 20 September 1997.
2. See Ken Berryman, 'An Institution Without Walls: The NZ Film Archive', (interview with Jonathan Dennis), *Filmnews* 133 (1987): 33.
3. One of the world's first film archives, the UK's National Film Archive was formed in 1935, and was a founder member of FIAF, the International Federation of Film Archives, begun in 1938. Within FIAF, AMIA (the Association of Moving Image Archivists) and SEAPAVAA (South East Asia/Pacific Audio-Visual Archives Association, of which the NZFA is a founding member), the NZFA works with the film archiving community in professional development, repatriation and exchange programmes.
4. See Berryman, 'An Institution Without Walls', 35.
5. Jocelyn Dodd and Richard Sandell, 'Social Roles and Responsibilities', *Including Museums: Perspectives on Museums, Galleries and Social Inclusion*, ed. Jocelyn Dodd and Richard Sandell (Leicester: Research Centre for Museums and Galleries, University of Leicester, 2001), 35.
6. See Steven D. Lavine, 'Audience, Ownership, and Authority: Designing Relations between Museums and Communities', *Museums and Communities: The Politics of Public Culture*, ed. Ivan Karp, Christine Mullen Kreamer and Steven D. Lavine (Washington D.C.: Smithsonian Institute Press, 1992), 144–45; Duncan Cameron, 'Marble Floors are Cold for Small, Bare Feet', *Museum Management and Curatorship* 12 (1993): 169; Constance Perin, 'The Communicative Circle: Museums as Communities', *Museums and Communities: The Politics of Public Culture*, 182.
7. See Berryman, 'An Institution Without Walls', 31.
8. Jonathan Dennis, 'Restoring History', *Film History* 6, no. 1 (1994): 120.
9. Ibid.
10. Jonathan Dennis, 'Nga Kaitiaki/The Guardians', *Te Ao Marama: Il mondo della luce. Il cinema della Nuova Zelanda*, ed. Jonathan Dennis and Sergio Toffeti (Torino: Le Nuove Muse, 1989), 125.
11. Berryman, 'An Institution Without Walls', 34. Influenced by André Malraux's *Le Musée Imaginaire* (Paris: Skira, 1947), loosely translated as 'Museum Without Walls', a concept which, as off.design.com has observed, 'has since gained wide currency as a useful shorthand for the diffusion of works of art beyond the museum'.
12. 'Organisational Profile' page on the NZFA website. Available at <http://www.filmarchive.org.nz/about/organisation.html>. The first Board of Trustees was headed by David Fowler, with Ron Ritchie as treasurer and included John O'Shea and Doug Eckhoff. Fowler's contribution to the establishment and initial development of the NZFA was considerable. Head of the NFU, he served as chair until 1984, but remained on the Board until his death in 1989. John O'Shea, perhaps the most important filmmaker in New Zealand during the 1950s and 1960s, also made a major contribution in this respect, serving on the Board from its inception until his death in 2002: he was, as Frank Stark observes, 'for many years the only non-Governmental representative of the vestigal notion of a film industry in New Zealand' (interview with Sarah

Davy, 28 January 2004). There have been five chairs of the NZFA's Board: Fowler, Eckhoff, Patsy Reddy, Mike Nicolaidi and Waana Davis.

13. Paolo Cherchi Usai writes of such film archivists: 'All of them pursued their own particular trajectories, with passion and a sense of adventure, with unstinting opposition to institutional bureaucracy, involved in personal conflicts, great projects and burning defeats'. Paolo Cherchi Usai, *Silent Cinema: An introduction* (London: BFI, 2000), 77. Dennis stood down as Director of the Film Archive in 1990.

14. Diane Pivac, 'Twenty Years Ago', *Newsreel* 47 (July 2001): 3.

15. The organisational recognition of the importance of publicity, vital for the NZFA's survival in its initial stages and beyond, was consolidated from the mid 1990s in the post of Publicist. Unlike most film archives, the NZFA has a dedicated publicist who is responsible for promoting its activities and helping to maintain its public profile. Additionally, the Friends of the Film Archive was founded in December 1983 to support and promote the work of the Archive.

16. The NZFA has a productive long-standing relationship with the Film Festival (now the New Zealand Film Federation Trust), which, from 1983, has included screenings of NZFA's restorations, including *The Adventures of Algy* (1925), *He Pito Whakaatu A Te Maori* (1919–23) and *Mana Waka* (1990).

17. In common with many of the world's film archives, the Archive's inflammable nitrate film elements have always been stored in an ex-military facility, in this case old ammunition bunkers at Shelly Bay in Wellington. From 1981–93 the safety film was held at the National Film Unit complex in Lower Hutt, which was also the initial base for the Archive's film preservation work.

18. The NZFA's film and video collection has grown from around 15,000 titles in 1992 to over 90,000 in 2003, and the Archive now services a national audience of close to 150,000 users a year, up from fewer than 10,000 in the mid 1990s. The Archive also holds 10,000 stills. This may be usefully compared with the size of the holdings of one of the largest film archives, the UK's National Film and Television Archive: 485,000 films and videos and 7 million stills. See NZFA Media Release 1 July 2002, 'Archive Move Announced', BFI website <http//:www.bfi.org.uk>, and NZFA website <http://filmarchive.org.nz/viewing.html> (accessed 15 February 2005).

19. In 1984–85 the NZFA curated a programme of films to accompany the Te Maori exhibition in North America, which later dominated its Travelling Film Show programme during its tour of New Zealand in 1986–87.

20. Arapata Hakiwai, 'The Search for Legitimacy: Museums Aotearoa, New Zealand—A Maori Viewpoint', *Proceedings of the International Conference on Anthropology and the Museum*, ed. Tsong-Yuan Lin (Taipei: Taiwan Museum, 1995), 290–91.

21. For a detailed Pakeha perspective on these issues, see Carol O'Biso, *First Light: A Magical Journey* (New York: Paragon House, 1989).

22. Dennis, 'Restoring History': 125.

23. Te Manu Aute evolved into Nga Aho Whakari, which represents Maori interests in film, television and video production.

24. As Witarina Mitchell, Mrs Witarina Harris starred in the early New Zealand film *Under The Southern Cross* (1929), and her position as kaumatua was established when she and the film were 'rediscovered' in 1982. Of great personal support to Dennis, she travelled extensively for the Archive as kaitiaki (guardian), to warm, support and give context to archival screening programs of Maori films, before she retired in 2000.

25. For a fuller account of this process, see Jonathan Dennis 'Taha Maori / The Maori Dimension', *Te Ao Marama: Il mondo della luce. Il cinema della Nuova Zelanda*, 133–39.

26. Merata Mita 'The Soul and the Image', *Film in Aotearoa New Zealand*, ed. Jonathan Dennis and Jan Bieringa (Wellington: Victoria University Press, 1996), 50–51.

27. Ibid., 52.

28. For Mita's full account of this project, see 'The Soul and the Image', 52–53. See also Geraldene Peters, 'Lives of their Own: Films by Merata Mita', in *New Zealand Filmmakers*, ed. Ian Conrich and Stuart Murray (Detroit, Wayne State University Press, 2007).

29. John O'Shea, 'A Charmed Life', *Film in Aotearoa New Zealand*, 17.

30. Cherchi Usai, *Silent Cinema*, 66.

31. Simon Cane, 'Conservation and Inclusion', *Including Museums*, 89–91.

32. As the NZFA's Taonga Maori Deposit Agreement states: 'The Film Archive and the depositor . . . agree that in choosing to place the materials under the mana tuturu regime, they are acknowledging that spiritual rights over the destiny of the deposited materials are being given to the named kaitiaki and their descendants'. *Taonga Maori Deposit Agreement*, 2.

33. NZFA, *Discussion Paper for the Draft Memorandum of Understanding* (n.d), 1. See also *Te Hokinga Mai O Nga Taonga Whitiahua*, an explanatory paper from the NZFA (n.d.).

34. Dodd and Sandell, 'Means to an End', *Including Museums*, 2.

35. The three previous heads were Jonathan Dennis (1981–90), Kate Fortune (1990–91) and Cheryl Linge (1991–93).

36. Frank Stark, email to Davy, 14 February 2004.

37. See the website for Shift, web designers for the NZFA website. 'Case Studies: The New Zealand Film Archive' available at <http://www.shift.co.nz/cases/nzfa.html>.

38. Stark, email to Davy, 14 February 2004.

39. With the exception of Christchurch, where the site is within the Christchurch Arts Centre at Te Puna Toi (Performance Research Project).

40. Until 1997, TVNZ had held the monopoly on television archiving. No commercial use is made of the television material archived by the NZFA. In partnership with television companies, the Archive works with producers to acquire master videos (or copies of) for this collection, as well as recording programmes off air.

41. The Film Centre was established in order to reconnect the Archive with audiences, which had dwindled from the early 1990s. Critically, it served as a testing ground for models of exhibiting moving images, informing the subsequent development of the Mediaplex. Film Centre exhibitions began in 1994 with $elling New Zealand, a multi-media monitor show of advertising, initially held at Wellington's City Gallery before touring the country.

42. One of the first artists to creatively re-use archival footage was Len Lye, in such films as *Trade Tattoo* (1936). When Dennis wrote to Lye in 1980 seeking support for the new archive, he replied 'Hope it aids creativity'. See Dennis, 'Restoring History': 126.

43. In addition to the ongoing SoundTracks series, the Archive also works with musicians to accompany screenings of silent films, as it has done since 1983, with the appointment of Dorothy Buchanan as Composer-in-Residence. This role has now broadened to include a range of musicians and composers.

44. '[Initially] nitrate, with its connotations of instability, fragility and volatile nature, offered the most potent symbols for the urgency of preservation'. Jane Paul and Diane Pivac, 'Seven Years on the Road—The New Zealand Film Archive's Last Film Search, 1992–1999', *This Film Is Dangerous: A Celebration of Nitrate Film*, ed. Roger Smither and Catherine A. Surowiec (Brussels: FIAF, 2002), 403. This article contains a full description of the project.

45. Paul and Pivac, 'Seven Years on the Road', 407.

46. Information provided by Frank Stark, interview with Davy, 28 January 2004.

2
Aesthetics and Form

7

The Space Between:
SCREEN REPRESENTATIONS OF THE
NEW ZEALAND SMALL TOWN

Ian Conrich

Location and space are culturally and socially significant issues in New Zealand, a country of such defining geographical uniqueness. New Zealand's land in total square kilometers is slightly greater than the UK, yet the population is considerably smaller and, in comparison to the UK, one-fifteenth of the size.[1] The current population of New Zealand is just over 4 million, with more than a million living in the largest city, Auckland. The country's five major urban centers combined—Auckland, Wellington, Christchurch, Dunedin, and Hamilton—contain around half the country's population.[2] Moreover, 1996 statistics showed that 80 per cent of New Zealand's population was urbanised; an extremely high figure that exceeded those for many other developed countries such as Japan, the US, and France.[3] Added to this must be the acknowledgement that by the late 1990s, 75 per cent of the population lived on the North Island and that New Zealand's population is concentrated around coastal areas.[4]

In a mountainous land—less than a quarter is below 200m—where vast regions of untouched natural beauty thrive, the rural and the wild is a dominant feature that only cedes occasionally to areas of urban concentration.[5] But dotted around the New Zealand landscape are small-town (and hamlet) communities, often located on a highway which, as it passes through, becomes the main street. These communities are, I would argue, distinct hubs for New Zealand's cultural and social identity; national identity appears here as the formation of an extensive series of identities determined locally.

The essence or presence of such community centers is reflected in local creative and artistic expression, in the literature of novelists and short story writers Ronald Hugh Morrieson, Frank Sargeson, Dan Davin and Bill Pearson; and in the paintings of Doris Lusk, Juliet Peter, and Dick Frizzell.[6] Within New Zealand cinema, small-town communities form a backdrop to the action in the films *Wild Man* (1977), *Goodbye Pork Pie* (1980), *Bad Blood* (1981), *Smash Palace* (1981), *Trespasses* (1984) and *In My Father's Den* (2004), with a number of other productions locating the small town as the narrative focus: *Skin Deep* (1978), *The Scarecrow* (1982), *Pallet on the Floor* (1984), *Came a Hot Friday* (1985), *Ngati* (1987), *Jubilee* (2000), *Magik and Rose* (2000), *Her Majesty* (2002), *Whale Rider* (2002) and *50*

Ways of Saying Fabulous (2005).[7] Three of these films are adaptations of
Morrieson's bleak novels of violence and sexual deviance; to include *Ngati*,
New Zealand's first Maori fiction feature, *50 Ways of Saying Fabulous*, a
story of adolescence set in the summer of 1975, and *Her Majesty*, a family
film depicting the 1953 visit of Queen Elizabeth II to the imagined New
Zealand small town community of Middleton, would mean six of the films
are set in the past. Of the remaining four productions, three—*Skin Deep*,
Jubilee (based on the novel by Nepi Solomon), and *Magik and Rose*—are
social comedies and set in the present, and it is these on which I wish to
concentrate this study of representations of the small town in New Zealand
film. Here, this article will employ the studies of small-town America on
film, to enable an approach to such images in New Zealand. In these post-
settler societies the small town can be microcosmic. It is also the space
between, neither of the city or the wild; a rural community, united with
others by a few simple transportation routes, that is linked to both the
larger urban developments and the surrounding farmland and bush.

The New Zealand Small Town

William J. Schafer is correct to observe that there are, in New Zealand,
small towns 'shoved together' that make 'definable cities'.[8] Beyond the
urban sprawl, however, New Zealand's many small towns appear spaced
and spread across a range of landscapes. And here, despite the separation,
there is a noticeable uniformity to the New Zealand small town. Passing
through one community to another there is a degree of predictability, yet
also a reassurance based on *a priori* knowledge of what the next town will
probably contain: the dairy (or convenience store), former bank or town
hall (now likely to be converted into the local museum, information centre
or a restaurant), a petrol station, a cafe, the war memorial, and possibly
lodgings for travellers.[9]

In a study by Kenneth B. Cumberland and James S. Whitelaw, the
'similarity of appearance' of New Zealand small-towns is reflected in their
own design of a 'generalised replica', a hypothetical 'Kiwitown', which has
a population of 'perhaps 2,500'.[10] Cumberland and Whitelaw construct
their 'Kiwitown' in detail, complete with town plan, and observe that there
are two forms of this settlement: the country town, which functions as
'a small rural service centre', with local traders and businesses linked to
the surrounding farmers and hinterland community through customer
allegiance and habit; and the special settlement, which is connected to the
exploitation or harnessing of a specific local resource, and serves primarily
a workforce population housed within the town's perimeters.[11] Within the
landscape, the latter settlement appears irregularly, as it is determined by
the location of the natural source. In contrast, the former is often spaced at
steady intervals in a manner that reflects local service distribution.

Vehicular transportation is essential for traversing this landscape and
for travelling from one settlement to another. And as Schafer writes, on the
road in New Zealand a car can quickly enter and exit a town 'like a human

projectile from a circus cannon. You're in town and then—zoom!—you pass a war-memorial arch . . . and you're in open countryside'.[12] An alternative function of the roads is the extent to which they offer an immediate escape from a small town that can appear limited and mundane. As I argued in an article on the New Zealand road movie, it is also an escape

> from the restrictions and confines of repressive authority and the many tightly structured communities . . . The country has been very much bound by committees, local boards and, at times, rigid moral values . . . These communities enforce conformity, respect and politeness which can suffocate expressions of individualism.[13]

Yet, individual expression in New Zealand small towns has been growing noticeably since the early 1990s, with local identity being proudly asserted through distinctive festivals, sizeable 3D art, murals and painted signage. Creative displays include the giant kiwifruit slice at Te Puke (the 'Kiwifruit Capital of the World'); the nine foot tall fibreglass carrot at the market garden town of Ohakune; the life-size two-ton concrete Moa at Bealey; and the open air gallery that is the town of Katikati with its forty or so murals capturing local history, which can be toured with the support of a brochure and by following a painted trail of yellow pukeko footprints.[14] These are the promotional efforts of enterprising townsfolk, or local folk heroes who, as Claudia Bell and John Lyall write, have 'defied expectations of conventional behaviour' and have 'put their town on the map'.[15]

New Zealand's settlements are sites of active social identity and this is reflected in the many local histories which are sustained through New Zealanders' almost obsessive practice of recording and publishing community experiences; of constantly organising reunions; and of celebrating an important town anniversary. Schafer writes that in New Zealand's town communities '[t]he sense of an immediate cultural past is strong', and it is in this discussion that he observes the many visible Victorian and Edwardian colonial villas and cottages, and the buildings constructed in the Art Deco style of the early twentieth century.[16] These historical buildings—a small town's architectural heritage—mark local Pakeha (European) settlement. They serve as solid reminders of the social past, and with many key civic and community constructions—the town hall, post office and original colonial home—transformed into the local museum or information centre, they remain of central importance to the small town's regional identity.

A town's facilities mark its independence, yet simultaneously create an apparent homogeneity with neighbouring settlements. As a post-settler nation, there are further apparent similarities with the American small town, though clearly there are also many differences. The distinctive nature of the American small town has been captured on film, in a great number of Hollywood and independent productions. Crucially, there has been research on this subject, where there has been none on the New Zealand examples. Here, as with the studies of the American small-town movie, issues of community, nation and cultural identity can be discerned in the screen representations of the New Zealand small town.

The Small-Town Movie—The American Example

There are two book-length discussions of the American small-town movie: the study by Kenneth MacKinnon (published in 1984), and the study by Emanuel Levy (published in 1991).[17] Strangely, given the similarities in subject focus, Levy's book fails to reference MacKinnon beyond the bibliography. Both books list the relevant films in an appendix and the examples are vast, ranging from the classics of Hollywood cinema such as *Fury* (1936), *It's a Wonderful Life* (1946), *Peyton Place* (1957) and *To Kill a Mockingbird* (1962), to the blockbusters of the 1980s such as *Gremlins* (1984), *Back to the Future* (1985) and *The Witches of Eastwick* (1987). More recent examples would include *Groundhog Day* (1993), *Pleasantville* (1998) and *The Truman Show* (1998).

MacKinnon's book, the more valuable of the two studies, notes that the American small-town movie may appear homogenous, yet there are clear provincial variations, with films set in the American South likely to portray social decay and racial tensions, and films located on America's East Coast, such as New England, prone to the depiction of the middle class life of the European settler. He views a number of thematic and ideological issues within the films, which he discusses at length, and sees the productions antithetically and as articulating social struggles.[18] MacKinnon's 'principal antithesis' which occurs 'more or less overtly, in every small-town movie', is between an image of utopia or an ideal and how the actuality, one of possible disharmony or dystopia, is perceived.[19] He writes that the American small-town ideal is founded on a 'promise of community, of decency, morality, normality and sanity [and] of democratic values'.[20] Yet it is interesting to observe that in a consideration of filmic representations of dystopia, the small-town movie offers many examples of a collapsing community. And within these movies the primary exploration of tension is within the family which, as MacKinnon observes, is a microcosm of the town, and the town community itself a microcosm of the nation.

Community is addressed in the films through public gatherings such as in a courtroom, or a town hall, and at rallies, festivities and annual celebrations; spaces that often serve to accentuate social division as opposed to cohesion. The town as a site of ritual, of flags flown and community song, is a storehouse of nationalism. Religion can bind the community, and whilst the church is a space of hymn-singing and address, it is also one of refuge and confrontation. Travellers and outsiders disrupt the community, creating suspicion and distrust and they can act as a catalyst between one neighbour and another. The outsider, or out-of-towner, could be from the city and may therefore bring to the small town a factor of the unfamiliar, for the better or worse of the community. The small town is independent and seemingly removed from other settlements, with the road or railway providing the link with the unseen outside. It exists between the country (nature) and the city, with movement into either a passage for individual development or reflection. The small town can, however, be impaired by its space between the city and the country, with the settlement open to both the effects of economic decline and population migration, and of a natural disaster, such as a flood or tornado.

The community is often repressive, and suffocating, with individualism challenged or extinguished by conformism, conservatism and authority. This can lead to the stifling of needs, such as those of a sexual or companionship nature, which then through frustration may lead to degeneration or violence. Individuals who appear different and exhibit idiosyncratic behaviour (eccentricity, senility, reclusivity, idiocy or insanity) are removed, or withdraw, from within the community. Such dissimilarity, as with individualism and the arrival of an outsider, threatens the town's homogeneity and perceived stability. Town morality, truth and the law are commonly upheld by key local figures—the lawyer, doctor, minister or newspaper editor—but discrimination and prejudice remain prevalent within these fictional small towns and this can be based on ethnicity, gender, sexuality, class and religious beliefs. Tensions extend further into the family home, often the site of dysfunction, intense drama and conflict: of oppressive and bullying parents, alcoholism, incest, seclusion and absent kinsfolk.

A traumatic experience often becomes in the small town film the drama in a narrative of remembrance; events recalled by a narrator who returns to the past. Such memory may be episodic, and the narrative possibly structured by changing seasons and passing years. Alternatively, depiction of transition may be as a nostalgic view of a way of life. Many small-town America films share themes, style and ideologies, but they do not constitute, as MacKinnon believes, a genre. Small-town films have never really been marketed as such. Publicity for these films has utilised distinctive iconography—the picket fence, tree-lined street and town square—though these are to assist a promotion's application of a more dominant and familiar genre image—for example, related to melodrama, comedy, science-fiction, horror or romance, to which the small-town movie has variously belonged. The three New Zealand small-town films— *Skin Deep*, *Jubilee* and *Magik and Rose*—which will form the focus in the following section, are examples of satirical drama and social comedy.

Three Communities

Perhaps the New Zealand small town is not too distinct in appearance if it can be used as a location for filming the American small town. Peter Jackson's ghost-comedy *The Frighteners* (1996), is supposedly set in the American town of Fairwater, yet it was filmed in the New Zealand South Island community of Lyttleton. Similarly, the horror film *Strange Behaviour* (1982), set in an American small town of Illinois, was filmed in the Auckland suburbs of Remuera, Epsom and Avondale.[21] New Zealand and American small towns do share a degree of common colonial wooden-frame residential and commercial design. Yet many New Zealand settlements clearly lack the familiar iconography of the larger American small towns—the fire station, town square, neat tree-lined streets, the red brick library and the pillar-fronted homes of the wealthy.

At the time of the Great Depression, in the 1930s, the identity of many an American small town of the mid-west was enhanced with the erection of a three-dimensional roadside object or sculpture, which served as an attraction (and as a bold community statement) for the passing traveller.[22] The idea was adopted by New Zealand small towns in the 1980s, during the country's economic recession; a cultural phenomenon, it has been spreading rapidly through communities since the early 1990s. And as an expression of local identity it is reflected in the New Zealand small-town film.

In *Jubilee*, the fictional town of Waimatua displays a giant fibreglass kumara (a sweet potato) as its roadside object. An image that is shown twice within the film's opening sequence, where we are informed that Waimatua is 'The Sweet Potato Capital of the World'.[23] The town in fact has supposedly two claims to fame, the other being Max Seddon (played by Kevin Smith) who left and became the captain of the New Zealand All Blacks rugby team. This is unmistakably a 'Kiwi Town', exporting notable local produce and a key player for the nation's favourite sport. Filmed around the North-West Auckland regions of Helensville and Riverhead, the settlement bears a partial resemblance to the town regions of Dargaville-Ruawai, the kumara-growing centre of New Zealand on the West coast of Northland, where at Ruawai a giant fibreglass kumara adorns a rooftop.

'Welcome to HOKITIKA. WILD FOODS CAPITAL OF THE WORLD', proclaims the road sign at the start of *Magik and Rose*, a film set in the actual town of Hokitika on the South Island's West coast. Here, local welcome signage announces a small town's identity or character, and emphasises a community slogan. In this Hokitika tale, further elevation of the local is evident in the large mural of a coastal scene (boats in a harbour), and the filming of part of the story at the mid-March Hokitika Wildfoods Festival, which has been an annual event since it began in 1990. *Skin Deep*, made in 1978 and prior to the surge in production of town roadside displays of art and creativity, ironically has its own noticeable statement of community identity—a large phallic-like barometer, known as 'Big Red', which records the local successes in fund-raising. Sited at the head of the main street, this barometer for the fictional local town of Carlton (filmed in Raetihi, on the North Island) appears to be equally measuring the rising pressure for an isolated male population in crisis, and the tensions of a community that is inherently dysfunctional. It is unquestionably the most dysfunctional town of the three films being considered here, and will therefore form the focus for the first part of this discussion.

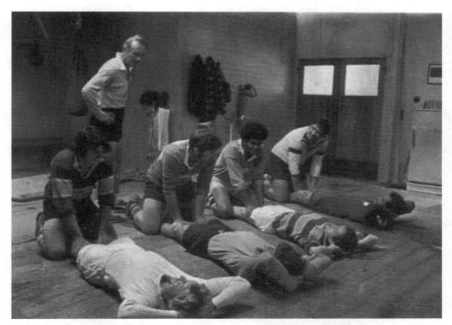

13. The homosocial space of the health club in *Skin Deep*, the epitome of small town dysfunction. Courtesy of the Ian Conrich collection of New Zealand cinema and visual culture.

Under the organisation of an all-male fund-raising committee of local businessmen (the 'Progressive Association'), a series of events are planned for *Skin Deep*'s town of Carlton—from the Axeman's Carnival (of competition log chopping) and professional boxing, to a sponsored run. The events illustrate, though, community division, with these examples of sport excluding female involvement. The entrants in the sponsored run are either men or boys, and the Axeman's Carnival and the boxing match appear more as celebrations of male prowess than as community strength. The men and women of Carlton are rarely seen together—the first thirty minutes of the film seem to almost suggest that there are no women in the town—and it is only at the Sunday church and the town hall dance near the film's end that the extent of local partnerships is suggested. Strikingly, the town accountant Phil Barrett (Grant Tilly), has a family, yet it is seen just once, briefly in a car as they drive home from church. Though even here, within the family car, there is division, with no interaction between the parents and the children and constant disagreement between Phil and his wife, Alice (Glenis Levestam).

Carlton is a town controlled by men and supportive of homosocial spaces. The city masseuse, Sandra Ray (Deryn Cooper), the film's central character who is hired to work at the newly created 'The Spa Health

Club and Sauna' (formerly 'Vic's Gym'), discovers that the local cafe's customers are solely men, who are drawn together at a back table and are content watching a televised professional wrestling match, a scheduled act of male bonding; the local bar is no better and is clearly a masculine space; whilst no woman ever visits the health club or sauna, a space where men (and local rugby players) gather and exercise in unison, performing synchronised sit-ups and press-ups, and practicing scrum formation. These homosocial gatherings are to be pitied by the viewer—the Axeman's Carnival, organised in the rain and with the support of a just-in-tune band, is watched by a woeful crowd; the men from the bar are often drunk; and the organised run is predominantly devoid of any cheering residents, the film avoids showing any competitors racing past the finishing line, and Vic Shaw (Alan Jervis), the owner of the local health club, completes the race suffering from a chest pain and just as everyone is going home. Association President Bob Warner (Ken Blackburn) badgers Sandra to include 'sextras', a topless massage and, eventually, masturbation in the services she offers, whilst Phil becomes obsessed with Sandra and wrecks the massage parlour in frustration. This is a town where despite its dominance masculinity is in crisis.

The town's target is to fund-raise NZ$20,000, money that is to be spent on a professional television advertising campaign to promote the area for business relocation and as a great place to live. *Skin Deep* reflects the economic recession in New Zealand in the late 1970s, where as Bob says 'in a small town like ours, in these troubled times, we've got to face up to the prospect of either growing or dying'. Like the Wildfoods Festival of Hokitika, and the giant fibreglass kumara in Waimatua, the aim of the small town of Carlton is to be 'put on the map', to be identified as a worthwhile destination. 'Goodbye Cities. Hello Carlton', is the town slogan proposed by the advertising executive, with the accompanying tune for the promotion extending an invitation to 'Come on out to Carlton'. Clearly, though, this is an unattractive settlement that cannot provide the promised community, and like the glossy posters of exotic destinations and beautiful bodies on Sandra's massage room wall, these myth-making media images disguise the truth. Worryingly, for such a dysfunctional place, the planned advertising campaign leads Bob to declare 'we're gonna make this little town of ours known up and down the whole damn country'.

Waimatua, in *Jubilee*, is also a dysfunctional community, one that is unable to organise the all-important reunion for its school's 75th anniversary. The town is far from being homogenous and is full of eccentrics—the chain smoker, the stammering butcher with his hand heavily bandaged from a work accident, and the lonely alcoholic, who declares 'people think I'm a crazy old bat'. The man who takes responsibility for organising the reunion is Billy Williams (Cliff Curtis), 'Silly Billy' as he is called by some, 'useless friggin' dork' by another, a Kiwi bloke who against the myth of the New Zealand male is incapable of doing things himself. For instance, Billy's wife Pauline (Theresa Healey) has to take a week off work so that their bedroom can finally be decorated; Billy's repeated token attempts at repairing the peeling bedroom wallpaper only lead to it falling down again.

Disillusioned with her domestic life (the home is 'a dump'), and a small town ('a one horse nowhere hick town') where nothing happens, Pauline talks enviously of 'all those people who went away and did something with their lives'. During the film's opening, where the image of the town is established, Billy as the film's narrator advises 'not a lot goes on in Waimatua', a statement which is reinforced at several points in the story by shots of the railway station. Here, no train is ever seen or heard, no passengers are observed waiting on the platform and the only activity on the tracks is a solitary dog crossing the lines. One shot of the railway station is followed by another of sheep grazing next to an empty rugby field. In these images, Waimatua appears as a static town where nobody seems to come or go and where, other than at the bar at the local hotel, there are few social or community gatherings. A handful of locals do assemble to make plans for the school reunion, but the meetings often descend into farce. It is not like Carlton, where the committee meetings are organised efficiently, though Carlton is a town where the decisions reached are undemocratic, and the many activities planned are for a collapsed community in which the womenfolk are marginalised.

Carlton's fund-raising is for 'the town's future', but as Phil, whose life 'is just a dead end', declares, 'what future?' His wife, Alice, later says 'everything's changed [in Carlton]. It used to be so good in this town . . . church used to mean something to people and we were so close'. The broad main street of Carlton seems to symbolise the distance between members of the town, whilst the piped easy-listening music, that plays outside the shops in an unsuccessful attempt to attract customers, shows the hollowness and mundanity of this particular community experience. Signs of small-town fatigue are shown in *Jubilee* by Billy's brother Potu (Hori Ahipene), who states that 'all of us [in Waimatua] are just holding on, hoping something might change, something good might happen'. Compared to Phil and Alice, who see town life as changed to a point of termination, there is however in what Potu says a belief that Waimatua will not be static forever. The jubilee festivities could be the tonic and Billy, as the Chair of the organising committee, is the local hero that the town needs—as Potu says 'someone to give them a reason to put a clean pair of undies on in the morning'. Billy as the hopeless hero is not quite the DIY Kiwi bloke, nor is he the enterprising New Zealander; he is, however, someone who 'has a go' at an opportunity. The massive tent, 'Big Bertha', that Billy rents for the jubilee may be inappropriate, but it serves as both a rallying flag for the local community to stop what they are doing and collectively help in erecting its vast frame, and as an umbrella under which the townsfolk can later celebrate their union.

Waimatua's 'Big Bertha' is a more fruitful and inspiring town erection than Carlton's home-made 'Big Red'. This phallic-shaped barometer which 'is pretty close to bursting point', with the fund-raising target being

14. The hopeless hero: Billy (Cliff Curtis) manages to inspire the town's anniversary celebrations in *Jubilee*. Courtesy of the Ian Conrich collection of New Zealand cinema and visual culture.

reached, stands at the head of the town's main street where it is dwarfed by the ever-present Mt Ruapehu (2797 metres high), New Zealand's multi-peaked active volcano which has erupted spectacularly on several occasions in the last hundred years. The tiny figures in the landscape, of the male competitors in the sponsored run, emphasise the insignificance of Carlton's townsfolk and their supposed community efforts, placed in the shadow of an awesome mountain.

If *Skin Deep* shows masculinity in crisis, then there is an argument that *Magik and Rose*, with its story of female infertility and unconventional sexual behaviour, is a film depicting women in crisis. True, the two central women, Magik (Alison Bruce) and Rose (Nicola Murphy), gain strength from their union and subsequent sharing of Magik's caravan, but this is as an escape or refuge from their deficiencies as mothers. Magik arrives in Hokitika searching for her daughter whom she gave up for adoption sixteen years before. When the daughter is found, though, Magik is rejected by the teenager, and it is not until the Wildfoods Festival at the film's end that the two enjoy a positive reunion. Rose, in contrast, has been struggling to conceive and is informed that she has a less than 1 per cent chance of bearing a child. Her desire for a baby, but an unwillingness to adopt, strains her marriage—to the local A.I. man (responsible for artificially inseminating cattle)—and she moves out of her unsatisfactory domestic space. The two childless women interestingly take refuge in a fake mystic's caravan, that can only deliver false futures. And whilst there

15. Relationships repaired as the eccentric townsfolk come together at the community's annual festival in *Magik and Rose*. Courtesy of the New Zealand Film Commission.

is strength in their union, ultimately, their domestic bliss is reliant on men—Rose returning to her husband, and Magik advertising for a sperm donor so she can have another child before she is too old.

As in *Jubilee*, the town of Hokitika in *Magik and Rose* may appear ordinary, even mundane, but it contains a series of eccentric characters—such as the farmer of snail eggs and Magik's chosen sperm donor, who is also a caller at the local barn dance, and the A.I. man, Rose's husband, who sings with her in a barbershop quartet, and dresses as a sheep for the Wildfoods Festival. The queue of men who reply to the enterprising advert for a sperm donor and who are then interviewed for their suitability illustrates, in montage, the range of peculiar men in just this one small town. But even against such oddity, the unconventional Magik cannot fail to be noticed. An ex-insurance salesperson from the South Island city of Christchurch, her appearance as a fortune-teller is certainly of another world. Magik feels that her appearance is so unconventional—her gaudy bathing-belle swimsuit, in particular—that she requests a clothes swap with the more formal Rose prior to her arranged meeting with her lost daughter.

Magik is the out-of-towner who is an alien maternal figure for her daughter; the catalyst who helps repair Rose's broken marriage; and the unsettled traveller who finds her own partner in the neighbouring resident of a caravan park on the town's edge. Sandra, in *Skin Deep*, is also from the city—'the wicked city'—and her independence immediately marks her as different from the town's housebound wives. The private vehicles in Carlton are practical pickup trucks and Land Rovers, commonly driven by the local men; Sandra, in contrast, drives her own unique sports car. Looking for the chance to settle in the country, Sandra arrives in town and locates herself in the box-room of a motel. She is perhaps the pioneer, the first of the many former city residents that the town wishes to attract in its drive for success and business generation. However, in this supposed land of new opportunity all she discovers is the town's inhospitality, malicious gossip and phone-call threats, hypocrisy, sexism and unhealthy imitation of city behaviour. She is the catalyst who brings to the surface the frustrated desires of the menfolk, and by the end of the film she is ejected from the dysfunctional community. In *Jubilee*, the sole visitor from the city is the Auckland-based rugby player, Max Seddon, returning to his home town for his school reunion. Max, dressed in black and wearing an expensive looking leather jacket, is as out of place within the community as the lifesize cardboard cut-outs of himself, promotional stands for his new book, which mechanically wave to everyone. The ex-boyfriend of Pauline, he presents to her the opportunity to escape the boredom of the small town and return with him to the big city. She decides to stay, though only after she has advised her daughter to follow her heart and leave with her young boyfriend for employment in the Hawkes Bay region. Of the three films, this young couple are the only small town residents who take the opportunity to leave for a new life elsewhere.

Conclusion

This is a study of just under a third of the key small-town New Zealand films identified at the start of the discussion. A consideration of the other films could lead to different conclusions, as almost all the other stories are located in the past; and Morrieson's particular style of small-town narrative drives three of the productions. In addition, *Ngati* and *Whale Rider* focus on Maori cultural values. As a body of social comedies addressing contemporary issues, *Skin Deep*, *Jubilee* and *Magik and Rose*, allow for a particular focus. However, if the study were to be extended, the local economy, cultural struggle and the stranger, or out-of-towner, would emerge as recurrent themes throughout most of the films.

In the three films chosen here for their contemporary settings, the small town community is repeatedly dysfunctional, or a site of personal disorder. There is general disillusionment with not only the small town way of life, but for the city dwellers Sandra, Max and Magik, there is also a desire to travel in a search for satisfaction. Certain characters return to the past, though beyond *Jubilee*'s simple narrative device of a school anniversary, none of the films establish, celebrate or engage with the immediate cultural heritage that Schafer had identified in New Zealand's small towns. Curiously, the settlements in these films exist in an historical vacuum. Like the American small-town film, the outside or neighbouring communities are unseen. *Skin Deep* does utilise the surrounding landscape to create a dramatic image; such moments, though, are few. And considering the rural expanse dwarfing the settlements in these films it is surprising that there have not been greater signifiers or images of the country than the odd farmer, and the hinterland drive to and from home.

Community identity is present in all three films where, most explicitly, the townsfolk gather for a local event. Carlton, in *Skin Deep*, organises the most events, ironically for a community that is divided. In contrast, in *Magik and Rose*, the Wildfoods Festival and the barn dances are very successful at uniting people. More spectacularly, *Jubilee*'s organised reunion brings a disconnected population together for a rare social occasion, where the party has space for a band, and a performance of the haka (a ritual Maori war dance). The evening culminates in a mass brawl, but this cannot hide the otherwise largely harmonious nature of the town. The local bikers are not as threatening as they appear and they are the key helpers in the erection of the tent. And though there are tensions in the marriage between Billy and Pauline—related to domestic and social expectations— their problems seem resolvable, particularly once Pauline has decided to stay in Waimatua and rejected the idea of escaping to Auckland with Max. Moreover, Pauline and Billy are a Pakeha–Maori marriage, and in this mixed community there is general harmony in the bi-racial relationships. Waimatua is a community without crime, vandalism or a youth problem. It is not like *Skin Deep*'s town of Carlton, where youths on bikes roam the main street at night, are blamed for the smashing of a shop window, and are possibly responsible for the destruction of a parade of potted shrubs (though a few local drunks are considered suspects). These misdemeanours are, however, less damaging to the town than the sexism, prejudice and hatred shown by the key figures in the community.

Thematically and ideologically, there are numerous points of similarity between the American and New Zealand small-town films. MacKinnon has argued that more or less every small-town movie contains an ideal/ actuality antithesis. This can be seen in a film such as *Skin Deep*, where the fund-raising should represent community achievement, shared ambition and togetherness, yet actually the community is impoverished, disillusioned and divided. And the planned commercial, to be paid for by the fund-raising, will present an ideal town that is far from the truth. In each of the three films there is however a recognition by the population of the reality of their situation where, contrary to the imaginary of the American small-town movie, life is far from connecting to an ideal. *Jubilee*'s town of Waimatua does briefly enjoy its festivities, yet the next day its milk factory and post office will still be closed, employment opportunities in the town low, and life will once again be mundane and uneventful.

Writing on *Skin Deep*, Nicholas Reid says that '[t]here are ample grounds for interpreting Carlton not just as the archetypal small town, but as a microcosm of New Zealand society'.[24] This is true, though when Reid says, '[*Skin Deep*'s] image of small towns is acerbic and unflattering' this raises the potential for reading the nation as dysfunctional.[25] In the film, at a meeting of the Progressive Association, a row of trophies and the New Zealand flag are placed just above the top table—the symbol of nation next to those of sporting achievement—and the anthem 'God Defend New Zealand' is sung by the men in attendance. If this is the image of a proud New Zealand then it is a narrow and exclusive representation of society. There is, however, a comparative scene in *Jubilee*, where a number of the townsfolk gather in the school classroom for the first meeting of the organising committee. To the side of the blackboard, there hangs a picture of the Queen—'Her Majesty Queen Elizabeth II. Queen of New Zealand'. On the opposite wall there are a number of posters celebrating rugby and the New Zealand All Blacks. And in the middle of this space of education, and surrounded by a small group of individuals—young and old, male and female, Pakeha and Maori—Billy, essentially the good citizen, has a go at a minor speech in which he speaks for 'Our Town'. As he does so, surrounded by symbols of Empire and nation, he offers a paradigmatic representation of the dynamics of the New Zealand small town.

This is a revised and updated version of an article, *The Space Between: The New Zealand Small Town and its Representation on Film*, which originally appeared in *Cultures of the Commonwealth* 9 (Spring 2003): 9–23.

Notes

1. The UK has a land area of 244,044 sq km; New Zealand has an area of 268,676 sq km. See *The International Geographic Encyclopedia and Atlas* (Berlin: Walter de Gruyter, 1979). The US Census Bureau estimates a 2005 population for the UK of 60,441,000, and for New Zealand a population of 4,035,000. <http://www.census.gov/ipc/idbsum/uksum.txt> and <http://www.census.gov/ipc/idbsum/nzsum.txt> (accessed 3 July 2005).
2. See Richard Le Heron and Eric Pawson, ed., *Changing Places: New Zealand in the Nineties*, (Auckland: Longman Paul, 1996), 284; and George Thomas Kurian, *Facts on File National Profiles: Australia and New Zealand* (New York: Facts on File, 1990), 124.
3. See Guy M. Robinson, Robert J. Loughran, Paul J. Tranter, *Australia and New Zealand: Economy, Society and Environment* (London: Arnold, 2000), 168.
4. Ibid., 167.
5. See Kurian, *Facts on File*, 124.
6. See, for instance, Ronald Hugh Morrieson's novels *Came a Hot Friday*, and *The Scarecrow*, Frank Sargeson's *Conversations with My Uncle*, and *A Man and His Wife*, Dan Davin's *Road From Home*, and Bill Pearson's *Coal Flat*; Doris Lusk's painting 'Overlooking Kaitawa, Waikaremoana', Juliet Peter's painting 'Geraldine', and Dick Frizzell's painting 'Town Square'.
7. Anthony McCarten's novel *Spinners*, about the uneventful small town of Opunake, and its visitation by space aliens, is currently being made into a film. There are also interesting made for television features, such as *The*

God Boy (1976), based on the novel by Ian Cross. For a discussion of this adaptation see Bill Lennox, *Film and Fiction: Studies of New Zealand fiction and film adaptations* (Auckland: Longman Paul, 1985), 96–112.

8. William J. Schafer, *Mapping the Godzone: A Primer on New Zealand Literature and Culture* (Honolulu: University of Hawai'i Press, 1998), 2.

9. Claudia Bell asks rhetorically, '[i]s there a town anywhere in New Zealand without a war memorial?', *Inventing New Zealand: Everyday Myths of Pakeha Identity* (Auckland: Penguin, 1996), 103. For a further discussion, see Chris MacLean and Jock Phillips, *The Sorrow and the Pride: New Zealand War Memorials* (Wellington: GP Books, 1990).

10. Kenneth B. Cumberland and James S. Whitelaw, *The World's Landscapes— New Zealand* (London: Longman, 1970), 146.

11. Ibid., 145, 151.

12. Schafer, *Mapping the Godzone*, 4.

13. Ian Conrich, 'In God's Own Country: Open Spaces and the New Zealand Road Movie', *New Zealand—A Pastoral Paradise?*, ed. Ian Conrich and David Woods (Nottingham: Kakapo Books, 2000), 34–35.

14. See Claudia Bell and John Lyall, *Putting Our Town On The Map: local claims to fame in New Zealand* (Auckland: HarperCollins, 1995); the video companion *Putting Our Town On The Map: local claims to fame in New Zealand* (directed by Shirley Horrocks, 1995); and the set of 10 stamps 'Town Icons', issued in the late 1990s by New Zealand Post. The pukeko is a brightly-coloured bird common in the wetter parts of New Zealand; the extinct Moa was a huge flightless bird that could grow to 3.5 metres tall.

15. Bell and Lyall, *Putting Our Town On The Map*, 10.

16. Schafer, *Mapping the Godzone*, 3. For a further discussion of colonial villas see Di Stewart, *The New Zealand Villa Past and Present* (Auckland: Penguin, 1992).

17. Kenneth MacKinnon, *Hollywood's Small Towns: An Introduction to the American Small-Town Movie* (Metuchen, New Jersey: The Scarecrow Press, 1984); Emanuel Levy, *Small-Town America in Film: The Decline and Fall of Community* (New York: Continuum, 1991).

18. See MacKinnon, *Hollywood's Small Town's*, 151–174.

19. Ibid., 152.

20. Ibid., 156.

21. The New Zealand films *No One Can Hear You* (2001) and *Exposure* (2000), were both filmed around Auckland city districts to look as if they were made in America. Interestingly, the parodic American small town movie *The Truman Show*, was scripted by New Zealander Andrew Niccol.

22. See Bell and Lyall, *Putting Our Town On The Map*, 13.

23. The claim that Waimatua is 'The Sweet Potato Capital of the World', is similar to the claim made by the New Zealand small town of Te Puke—'The Kiwifruit Capital of the World'.

24. Nicolas Reid, *A Decade of New Zealand Film: Sleeping Dogs to Came A Hot Friday* (Dunedin: John McIndoe, 1986), 44.

25. Ibid.

8

Beyond Materialism?:

SPIRITUALITY AND NEO-UTOPIAN SENSIBILITY IN RECENT NEW ZEALAND FILM

Ann Hardy

In New Zealand cinema, the years surrounding the millennium, those immediately before the release of the first part of *The Lord of The Rings* trilogy, were distinguished not by a single film but by a series of modest productions from directors undertaking first or second feature films. Within these two dozen or so relatively 'minor' films, some critically appreciated, most unfortunately commercially unsuccessful,[1] there is a discernable sub-group of features that investigate a series of shared concerns while flirting with the boundaries of cinematic realism. The group includes *Memory and Desire* (1998), *Saving Grace* (1997), *Channelling Baby*, (1999), *Magik and Rose* (2000), *The Price of Milk* (2000), *The Irrefutable Truth About Demons* (2000) and *Snakeskin* (2001). Several factors link these productions, in all of which the marvellous intrudes into everyday life. While exhibiting the imprint of the character-focused 'psychodrama' genre first identified as significant in New Zealand cinema by Roger Horrocks in 1992,[2] they are also reminiscent of the fantastic, mystical vision of New Zealand once the province of director Vincent Ward. Ultimately, however, these films differ from Ward's work in seeking younger, more cynical audiences than the art-house clientele he typically addressed.

At a most basic level the similarities in these films concern the vicissitudes of heterosexual pair-formation: falling in love, being unable to sustain love, dealing with an incompetent, deluded or dangerous partner. Four of the seven films are directed by women, and the most active character in all but one of them is female. However, the significance of these features comes in the form of the opposition the lovers face, since, in the majority, the obstacle is not so much human or material, as supernatural, and the battle to reassert control is therefore one that is psychic, or spiritual. In *The Irrefutable Truth About Demons* the adversary is a horde of demons, in *Snakeskin* it is no less than the Devil himself in the guise of an American drifter who indulges the heroine, Alice's (Melanie Lynskey), craving for sex, drugs and adventure. In *Saving Grace* one of the two protagonists appears to have the ability to perform miracles and claims to be an avatar of Jesus Christ. In *The Price of Milk*, although a human rival steals away Lucinda's (Danielle Cormack) husband, the real narrative force of the film is the power exerted by an elderly Maori woman who gains control over the couple by stealing the quilt from their marital bed. In *Channelling Baby*, a narrative about a relationship destroyed by bad luck and obsession, a mother's yearning for her dead child seems to initiate contact with her from beyond the grave, while in *Memory and Desire* the ghostly presence is that of a newly-wed, impotent, husband; his death by drowning is the catalyst for a solitary purgatory of grief and reparation undertaken by his young widow. *Magik and Rose*, on the boundaries of the territory mapped here, explores the appeal of the supernatural through a central character that practises fortune-telling but, ultimately, finds its narrative resolution within a humanist rather than mystical paradigm.

The thematic territory of these narratives is psychic and spiritual partly because it is specifically not religious; that is, the films deal with non-material explanations for life-events but they do not represent, in a manner which constitutes an endorsement of them, the tropes of Christianity, or of any other religion for that matter. In this, they are consistent with the generally secular, sceptical traditions of European New Zealand filmmaking and film criticism. Apart from a handful of exceptions (films by Merata Mita [*Mauri*, 1988] and Barry Barclay [*Ngati*, 1987; *Te Rua*, 1991], the work of Vincent Ward, and Leon Narbey's *Illustrious Energy* [1988], a film about the worldview of Chinese goldminers), the majority of New Zealand films which raise the topic of religion do so in order to lambast it as hypocritical or to challenge it as a crutch for the immature. For instance, *The God Boy* (1976), *Utu* (1983), *Trespasses* (1984), *The Quiet Earth* (1985), and *The End of the Golden Weather* (1991), are all examples of this ambivalent, if not hostile, attitude to religion. Certainly, in this recent set of films, *Saving Grace* employs explicit elements of the Christian myth, while *Snakeskin* and *The Irrefutable Truth About Demons* draw upon notions of embodied evil; but none of these parallels are elaborated with a degree of commitment sufficient for the films to be seen as features that attest to religious belief. Rather, these somewhat fey movies are local variants of a contemporary trend in Western filmmaking: the secular film which finds its subject in aspects of life that cannot be readily quantified and commodified, nor dealt with by brute force or worldly power. Instead, the characters in these films, threatened by adverse circumstances, try and deal with them through practices of indirect manipulation of their environment, or of emotional or imaginative transcendence of it. Yet this angle of approach does not entail that all these films present a form of advocacy for spirituality—indeed, *Magik and Rose*, and parts of *Channelling Baby*, debunk the paraphernalia of New Age spiritualism, while the sub-*Matrix* philosophising of *The Irrefutable Truth About Demons* seems meant to be taken in a spirit of irony.[3]

Socio-cultural Contexts

The films discussed here were developed over a production period of two to three years each within an overall time-range stretching from 1996 to

16. A demonic presence within the everyday: Le Valliant (Jonathon Hendry), the leader of a satanic cult, in *The Irrefutable Truth About Demons*. Courtesy of the New Zealand Film Commission.

2001. This followed the end of a period of fifteen years in which politics in New Zealand was distinguished by successive governments' fervent implementation of measures based on neo-liberal or New Right economic theory. The divisive social effects of the consequent labour-market rationalisation are well documented but there was also a more abstract, yet powerfully general, effect of the adoption of free-market economic policies: the tendency for a range of discussions relating to cultural practices to be subsumed under discourses of 'efficiency', 'growth', 'value for money' and individual 'choice'. As a consequence it became difficult to operate in the public sphere without employing the vocabulary of neo-liberalism.[4] By the middle of the 1990s, however, gaps had developed between government policy and public opinion, and previously marginalised discursive formations were scrutinised for their potential to offer alternative public goals and vocabularies. These included discourses of art and culture, liberal discourses of nationalism, and, of particular relevance to this work, discourses of 'values', spirituality and, to a lesser extent, of religion; areas of life which had been least identified with economic rationalism, and had on occasion, been in a position of open conflict with it.[5]

It is selections from within this latter grouping of languages and narratives, in which the spiritual and the non-material can be developed as an alternative to pragmatic, materialist politics, that are being mobilised in the films under discussion. In particular, it is the strategies of utopianism, where a wishful dynamic underpins the narrative, allowing a tale to function simultaneously as entertainment and as a vehicle of social critique, that animate these features' relationship to the cultural context of their production.

Utopianism

Utopianism is particularly relevant to the discussion of forms of New Zealand cultural production because the country has long attracted utopian projections of the imaginary 'good place', where it is possible to make a fresh start at creating an ideal community in a benign, beautiful natural environment.[6] At their most banal these projections have been assimilated into visual representations of national identity: they form the background both for tourist marketing campaigns and for local cinema production, even when, as noted in Sam Neill and Judy Rymer's 1996 documentary *Cinema of Unease: A Personal Journey by Sam Neill*, New Zealand films often deal with the failure of settlers to live up to the promise of the environment. The recent pressure to make films that reach a global market, while still retaining a sense of a discernable national identity, has reinforced the likelihood that utopian representations will continue to be employed. In the films under discussion, however, this utopian sensibility is extended beyond the traditional use of landscape into the wider texture of the plot, where the lead characters, in the majority Pakeha (European) New Zealanders, strive to achieve a state beyond unease, to achieve a sense of spiritual belonging in the environment, whether it be rural or urban.

According to Lucy Sargisson, several forms of ideal or utopian society have influenced literary, and more recently cinematic, tradition.[7] The first is known as 'Cockaygne', from the medieval poem about a land of the same name: 'In this place desires are instantly gratified; [. . .] it is a hedonistic paradise'. The second form of ideal society is 'Arcadia', a pastoral setting of natural abundance to which are added morally or aesthetically motivated humans. The third type is 'The perfect commonwealth', a society with a prescriptive moral order, perfectly realised by all of its members, while the fourth is 'The Millennium', a society in which 'men and women are transformed, usually for the better, by an external force'.[8] The fifth and final type of ideal society, which functions in balance without need of external or supernatural assistance, accepting the limitations of both its environment and its citizenry, is what J.C. Davis, upon whom Sargisson draws, identified as a paradigmatic 'Utopia'.

A specific style that may be used to embody utopian vision is that of magic realism, in which 'the supernatural, the mythical, or the implausible are assimilated to the cognitive structure of reality without a perceptive break in the narrator's or character's consciousness'.[9] Originally associated with Latin American writing, the epithet 'magical realist' is now applied more generally to works that challenge 'the scientific and materialist assumptions of Western modernity', specifically the attitude that reality 'is knowable, predictable and controllable'.[10] Additionally, magic realism has

17. New Zealand as a potentially utopian space: Sayo and Keiji's expression of passion and liberation in *Memory and Desire*. Courtesy of the New Zealand Film Commission.

sometimes been viewed as a postcolonial fictional mode that introduces the inexplicable into everyday life in order to subvert the rational regimes of Western colonisation.[11] While postcoloniality is a vexed term in the New Zealand context, a magic realist style is used in segments of all the films discussed here with the exception of *Magik and Rose*.[12]

These forms of imaginative ideal and technique then, especially the first two varieties of utopianism focused on the satisfaction of sensual and emotional desire, are both a context and hermeneutic for this body of films. In the terms of this argument, *The Price of Milk* (set on an idyllic dairy farm) and *Magik and Rose* (culminating in the Wildfoods Festival on the South Island's West Coast) are Arcadian fictions, with a touch of Cockaygne, since the fulfillment of the protagonists' sensual desires is the spine of the plot. *Snakeskin* also, in part, delineates such a world: revelling in mountain scenery, seductive company, and the effects of drugs, its protagonist, Alice, proclaims: 'if I had to rest here for eternity, it's not so bad'. However, *Snakeskin's* play with notions of utopia is self-reflexive and the film eventually descends into utopia's opposite, the dystopia of a rural economy based on the slaughter of animals. *Channelling Baby* also begins in Cockaygne: a sun-soaked, colourful, sensually expressive recreation of the 1970s, a state to which the exiled lovers keep seeking a return. In *Memory and Desire*, the New Zealand of newly-wed Keiji (Eugene Nomura) and Sayo's (Yuri Kinugawa) experience is potentially an ideal place too, where the class distinctions of Japanese society cannot repress them. However, the narrative has to move through tragedy and into a 'millennial' realm of transformative force (the wild powers of nature, the intervention of a ghostly lover) before Sayo can achieve an individualised form of freedom. *The Irrefutable Truth About Demons* is a dystopian version of urban New Zealand, (populated by blood-letting ghouls), yet evinces such enthusiasm for this vision that it represents a realm of sensual satisfaction all of its own.

The third and fifth types of ideal society—the commonwealth and the Utopia proper—that is, the more overtly political forms of utopian organisation, do not feature heavily in these films. Paradoxically, however, this absence confirms the significance of the global and local ideological pressures that shape the New Zealand film industry. Writers and directors may, personally, be idealistic, but opportunities to access the money available to finance filmmaking are rare. It is generally both prudent and in tune with the local zeitgeist therefore, to craft stories that bring together the safely mythical and the safely personal, as these films do, rather than operating in the exposed middle ground of overt reference to specific social practices and specific institutions. While the films based on Alan Duff's novels (*Once Were Warriors* [1994], and *What Becomes of the Broken Hearted* [1999]) are exceptions it is typically safer to play with concepts of 'figures in a landscape' (whether paradisaical or fallen) than it is to confront actual political, ideological and economic conflicts within New Zealand society.[13]

Nevertheless, to note this tendency towards the 'soft sell' of much recent New Zealand film is not to condemn it as without political relevance. Rather it is to note that filmmakers work within the practical and ideological limits of a given culture at a given time. For in utopianism, as in magical realism, the dynamic underlying a fanciful surface may still be one, according to Tom Moylan, of discontent:

> [Utopian thought] is, at heart, rooted in the unfulfilled needs and wants of specific classes, groups and individuals in their unique historical contexts . . . Utopia negates the contradictions of a social system by forging visions of what is not yet realised either in theory or practice. In generating such figures of hope, utopia contributes to the open space of opposition.[14]

Utopian texts may establish, or refer to, very different types of imagined communities, says Moylan, but 'the shared quality in all of them is a rejection of hierarchy and domination' accompanied by the celebration of emancipatory ways of being.[15]

Differing Relationships to Utopian Concepts

The films discussed here do not all locate Utopia in the same place. For instance, Alice, in *Snakeskin*, is bored rigid with her life in small town New Zealand: her version of Utopia is a pastiche of ideas taken from American movies. The ironic, slippery tone of *Snakeskin* subsists then in the introduction of elements from Alice's movie dream world into the sublime, touristic landscape of the Southern Alps that provides the film's visual power. The two states coexist for much of the film until, through an act of violence, Alice manages to incorporate 'America' into her body and spirit. At the film's conclusion she stands, snakeskin-clad, beside the road on a West Coast cliff top, with an eerie light in her eyes as she flags down the next group of gullible locals. The many levels of association orchestrated in this final sequence emphasise the mixture of cynicism and celebration with which writer/director Gillian Ashurst has treated her topic, since, in *Snakeskin*, Utopia is an intertextual state that references the virtual worlds of the media as much as any physical conditions of existence. For instance, the appearance of a yellow Mini at this point is not only a homage to the iconic 1980 Kiwi road movie, *Goodbye Pork Pie*, it also serves as an ironic evocation of the brand of joyous, anarchic (male) nationalism that the earlier film embodied. Similarly, *Saving Grace* is a film in which Utopia remains very much an imaginative ideal, a 'no place' which eludes the protagonists, Grace (Kirsty Hamilton) and Gerald (Jim Moriarty). In such a space the two need not fear poverty or loneliness, and could, moreover, escape death. It is this desire for a realm of immortality that gives rise to Gerald's dubious conviction that he is Christ and that death cannot touch him.

In dealing with themes expressed as the private concern of an individual or a couple, these films therefore exhibit the relatively apolitical temper of American utopianism, which, compared to British forms for instance, Nan Albinski found to be concerned with a 'belief in social rather than political change, in internals rather than external influences and in religious and moral rather than secular evolution'.[16] Still, the films do criticise certain aspects of social organisation, albeit obliquely. Their discontent focuses on three major areas: the rejection of the primacy of economic values, the exploration of a continuing sense of tension around Maori–European ethnic and cultural issues, and the enduring feeling that gender relations still need adjustment if the 'good society' is ever to be attained. These are rather the usual suspects—but, in addition to growing concern about issues of environmental sustainability, continue to be significant categories of debate in the public sphere of Aotearoa/New Zealand.

Discourses of Maori spirituality
The vexed and often controversial issue of 'Maori spirituality' features prominently in *Snakeskin*, *The Price of Milk*, and to a lesser extent, by virtue of casting decisions, in *Saving Grace*. In recent years, a model of Maori society as different from, and indeed superior in some ways to European culture, has occasionally been employed in imagining New Zealand.[17] While the difficulties involved in claiming that any culture is inherently unitary in nature are obvious, a key aspect of this idealisation lies in a perception that Maori society is more focused around 'spirituality' than European culture, a spirituality which in practice seems to be a fusion,

or co-existence of, pre-colonial indigenous beliefs and influences from Christianity.[18] From the European side attributing an original, untainted spirituality to Maori is perhaps part of a complicated, ambivalent process of acknowledging past and ongoing oppression, and there is also a nostalgic tendency among those interested in New Age spirituality to look for inspiration in the worldviews of indigenous peoples considered to have been less corrupted by the forces of modernisation. Paradoxically, however, any reification and idealisation of Maori spirituality may additionally be useful in supporting Maori aims for political and cultural decolonisation. For instance, Hauraki Greenland identifies the conscious development of a discourse of spirituality in the radical ideologies of Maori protest groups in the 1960s and 1970s, whereby claims for the return of alienated land were supported by an argument that rejected the moral basis of Pakeha society. According to Greenland, 'a contrast was drawn between two allegedly conflicting approaches to land—one emotive and communal (Maori), the other artificial and exploitative (Pakeha)'.[19] Pakeha were typified as predators while Maori were credited with spiritual integrity due to their closer links with the land. In New Zealand culture one effect of these dichotomous constructions has been to characterise European New Zealanders as being without a positive sense of spirituality, ensnared in materialism.

For their part, Pakeha filmmakers are often more comfortable dealing with spiritual matters through Maori characters. For instance, *Saving Grace*, which began life as a play written by Duncan Sarkies, had always revolved around a bi-racial couple, but on-screen the Maori female/Pakeha male casting of the play was reversed, with Maori actor Jim Moriarty playing the part of Gerald/Jesus. There was no explicit reference to ethnicity in the dialogue, but interviews done with the production team indicated that they were aware of, and pleased by, the challenge that Moriarty's performance of the role offered to conventional notions about Christ's identity.[20] Moreover, a personal fusion of Maori, Christian and other spiritual beliefs explicitly informed Moriarty's understanding of the role, which he perceived both as 'right for his spirit' and as providing a sense of 'moral integration' for the audience.[21]

In *Snakeskin* and *The Price of Milk*, however, the focus is less on the mana (power/presence) of a lead performance, than on secondary characters embodying Maori/European tensions about the ownership and guardianship of land. Both films deal with this dynamic in a similar, allegorical manner. Not long after Alice (in *Snakeskin*) and her companions begin a journey through the Southern Alps, they meet with a nameless elderly Maori woman (Katerina Davis) and her son, Tama (Gordon Hatfield). The woman warns Alice not to 'cross that land' since it has been the site of recent deaths. Moreover Tama, offended by the plastic tiki (carved representation of an ancestor) hanging in the travellers' car—an act of cultural appropriation—tells them: 'You're on my land now'. As darkness falls the group come to a fork in the road: 'This land is tapu' (sacred), Tama again asserts. The travellers make the wrong choice as to direction and their bad luck mounts, eventually provoking a deadly conflict amongst the main characters. However, although the warnings of the tangata whenua (the people of the land) are thus vindicated, the focus of the film ultimately shifts back to Alice and her journey of self-discovery. There is therefore no resolution of the sub-plot involving the Maori characters, but there is nevertheless a strong sense pervading the film that the land is haunted by the spirit of bad faith, and by the energy of revenge.

The Price of Milk also features a nameless Maori matriarch and a group of her younger male kin, this time wearing jackets with the logo of the 'Waimatuku Golf Club' (perhaps a double allusion to the 'patches' worn by gang members and to a famous land dispute from the 1970s, the reclamation by local Maori of the land comprising the Raglan golf course). The old woman (Rangi Motu) is obviously magical. Despite being hit by Lucinda's car she gets up and disappears into the bush, and when Lucinda is torn between love for her partner Rob (Karl Urban) and a bargain made with the old woman, the woman appears outside her house, strangely advancing and retreating as Lucinda repeatedly changes her mind.

The Price of Milk pivots on a system of visual metaphors related to land, to theft and to reparation. The opening shots depict an idyllic landscape which morphs into a patchwork quilt under which dairy farmers Rob and Lucinda are sleeping. The quilt is peeled away from them by the Golf Club boys, who take it to keep the old woman warm, since she is preternaturally cold (having been robbed of her land in the first place?). Subsequently, the protagonists become involved in an escalating series of material and spiritual deals until finally the old woman is satisfied. She returns the quilt/landscape to Lucinda and Rob—although her final admonition is that it is only on loan and she may want it back some day—a line implying that an ideal relationship to land is one where later immigrants regard themselves as tenants or guests on Maori land rather than having ownership rights to it.

None of the films discussed here address the troubled relationship between colonisers and colonised directly; instead it is poked at and pointed to in search of a low-key and harmonious solution.[22] The resulting vision in *The Price of Milk* seems to be genuinely utopian in that a respectful sharing of land, on Maori terms, is envisaged. In *Snakeskin* however, the indigenous vision is ultimately used as mere story-colour, sacrificed in favour of an ending that endorses an Americanised form of individualism, while in *Saving Grace* the opportunities suggested by casting a Maori actor as Jesus are passed over in what also ultimately becomes another story about a white woman's self-development. These features point to the increasing awareness of issues regarding land ownership and Maori spirituality within general filmmaking culture in New Zealand, but they also suggest that, as well as referencing utopian visions of a postcolonial

18. The quilt as object of cultural exchange and a spiritual relationship to ownership of land in *The Price of Milk*. Courtesy of the New Zealand Film Commission.

culture, such awareness is still often subservient to the interests of non-Maori writers and directors, rather than constituting an open, whole-hearted, negotiation with the indigenous worldview.

Women's Spirituality

Another significant element of the spirituality movement in New Zealand since the 1970s has been the creation of forms of ritual by and for women. Like Maori spirituality this is a movement mixing personal preferences with political positioning, in that women's spirituality groups are typically informed by second-wave feminist critiques condemning the patriarchal nature of dominant religious traditions. However, since the makers of these films are targeting younger generations of audience, for whom a classical feminist worldview might either not be attractive, or for whom gender equality is sometimes assumed to be a given, explicit links between feminist politics and spirituality are not foregrounded in these works.

Nevertheless, some level either of feminist understanding, or on occasion, a revisionist view of women as intrinsically linked to nature, whimsicality and spirituality, is fundamental to these post-1996 features. The fact that six out of the seven films have a female protagonist has already been noted since, even when paired with a charismatic male lead, it is the female's actions and desires that tend to shape the plot. For instance, in both *Channelling Baby* and *The Price of Milk* Danielle Cormack is presented as a love-goddess, motivated primarily by her emotions and instincts: in

Channelling Baby, she makes her first appearance in a van decorated with a huge painting of a Botticelli Venus. However, the cinematographers of the other films (*Magik and Rose, The Irrefutable Truth About Demons, Saving Grace, Memory and Desire, Snakeskin*) are less awestruck with the appearance of their leading ladies. Instead, the characters are admired for their energy and courage, even when (as with Alice, Sayo and Grace) they take the action into the mythical realm of death and resurrection—a role that is traditionally reserved for a male hero. In these films, a relationship with a male is an important aspect of the plot, but such alliances are typically presented through a conscious exploration of ever-changing power relations rather than charting the final achievement of either dominance or subservience. While four of the films end with humour in the formation or reconciliation of couples, three of them (*Saving Grace, Memory and Desire, Snakeskin*) portray the male as ultimately dispensable, and the female protagonist capable of self-reliance: only in *The Irrefutable Truth About Demons* is a male hero actually triumphant. Although there are other films made during this period in which male styles of being are still valorised, such as *Stickmen* (2000) with its focus on three male pool hustlers, those identified as favouring a spiritual rather than a material economy suggest that an 'ideal society' is one in which men and women would share authority, or paradoxically, would be one in which women have the greater power to shape themselves and the circumstances of those around them.

Utopia for Sale

The production of a group of recent New Zealand movies with spiritual overtones is an occurrence that is likely to have been multiply determined. There is, at present, a visible international tendency for filmmakers to have greater recourse to story-material about values, spiritual beliefs and supernatural causation. This trend may merely be part of the cycles of fashion and novelty that shape the global film industry, but it may also be evidence of what has been theorised elsewhere as a paradigm shift in the nature and location of religiosity—away from institutional religion and towards more localised, even individual, expressions of spirituality, which in their turn find their way into contemporary story-telling.[23] A third possibility, which has been outlined in this chapter, is that in New Zealand, in the latter half of the 1990s, a cultural dynamic developed whereby discourses of spirituality, allied with, and sometimes blurring into, discourses of art and nationhood, comprised one strategy of opposition to the status quo. The New Zealand film industry, mirroring the predominant political quietism of New Zealand society, does not have a strong tradition of explicitly political fiction filmmaking (although the situation is somewhat different in the documentary field), but found cause to employ this increased interest in spirituality. In so doing the industry permitted itself to explore social issues indirectly, largely by imagining utopian alternatives to present arrangements. These imaginings were not necessarily radical—

they seemed to consist, rather, of preliminary musings about the possibility of addressing some of the structural inequalities of New Zealand society. Excessive materialism and gendered worldviews were two issues addressed with some regularity in the groups of films considered, but overall, the contestation between Maori and European myths of identity stood out as the area investigated with the most fascination. In this regard, while the particular films discussed may have had only a modest impact on audiences at the time, they appear now to have been precursors of later developments. For instance, a consideration of television is outside the scope of this analysis, but the tales of supernatural aspects of the Maori world presented by the television series *Mataku* (2002) have latterly provided a space for the reassertion of indigenous understandings of identity, place and the spiritual links between them. The series, developed by Maori writers and producers, while operating within popular culture as entertainment, also wove subtextual political messages of considerable force into each half-hour narrative.

In contrast, two further film projects, both in a 'spiritual' genre, although very different in scale, have taken the tension involved in utopian imaginings of New Zealand through into the first decade of the twenty-first century. Niki Caro, the director of *Memory and Desire*, made *Whale Rider* (2002), a film based on Witi Ihimaera's novella of the same name, which re-tells a Ngati Porou ancestral myth about a human who befriends the great spirits of the sea. Featuring a young female protagonist, the production engages with both feminist and indigenous spirituality and marked the first time in many decades that a crew composed predominantly of European New Zealanders had worked on such a key Maori text, albeit with the support of the local people to whom the myth belongs.[24] The film version of *Whale Rider*, which, in comparison to the original literary work, has had its political and erotic elements pared back in order to tell a story of universal appeal,[25] has found significant success with international audiences as well as in New Zealand, but has nevertheless been the subject of a passionate debate in the industry magazine *Onfilm*, led by Barry Barclay, about the dangers of (even well-meaning) cultural appropriation.[26] Furthermore, Peter Jackson and the team making *The Lord of the Rings* trilogy (2001–03) have not so much negotiated with a Maori worldview as replaced it with a complete mythological system imported from Europe via J.R.R. Tolkien's Britain. The transformation of New Zealand into the sublime landscape of Middle Earth, where the heroes and benign spiritual beings are fair-skinned and blue-eyed, while the demons are of darker hue, is not just another exploration of utopia and its enemies, it is also a fictional re-colonisation of considerable magnitude.

The hitherto small New Zealand film industry has long been looking for ways to position itself in a sustainable 'niche' within the global market, with stories that are local yet appeal to worldwide audiences. With tales that feature a still-beautiful environment, linked to populist concepts of spirituality that often draw on Maori exoticism, and are filmed in magical realist style, (or, the case of *The Lord of the Rings*, as state-of-the-art fantasy) the industry may have found such a niche product, which repackages the whole country as utopian 'other' to a disenchanted world. From such a viewpoint the earlier films—*Memory and Desire, Saving Grace, Channelling Baby, Magik and Rose, The Irrefutable Truth About Demons, The Price of Milk*, and *Snakeskin*—are merely minor, and partial, precursors to the later successes of *The Lord of the Rings* and *Whale Rider*. Alternatively, however, these films can be seen as offering valuable engagements with the difficulties of constructing diverse views of national identity, especially the concerns of Pakeha New Zealanders, in a manner that is not as readily discernable in the market-savvy confidence of the two later projects. It would be a shame if those smaller experiments in imagining an alternative Aotearoa/New Zealand were to be largely occluded by the greater public presence of their successors.

Notes

1. For a discussion of the lack of success of films during this period see Greg Dixon, 'The Great Unwatched', *North & South* (January 2001): 66–74, and Frances Walsh, 'Lord . . . what next? Why our films don't have a better hit rate', *Listener* (March 9, 2001): 16–19.
2. See Roger Horrocks, 'The Tradition of the New', *Film in Aotearoa New Zealand*, ed. Jonathan Dennis and Jan Bieringa (Wellington: Victoria University Press, 1992), 57–88.
3. *Holy Man* (1998), *What Dreams May Come* (1998), *American Beauty* (1999) and *Amelie* (2001), are but a few of the many international films in the last decade that have operated in similar territory.
4. For discussions of neo-liberalism from a leftist perspective see Jane Kelsey, *The New Zealand Experiment* (Auckland: Auckland University Press with Bridget Williams Books, 1997), and Bruce Jesson, *Only Their Purpose is Mad* (Palmerston North: Dunmore Press, 1999).
5. For example, in September 1998 the Anglican Church organised a nationwide protest march or 'Hikoi of Hope', during which stories of poverty and deprivation were collected and presented to the government at the Hikoi's destination in Wellington.
6. See for instance Samuel Butler, *Erewhon, or, Over the Range* (London: Grant Richards, 1901 [1872]); Martin Blythe, *Naming the Other: Images of the Maori in New Zealand Film and Television* (Metchuen, N.J: The Scarecrow Press, 1994) and *New Zealand – A Pastoral Paradise?*, ed. Ian Conrich and David Woods (Nottingham: Kakapo Books, 2000).
7. Lucy Sargisson, *Contemporary Feminist Utopianism* (London: Routledge, 1996).
8. Ibid., 15–16.
9. Peter Standish, cited in Joan Mellen, *Magic Realism* (Detroit, New York: Gale Group, 2000), 1.
10. Lois Parkinson Zamora, 'Magical Romance/Magical realism', *Magical*

Realism: Theory, History, Community, ed. Zamora and Wendy B. Faris (Durham N.C: Duke University Press, 1995), 498.

11. Amaryll Chanady, *Magical Realism and The Fantastic: Resolved versus Unresolved Antinomy* (New York: Garland, 1985).

12. For instance, Powhiri Rika-Heke argues that, from a Maori point-of-view, there has never been an end to colonialism in New Zealand, so the term 'postcolonial' lacks valid reference. See 'Tribes or Nations? Post or Fence? What's the Matter with Self-definition?', *Not On Any Map: Essays on Postcoloniality and Cultural Nationalism*, ed. Stuart Murray (Exeter: University of Exeter Press, 1997), 170–81.

13. By contrast, the last few years have seen a slew of Australian films—*The Castle* (1997), *The Man Who Sued God* (2000), *Rabbit-Proof Fence* (2002), *The Bank* (2002)—that do feature societal conflicts between the 'ordinary' person and the forces of Law and Capital. In those circumstances the focus expands beyond instances of personal spirituality to include exploration of the morality and values of larger sections of the community.

14. Tom Moylan, *Demand the Impossible: Science Fiction and the Utopian Imagination* (London: Methuen, 1986), 1–2.

15. Ibid.,1–2.

16. Nan Albinski, *Women's Utopias in British and American Fiction* (London: Routledge, 1988), 5.

17 See Blythe, *Naming the Other*, 142, 146, and 149.

18 Te Pakaka Tawhai, 'Aotearoa's Spiritual Heritage', *The Religions of New Zealanders*, ed. Peter Donovan (Palmerston North: Dunmore Press, 1990), 11–19. Tawhai describes a system of korero tahito, or ancient explanations for aspects of existence. Korero tahito include extensive creation myths and a pantheon of deities which inhabit nature, influencing human activities. Concepts of mana (influence, power, status), tapu (sanctity, sacredness), utu (revenge and recompense), were also common as organising principles for everyday life. He suggests it is likely that involvement with Christianity has not entirely superseded the relevance of korero tahito—instead, Tawhai claims, the two worldviews continue in co-existence, especially in situations where people gather for ceremonial occasions.

19. Hauraki Greenland, 'Maori Ethnicity as Ideology', *Nga Take*, ed. Paul Spoonley (Palmerston North: Dunmore Press, 1991), 93.

20. See Ann Hardy, 'Sites of Value? Discourses of Religion and Spirituality in the Production of a New Zealand Film, and Television Series', unpublished Ph.D thesis (Hamilton, New Zealand: Waikato University, 2003).

21. Jim Moriarty, interview with author, 10 July 1997.

22. Perhaps this is because, as Allan Webster points out in his 2001 study of value-cultures in New Zealand, half of the country's ethnically Maori population consider itself to be primarily 'New Zealanders', and share the values of the nation's majority culture. However, there is another 7 per cent of the population, a rapidly growing group, which considers itself to be Maori before identifying with New Zealand. This group's attitudes to government, to the allocation of resources, and to the value of religion are distinctive when

compared to those of the 46 per cent, more secular, more contented, portion of the population who identify as New Zealanders. See Allan Webster, *Spiral of Values: the Flow from Survival Values to Global Consciousness in New Zealand* (Hawera: Alpha Publications, 2001).

23. See Catherine Albanese, 'Religion and American Popular Culture: An Introductory Essay', *Journal of the American Academy of Religion* 62, no. 4 (1994): 733–42; Paul Heelas, *The New Age Movement* (Cambridge & Oxford: Blackwell, 1996); Robert Wuthnow, *After Heaven: Spirituality in America Since the 1950s* (Berkeley, Los Angeles, London: University of California Press, 1998); Linda Woodhead and Paul Heelas, *Religion in Modern Times* (Oxford: Blackwell, 2000).

24. Witi Ihimaera, 'Whale Rider Thunders into Toronto', *Onfilm* 19, no. 10 (October 2002): 5–6.

25. Kerry Doole, 'Whale Rider Makes Huge Splash at TIFF', *Onfilm* 19, no. 10 (October 2002): 5–6. In this account of the film's reception at the Toronto International Film Festival, Caro describes the principles that guided her in the adaptation of the material from novella to film.

26. There was a three-sided debate between Barclay, Alan Brash (writer/producer with Shoot First Productions) and Carey Carter, producer of the *Mataku* series, on the issue of who has the right to make films based on Maori material, carried out in the February, March and April 2003 issues of *Onfilm*. See *Onfilm* 20, no. 3 (2003): 11; 20, no. 4 (2003): 11; 20, no. 5 (2003): 11.

9

The Adaptation of New Zealand Literature to Film:
A CASE-STUDY APPROACH

Brian McDonnell

In the first ten years after the establishment of the New Zealand Film Commission in 1978, in excess of 50 feature films (excluding documentaries and completely foreign-financed projects) were produced. Of these, approximately 25 per cent were adaptations of local works of fiction: for example *A State of Siege* (1978), *Sons for the Return Home* (1979), *The Scarecrow* (1982), *The Silent One* (1984), *Other Halves* (1984), *Pallet on the Floor* (1984), *Among the Cinders* (1984), *Came a Hot Friday* (1985) and *The Quiet Earth* (1985). In addition, *Sleeping Dogs*, the breakthrough film of the contemporary era, was an adaptation made in 1977, just before the Interim Film Commission was established, and the above list is further augmented by *Middle Age Spread* (1979), adapted from a local play, *Sylvia* (1985), from the autobiography of writer Sylvia Ashton-Warner, and *Footrot Flats: The Dog's Tail/Tale* (1986) from a comic strip. In the sixteen years since 1988, the percentage of adaptations has dropped but remains significant (approximately 21 per cent).

Why were literary adaptations so popular in New Zealand's New Wave of filmmaking? The main reason was a purely pragmatic one. In a country new to sustained feature film production, there were in those years few experienced scriptwriters and little confidence in original scripts within the fledgling film investment market. Those considering committing money to film production were more likely to be tempted by a project whose instigators could hold up an already published and successful novel. As Brian McFarlane points out in his study *Novel to Film*, an analysis of adaptation processes, adapters can seek to invest a new film project with the 'popularity' and 'respectability' of the original book.[1] Since at least the 1950s local novels had achieved overall acceptance with many New Zealanders. Local films, however, did not achieve similar acceptance in the culture until arguably the early 1990s, and thus adaptations of local literature helped to sell film ideas in the intervening period. Adaptations thus became a crucial component in the formation of an organised film culture in New Zealand. Once the industry found its feet during the mid to late 1980s, this reliance gradually began to diminish as local screenwriting skills emerged, but the various strengths of adaptations continue to persist in the contemporary film culture.

The three case studies chosen here from those adaptations of the first ten years after 1978 (*Sons for the Return Home*, *Other Halves* and *Came a Hot Friday*) not only serve the purpose of providing detailed information on the process of particular cinematic adaptations, but also highlight broader aspects of the New Zealand cultural environment at the relevant times of production. In his study *Film Adaptation*, James Naremore calls for adaptation studies to take an interest in issues other than formal ones, to investigate 'economic, cultural and political issues' and to take note of the commercial and industrial apparatus and audience.[2] That call will be answered here, though scrutiny will also be given to more traditionally aesthetic and formal issues such as narrative structure and thematic emphasis.

Sons for the Return Home (1979)

For cultural as well as formal reasons, *Sons for the Return Home* stands out as a very distinctive example of the adaptations of the late 1970s and early 1980s. Writer Albert Wendt is Samoan, and *Sons for the Return Home* (1973), his first novel, was semi-autobiographical (Wendt himself moved from Samoa to New Zealand to further his education) as it traced the geographical and identity shifts of a young Samoan man who travels to New Zealand and begins a relationship with a Palagi (European) woman. The producers of the film version had to walk a difficult cultural and aesthetic path in bringing this work to the screen and, according to statements by producer John O'Shea, the tensions involved were not fully resolved. As will be demonstrated below, the film remains problematic, both in its internal formal structures and in its social and political ramifications.

Sons for the Return Home was the first novel by a Samoan ever published in English and the first novel to deal with race relations in New Zealand from a Pacific Islander's perspective. Furthermore, the film version of the novel was the first New Zealand feature to deal with the experiences of those Pacific Islanders who came to New Zealand in the mid-twentieth century seeking a better material life, and who now form an important group in society. For these reasons, much of the initial attention of commentators on both novel and film was centred on the social contexts of the works—so much so that it was difficult in the 1970s and 1980s to assess either text in terms of its aesthetic qualities.

Sons for the Return Home was seen by several critics as a postcolonial novel,[3] especially in the sociologically rich section of the book describing the protagonist's judgments of newly independent Samoa on his return to the country. Samoa was New Zealand's own colonial adventure in the first half of the twentieth century, the islands being ruled until 1962 by what subsequent historians have considered a sometimes outrageous New Zealand administration.[4] Wendt's novel is the story of the maturing of an unnamed young Samoan man brought to New Zealand (the metropolitan centre, as it were) by his parents when only four years old and thus cut off from his Samoan roots. He is also alienated from the New Zealand society in which he grows up and feels himself a permanent exile not truly belonging anywhere. His love relationship with the (also unnamed) Palagi girl falls apart at the end of the novel. Called an 'impatient rebuttal of all Polynesian stereotypes' by Roger Robinson, the boy is adept in sporting and academic spheres, stoical, coolly silent, macho and brutal.[5] The novel's conclusion leaves him displaced, literally suspended between two worlds in an aircraft over the Pacific.

While the original novel was written by a Samoan, almost all the people working on the film version were white New Zealanders, and Wendt said at the time of the film's release that he had nothing to do with the adaptation of his novel.[6] The novel, then, is a Samoan view (both of Samoa and New Zealand), but the film is largely a Palagi interpretation of a Samoan view, with Wendt's Polynesian vision being filtered through the New Zealand sensibilities of writer/director Paul Maunder and his collaborators. As well as the many other complications always present when translating a novel into screen form, there is also in this case the further issue of cultural translation. The adapters were not only attempting to render Wendt's poetic prose in cinematic equivalents but also to convey through their eyes his views of both present-day New Zealand and Samoa and of the older cultural heritage of the protagonist's forebears in Samoa.

Anti-capitalist and left wing, director Maunder liked his art to be political, even didactic in a Marxist sense. He told the Australian journal *Cinema Papers* that he wanted in all his work to be critical of white New Zealand society: 'Europeans should feel guilty about our colonisation. If the guilt is not comprehended, then it remains as an unsettling pattern and feature of life in New Zealand'.[7] But, paradoxically, in *Sons for the Return Home* he wanted the representation of the main Palagi character (the girl) to be more sympathetic than he felt it was in the novel, and so he changed the novel's theme of an alienated man into a parable of the meeting of two cultures.

Maunder had long wanted to adapt Wendt's novel because of its potential as a love story bolstered by the exotic interest of its Samoan aspects. He told *Cinema Papers* that the difficulties in adapting the book came from its 'two strands: a sociological one which follows the family and its experiences, and the love story. The biggest problem was to unify the whole thing'.[8] Maunder did not like the separation of the novel's narrative sections: i.e., the New Zealand narrative occurring first, followed by the Samoan sequences. For reasons of narrative development, he wanted to combine the two, and perhaps also for commercial reasons he desired that the visually exotic Samoan locales should be on screen as soon as possible. For purely pragmatic reasons he gave to the novel's unnamed chief characters the names Sione (Uelese Petaia) and Sarah (Fiona Lindsay).

However, showing Sione in Samoa very early in the film and then having him remember his New Zealand experiences required the use of flashbacks.

19. The meeting of two cultures: Sarah and Sione (bottom left) socialising at a Samoan gathering in Wellington in a scene that was eventually not used in *Sons for the Return Home*. Courtesy of the New Zealand Film Commission.

Maunder also added crucial scenes that accentuated the political nature of the story, two examples being a dramatisation of 1970s' dawn raids by New Zealand police on immigration overstayers, and framing scenes, set in London, inserted at the beginning and end. These London scenes are not in the novel at all and serve mostly to internationalise the film, to present its issues in such a way that a British audience might understand them more readily, and to bring in the issue of class as an analogue to the issue of race. Imelda Whelehan has said of film adaptations in general that any sense of an historical period in an adaptation always 'coalesces with the period in which the adaptation is made'.[9] This is certainly true of the immigration raids added to the script. Historically, these events had occurred between the publication of Wendt's novel and the film's production. They became a talking point of the late 1970s for liberal New Zealanders, and their inclusion underlines Maunder's attempts to invest the film with a commentary on contemporary race relations, even allowing for their absence from Wendt's original composition.

The same cannot be argued for the additional scenes located in the UK. In the film's opening, working-class London pub drinkers surround Sarah and ask her about New Zealand. She says it is not the paradise they might expect. It has its own exploitation: of Maori and of Pacific Islanders. An international audience is thereby given a set of moral parameters within which to place their reading of the film: they are about to see a story of oppression. At the film's end Sarah is seen taking part in a Trafalgar

Square protest rally, as if she has been politicised by the events of the film. These additions caused producer John O'Shea to take his name off the film's credits after major disagreements with Maunder. He told colleagues that he disagreed with the director's cut and that Maunder was imposing his Marxist view on the film and cutting the heart and warmth out of it. He noted that the film was 'politically and sexually unsubtle', far less subtle than Wendt's novel.[10]

The film adaptation of *Sons for the Return Home* then combines a personal love story with a political strand depicting the deleterious results of colonialism. In so doing the film is less unitary than it might have been had it chosen to foreground the love story and emphasise scenes involving the two leads, or further concentrated on depicting the oppression of Pacific Islanders in general by including more sequences such as those depicting the immigration raids. As it stands, the film is an awkward mixture of approaches because it tries to achieve too much. This was a pervasive trait of New Zealand film adaptations of the late 1970s and early 1980s: only *Came a Hot Friday* steered away from such a policy by deliberately limiting its intentions, cutting the coat of its literary adaptation to suit the cloth of its cinematic ambitions.

Wendt was reluctant at the time of the film's release to be critical but he did admit he found the production 'heavy with social comment and messages. I would have liked a more lyrical treatment—it's a love story after all'.[11] It is possible to agree with his (and O'Shea's) misgivings and find further faults. Overall, the time-juggling plot structure only served to emphasise a lack of clarity in the presentation of the film's themes. The novel's plot runs relatively chronologically but the film is more disjointed, resulting from the decision to intercut constantly from the 'present' in Samoa to the 'past' in New Zealand. This results in twelve flashbacks (an uncommonly large number) and six flashbacks-within-flashbacks, which become very confusing. Maunder does, however, give the two geographical settings different visual styles and colour values which work effectively as visual expressions of the thematic contrasts between the locations. The Wellington scenes are dominated by cold greys and blues, combined with a number of shots of sterile buildings. Samoa, by contrast, is a place of warm colours: rich vegetation, flowers, firelight and a bright sky. In terms of image, the distinction between a potentially hostile New Zealand and a more accommodating Samoa is clear.

In 1990, another Wendt adaptation reached the screen: *Flying Fox in a Freedom Tree*, directed by Martyn Sanderson and filmed in Apia, Samoa's capital city. The film does not always cohere as a fully realised work of art, but it does show the integrity of Sanderson's intentions in attempting to help increase inter-cultural understanding. *Flying Fox in a Freedom Tree* was adapted from Wendt's 1974 novella of the same title (also developed into the second section of his 1979 novel *Leaves of the Banyan Tree*) which dealt with a subject dear to him: that of the outsider, the man who must make his own path between tradition and new ways. Utilising the metaphor of the flying fox itself (a fruit bat), the protagonist Pepe (Faifua Amiga Junior) must learn to hang suspended, balancing his core concepts of identity and belonging with the changes that have come to Samoa.

Pepe and his friend Tagata (Richard von Sturmer) must chart their own individual life courses against the weight of the old fa'a Samoa (Samoan way of life) and the new commercialism of the city. Within the contemporary complexities of Samoa's postcolonial society, they have to forge their own values or risk being trapped within either an aggressively capitalistic society (signified by Pepe's father) or a traditional culture in danger of becoming static and meaningless. Unlike the production of *Sons for the Return Home*, Wendt was consulted on each draft of the script for *Flying Fox in a Freedom Tree*. The result is that the film's cultural politics and depiction of the consequences of colonial history are closer to those portrayed in the original literary text than in the earlier film, and suffer less from the addition of extra material.

Other Halves (1984)

The second case study in this analysis is the adaptation of Sue McCauley's 1982 novel *Other Halves*. This is also the story of an inter-racial love affair, a popular subject in New Zealand film up until the 1980s (see, for instance, *Broken Barrier* [1952] and *To Love a Maori* [1972]), but unlike previous manifestations the narrative places more emphasis on the woman's point of view. *Other Halves* illustrates well the reliance film producers in a small film market such as New Zealand (currently with a population of only 4 million people) must have on selling their stories overseas in order to assist profitability, a financial imperative not always fully understood by overseas critics. Such pressure can result in any literary adaptation altering the original story in ways designed to make it more understandable for international audiences, an issue exemplified also by the later case of Lee Tamahori's *Once Were Warriors* (1994), adapted from Alan Duff's 1990 novel.

The adaptation of *Other Halves* was unique for the period in question in that the author also wrote the screenplay.[12] That fact, of course, did not stop other, later, changes in emphasis by producer and director as described below. The original novel has a comparatively straightforward plot. Liz Harvey is an unhappy middle-class Pakeha woman in her thirties living in Christchurch in 1973. She suffers a nervous breakdown and while recuperating forms an attachment with a 16-year-old Maori boy Tug Moreton. The story follows their relationship as they struggle against unsympathetic social welfare, justice and health bureaucracies and an uncaring society. They travel north from Christchurch to an island near Auckland and the novel ends optimistically with their happy future together seeming a likely eventuality. Liz is the central consciousness of the novel (unlike the film which has a more even-handed emphasis on the two main characters) with Tug always being seen from her point of view, and the novel is very much the story of Liz and her growth as a person, particularly her education (through her relationship with Tug) in how the 'other half' lives in New Zealand. McCauley thus sets up a contrast between the two classes—the comfortable bourgeoisie versus the marginal street gangs—as two separate cultures. Liz was already becoming an outsider in middle-class culture but previously had nowhere to go in her alienation: now she sees an alternative culture to join. She gradually comes to see that her middle-class perspective is inadequate, symbolically rejecting the strictures of law and order when shoplifting items from a Woolworth's store. The novel presents a negative general view of the middle class as made up of people whose emotions have atrophied, who are pretentious and uncaring.

Other Halves fell on surprisingly fertile ground in early 1980s' New Zealand and became both a literary and a sociological event, winning both the 1982 James Wattie Book of the Year Award and the 1983 New Zealand Book Award for Fiction. The novel was a fictional intervention into New Zealand culture at a transitional time: after a decade of feminist activism and a growing ethnic and political renaissance among Maori, and just before the launch of the neo-liberal agenda of the Lange-Douglas Labour government in 1984. Clearly there was a ready national audience at that moment for such a story, which combined features of Mills and Boon romance with liberal and feminist ideas. The novel's original editor, Marcia Russell, lived with film producer Tom Finlayson, introduced him to the book, and his production company subsequently bought the film rights. Finlayson said he chose *Other Halves* as a potential film property because 'it was an international story. It could be set in Liverpool, Chicago, London or New York'.[13] He told a television interviewer that, out of all the possible aspects of the novel including its social themes, they had chosen to film the love story.[14] The film's script eliminated the idea of real poverty from the novel, instead putting less emphasis on class and more on the potential resolution provided by romance.

The change in emphasis between the novel and film highlights key questions about the presentation of cultural and racial issues for a cinematic audience in a society that, by the early 1980s, was growing more used to seeing its own social narratives on screen. The novel's climactic shoplifting scene was removed from the film: Liz's (Lisa Harrow) rebellion from middle-class values is thus reduced to her telling her boss to 'shove' his job. Unlike *Once Were Warriors*, *Other Halves* does not seek to overtly discomfort its target middle-class audience, a situation which would have been the case had the novel's ending been used. The film, moving away from Liz's point of view, focuses more on Tug (Mark Pilisi) and on the gang context, adding a certain glamour to the crime depicted with a view to an international audience. At the time of the film's release, McCauley voiced her misgivings about these changes and said she would have preferred to 'have been involved with a gritty, low-budget film full of integrity . . . but the commercial gloss I think I can see the rationale for',[15] though she did later retract these criticisms somewhat.[16] Overall she was

20. The inter-racial relationship that dissolves social barriers: Tug and Liz in *Other Halves*. Courtesy of Brian McDonnell.

ambivalent about the resulting film, remaining uncomfortable that the film could be so palatable to middle-class audiences.

The significant difference between book and film in terms of target audience was an adaptation issue of particular importance in the New Zealand film industry in the 1980s. The book was aimed at a local audience, the film at an international one for clear commercial reasons. The film's gang members may not be realistic New Zealand figures to local audiences but can be read internationally by the employment of generic characteristics (type of car, clothes and drinking habits) in the depiction of urban crime. A surprise to the producers was the film's popularity with young Polynesians. Local audiences surveyed in 1985 were a mix of older, Pakeha people who might have read the novel and a younger group of teenagers, unemployed people, school kids, often Polynesian. The latter sympathised with Tug throughout the film and became restless when Liz's problems were dominating the story.[17]

Some reviewers nonetheless found that *Other Halves* misrepresented Polynesians: 'The film's slickness is dishonest . . . the street kids are just convenient props on which to hang this year's rage for tribal fashions . . . they are cute poor, cute criminals, cute druggies (they pop pills rather than sniff glue)'.[18] At the same time, it must be acknowledged that, by the mid 1980s, Auckland street kids were copying the external lifestyle trappings of African–American communities: ghettoblasters, Cuban shades, Afros, graffiti, sweatshirts, baseball caps and basketball shoes. The film itself makes little comment about racial politics except to point towards an idea of personal reconciliation as the answer to social division.

Such reconciliation between individuals, and sensitivity to the problems of others, is seemingly enough. Liz could be viewed critically as someone who uses Tug (in the film he is a Niue Islander—as is Pilisi—rather than a Maori as in the novel) for her own gratification in a radical chic way. The film suggests that their concluding sexual *rapprochement* is sufficient to dissolve class and ethnic barriers. There is no dramatic action at the end to show a change in Liz, comparable to the shoplifting in the book. Thus she does not have the same political development, and is still tied to her middle-class values and attitudes. In addition, in formal terms the ending is problematic because it peters out in a long montage sequence instead of building to a satisfying climactic scene.

Critics of the time also puzzled over exactly to which genre the film belonged.[19] It was made partly as a slice-of-life, quasi-feminist, realist picture of a middle-class woman in contemporary society, partly as a stylised street film stressing urban danger and excitement, partly as a love story with political/ethnic aspects, and partly as a liberal political film depicting the plight of Tug. The filmmakers believed that international audiences in the mid 1980s were not ready for a gritty, geographically and historically specific expose of a violent Polynesian underclass life. Such audiences had to wait for *Once Were Warriors* to see anything approaching that depiction.

Came a Hot Friday (1985)

One novelist—Ronald Hugh Morrieson—stands out in New Zealand's New Wave filmmaking because three of his four novels were turned into films during the early period of the revolution in local production (*The Scarecrow* [1963], *Came a Hot Friday* [1964] and *Pallet on the Floor* [1976]— the exception is his 1974 novel *Predicament* which remains unadapted). Morrieson's first novel *The Scarecrow* was adapted in 1982 by director Sam Pillsbury and a film version of his last, unfinished, novel *Pallet on the Floor* was produced in 1984 and eventually released theatrically in 1986. If there could be said to exist an historical progression in the commercial and aesthetic success of literary adaptations over the decade under study, then films made from Morrieson's novels offer an ideal example of this process.

In its final 90-minute form, Pillsbury's *The Scarecrow* shows signs of the difficulties its makers experienced in trying to include numerous characters and incidents from a complex novel in such a brief running time. Instead of jettisoning scenes or paring down the plot, the filmmakers merely shortened each scene so that it became like a series of montages. The film's plot is a disturbing mix of youthful high jinks, serial killing and necrophilia, reflecting Morrieson's thematic interests which were equally divided between the more light-hearted aspects of adolescence and a frightening examination of extreme sexual violence.[20] This mix of grimness, violent impulses and rollicking humour is present in varying proportions in all Morrieson's four novels but becomes progressively darker in the later novels *Predicament* and *Pallet on the Floor*, and in the posthumously published short stories.

With the adaptation of *Came a Hot Friday*, however, scriptwriters Ian Mune and Dean Parker were far more ruthless than the adapters of *The Scarecrow*. They cut out extraneous material, especially by highlighting the qualities of the novel they saw as life-affirming rather than the darker side of Morrieson. Mune, who directed the film, and who is recognised as a skilled adapter of New Zealand literature, has noted: 'With *Came a Hot Friday*, the script underwent some massive changes. The story was so spread-eagled and sprawling, it wasn't working. So we tried for the sharp linear pace of American movies until what we had was a terrible story of black negation, the characters were horrible people, greedy, avaricious, ugly and awful'.[21]

Thus, while the first two Morrieson adaptations mentioned encountered difficulties handling the bipolar tone of his writing, the cinematic version of *Came a Hot Friday* chose a radical but effective solution to this problem: jettisoning almost completely the darkest and most troubling aspects of that book's storyline. The plots of both book and film follow the antics of two con men (Wes Pennington [Peter Bland] and Cyril Kiddman [Philip Gordon]) as they attempt a scam on rural bookmakers while drinking, carousing and gambling with the denizens of a small North Island Taranaki town. Towards the story's end, they contest a large sum of dubiously acquired money with gambling hall owner Sel Bishop (Marshall Napier), and with an eccentric Maori obsessed with things Mexican who is known as the Te Whakinga (in the film the Tainuia) Kid (Billy T. James).

A typical example of the difference in the film's tone compared to that of the novel is found in its opening. The first chapter of the novel juxtaposes two views of gambling (light and dark), depicting one character Morrie Shapelski, who gets in gambling debt so deeply that he agrees to commit arson. An old man, Pop Simon, consequently is killed in the fire, and Morrie is permanently psychologically damaged. By way of contrast, Wes and Cyril's actions exhibit a positive sense of gambling as a hedonistic adventure. The film version retains only this upbeat emphasis, with the hectic early scenes co-opting the viewer into the adventures of the lead characters. Unsurprisingly given such specific details of its adaptation, the film has been widely praised as energetic and fast-paced. Writing shortly after the film's release, Nicholas Reid noted that '*Came a Hot Friday* is, bar none, the funniest, liveliest, most exuberant film ever made in New Zealand'.[22]

The novel's ending is also much darker than that of the film, with the violent death of Sel Bishop and a vicious spade attack by Wes on a bookmaker. In the literary narrative, Cyril and Wes merely fade away, leaving the final scene to the Kid who watches the stolen money disappear into a river. The film retains this river scene, but then presents an epilogue with a view of a wistful Anzac Day parade which enables a light-hearted farewell to most of the characters. Wes observes to Cyril: 'That's the

21. Cultures combined: The Maori Tainui Kid (Billy T. James), the 'Mexican bandito gone New Zealand bush' in *Came a Hot Friday*. Courtesy of the Ian Conrich collection of New Zealand cinema and visual culture.

weekend cut', as if they experience this sort of escapade all the time. They then speed off to their next adventure. Compounding this trend, the film brings in tantalising glimpses of Billy T. James (the leading New Zealand television comic of the period and a clear box office draw) as the Kid much earlier, and makes more of him as a character overall, than does the novel. As one reviewer noted: 'Billy T. James, as the Tainuia Kid, is one of the most original characters seen on the local screen, a blend of frenetic Zorro and Mexican bandito gone New Zealand bush'.[23] Perhaps unconsciously, Morrieson had made the Kid of the novel a representative of Maori reaction to Hollywood films of the 1930s and 1940s, his life located awkwardly between traditional life on the marae (Maori meeting place) and the assimilative forces of European townships. In so doing, Morrieson forged an identity out of the ethnic minority secondary characters of Western films he watched at Saturday matinees. The Kid's dark, ugly, animalistic brother (a troubling presence in the book) is, however, totally absent from the film.

Until the phenomenon of *Once Were Warriors* (which grossed $NZ6.6 million), *Came a Hot Friday*, taking over $NZ1 million locally on first release, was by far the most commercially successful literary adaptation in New Zealand.[24] Its rollicking comedy was well received critically by reviewers at the time of release: 'There's no mistaking novelist Ronald Hugh Morrieson territory—small-town, post-war (1949) Newzild, where the outside world arrives as parody, flashy and phoney, with feet of clay already cracking. . . . [the filmmakers] also lighten the tone; Morrieson's obsessions with sexuality and crime are reduced to plot mechanisms, but his ebullient comedy blossoms on screen'.[25] By opting for narrative pace, clear characterisation and straightforward humour instead of an adaptation that is a faithful rendition of the novel, Mune and his collaborators struck a chord with New Zealand audiences of the 1980s in a way other adapters had not been able to achieve.

Conclusion

The average cost of publishing and launching a new novel in New Zealand in the 1980s was between $15,000 and $20,000, but a new feature film at that time was unlikely to be made for less than $1 million plus release (marketing and distribution) costs.[26] Filmmakers and investors therefore had to consider the commercial potential of any production project, and source novels were likely to be reworked not only in terms of the needs of the film medium but also in terms of attracting as wide an audience as was possible. Faithful adaptations of local novels, which in Australia or the UK might appear as a mini-series on national television, have rarely appeared in New Zealand (*The God Boy* in 1976 and several Ngaio Marsh mysteries in 1978 being the main exceptions).

In addition to such obvious commercial concerns, technical skills in direction, cinematography and editing developed in the New Wave of filmmaking before a comparable skills base was established in screenwriting. Adaptations of local short stories and novels therefore helped the film industry by providing the props of pre-existing stories and by giving scripting experience to filmmakers (such as Roger Donaldson and Vincent Ward) who later went on to write successful original scripts for features.[27] What most popular directors and scriptwriters learned in the early 1980s were certain storytelling skills in terms of pacing a feature film, interweaving characters without confusing the audience and avoiding overcrowding scripts.

In terms of the adaptations discussed here, *Sons for the Return Home* stresses the additional pressures of cultural translation, given its status as a Samoan novel filmed by New Zealanders. The book had a sprawling structure; this problem had to be thought through and the structure altered. The result was unsuccessful in one respect: the overall time structure was compressed and the film wove together past and present in a sometimes bewildering manner. The film's mixture of the personal and the political was also uneasy: the director differed markedly in his aims and style from the novel's author and later clashed with the producer. These pressures are visible in the finished film, in its confusing structure and in the deadening effect of Maunder's polemics.

The makers of *Other Halves* started out with a source novel that was strongly local in flavour, but they chose to highlight those aspects likely to interest an international audience—in particular, what producer Tom

Finlayson termed the 'sophisticated' viewers of the large cities of Western Europe and North America.[28] This objective influenced the visual style and, when New Zealanders saw the film, they sometimes reacted with resentment and confusion. Commercial pressures seemed to outweigh the original social message; in the end it became more of a personal story aimed at the same middle-class audience whose values were called bogus in the novel. The film did, however, provide New Zealanders with a picture of a class-divided society different from the egalitarian myths seen in much of the popular culture at the time.

The shakedown early period following the setting up of the Film Commission led eventually to changes in the tax environment in 1982, putting pressure on films to be more profit conscious, with the result that a certain kind of filmmaker, skilled in the strategies of commercial survival, emerged.[29] Such filmmakers came to have the greatest influence on the style of literary adaptations. Mune, with his attitude of: 'Get to know the book thoroughly, and then throw it away', is a representative example.[30] In the case of *Came a Hot Friday* the adapters were faithful to only the one aspect of the novel they wished to adapt. After considerable discussion and argument about Morrieson as a 'manic-depressive' writer, they chose to use only the manic (comic) side of the novel. Mune believed it was possible to produce a more successful adaptation by not attempting to be comprehensive.

The New Zealand film industry thus learned certain hard lessons in the period 1978–87. In formal terms it learned, for example, that it could not treat a novel as a very long screenplay and try to make a film from it directly. Adaptation was found not to be the total answer to the problem of a lack of experienced scriptwriters because the need for adaptation skills equals those required to write an original script. Today, after a long period of building up experience and fostering training through scripting workshops and the establishment of formal education courses in scriptwriting, there is greater confidence shown in original material as the blueprint for film production. Nevertheless, local novels still sometimes make very successful films, as is attested by the unprecedented success, both nationally and internationally, of *Once Were Warriors* and *Whale Rider* (2002), which have each grossed over $NZ6 million in local box office receipts. These two characteristics, greater talent in original scriptwriting and the continued marketability of the literary adaptation, manifest in the current film production culture are not, however, mutually antagonistic. In fact, as the appendix below demonstrates, there has been a flurry of adaptation projects in development since the success of *Whale Rider*, with both contemporary works of fiction and more classic novels being translated into cinematic form. Indeed, with the production rate of both literary works of fiction and feature films made in New Zealand during the early years of the new century being far greater than in the 1970s and 1980s, there is at present ample room for both original and adapted screenplays to find acceptance.

APPENDIX: New Zealand Literature to Film (Feature and Television) Adaptations since 1976

Year	Title of Film	Director	Adapted From	Author	Form
1976	*The God Boy* (television film)	Murray Reece	*The God Boy*	Ian Cross	novel
1977	*Sleeping Dogs*	Roger Donaldson	*Smith's Dream*	C.K. Stead	novel
1978	*Died in the Wool* (television film)	Brian McDuffie	*Died in the Wool*	Ngaio Marsh	novel
1978	*Colour Scheme* (television film)	Peter Sharp	*Colour Scheme*	Ngaio Marsh	novel
1978	*A State of Siege*	Vincent Ward	*A State of Siege*	Janet Frame	novel
1979	*Middle Age Spread*	John Reid	*Middle Age Spread*	Roger Hall	stage play
1979	*Sons for the Return Home*	Paul Maunder	*Sons for the Return Home*	Albert Wendt	novel
1980	*Beyond Reasonable Doubt*	John Laing	*Beyond Reasonable Doubt*	David Yallop	investigative non-fiction
1982	*The Scarecrow*	Sam Pillsbury	*The Scarecrow*	Ronald Hugh Morrieson	novel
1984	*The Silent One*	Yvonne Mackay	*The Silent One*	Joy Cowley	children's novel
1984	*Pallet on the Floor*	Lynton Butler	*Pallet on the Floor*	Ronald Hugh Morrieson	unfinished novel
1984	*Among the Cinders*	Rolf Haedrich	*Among the Cinders*	Maurice Shadbolt	novel

Year	Title of Film	Director	Adapted From	Author	Form
1984	*Other Halves*	John Laing	*Other Halves*	Sue McCauley	novel
1985	*Came a Hot Friday*	Ian Mune	*Came a Hot Friday*	Ronald Hugh Morrieson	novel
1985	*The Quiet Earth*	Geoff Murphy	*The Quiet Earth*	Craig Harrison	novel
1985	*Sylvia*	Michael Firth	1. *Teacher* 2. *I Passed This Way*	Sylvia Ashton-Warner	autobiographies
1986	*Footrot Flats: The Dog's Tail Tale*	Murray Ball	*Footrot Flats: The Dog's Tail Tale*	Murray Ball	comic strip
1987	*Starlight Hotel*	Sam Pillsbury	*The Dream Mongers*	Grant Hindin-Miller	children's novel
1988	*A Soldier's Tale*	Larry Parr	*A Soldier's Tale*	M.K.Joseph	novel
1989	*Champion* (television film)	Peter Sharp	*Champion*	Maurice Gee	children's novel
1990	*Flying Fox in a Freedom Tree*	Martyn Sanderson	*Flying Fox in a Freedom Tree*	Albert Wendt	novella
1990	*An Angel at My Table*	Jane Campion	1. *To the Is-Land* 2. *An Angel at My Table* 3. *The Envoy from Mirror City*	Janet Frame	autobiographical trilogy
1991	*The End of the Golden Weather*	Ian Mune	*The End of the Golden Weather*	Bruce Mason	one-man stage play

Year	Title of Film	Director	Adapted From	Author	Form
1991	*Chunuk Bair*	Dale G. Bradley	1. *Once on Chunuk Bair* 2. *Gallipoli, The New Zealand Story*	Maurice Shadbolt; Chris Pugsley	stage play non-fiction history
1992	*Moonrise*	David Blyth	*Moonrise*	Michael Heath	radio play
1992	*Alex*	Megan Simpson	*Alex*	Tessa Duder	teenage novel
1993	*Bread and Roses*	Gaylene Preston	*Bread and Roses*	Sonja Davies	autobiography
1994	*Once Were Warriors*	Lee Tamahori	*Once Were Warriors*	Alan Duff	novel
1996	*Flight of the Albatross*	Werner Meyer	*Flight of the Albatross*	Deborah Savage	juvenile novel
1997	*Saving Grace*	Costa Botes	*Saving Grace*	Duncan Sarkies	stage play
1998	*Memory and Desire*	Niki Caro	*Of Memory and Desire*	Peter Wells	short story
1998	*Heaven*	Scott Reynolds	*Heaven*	Chad Taylor	novella
1999	*What Becomes of the Broken Hearted?*	Ian Mune	*What Becomes of the Broken Hearted?*	Alan Duff	novel
2000	*Jubilee*	Michael Hurst	*Jubilee*	Nepi Solomon	novel
2001	*Clare* (television film)	Yvonne Mackay	*Fate Cries Enough*	Clare Matheson	autobiography
2001	*Rain*	Christine Jeffs	*Rain*	Kirsty Gunn	novella
2002	*Whale Rider*	Niki Caro	*The Whale Rider*	Witi Ihimaera	novel

Year	Title of Film	Director	Adapted From	Author	Form
2003	*Skin and Bone* (television film)	Chris Bailey	*Foreskin's Lament*	Greg McKee	stage play
2004	*In My Father's Den*	Brad McGann	*In My Father's Den*	Maurice Gee	novel
2004	*Fracture*	Larry Parr	*Crime Story*	Maurice Gee	novel
2004	*Spooked*	Geoff Murphy	*The Paradise Conspiracy*	Ian Wishart	novel
2005	*50 Ways of Saying Fabulous*	Stewart Main	*50 Ways of Saying Fabulous*	Graeme Aitken	novel
2006	*No. 2*	Toa Fraser	*No. 2*	Toa Fraser	one-woman stage play
2006	*Out of the Blue*	Robert Sarkies	*Aramoana: Twenty-two Hours of Terror*	Bill O'Brien	non-fiction
2009	*The Vintner's Luck*	Niki Caro	*The Vintner's Luck*	Elizabeth Knox	novel
2009	*Under the Mountain*	Jonathan King	*Under the Mountain*	Maurice Gee	children's novel

As of 2008, the following film projects are at varying stages of script development:

TITLE OF FILM	DIRECTOR	ADAPTED FROM	AUTHOR	FORM
Mahana	Andrew Bancroft	*Bulibasha*	Witi Ihimaera	novel
Death of a Superhero	Anthony McCarten	*Death of a Superhero*	Anthony Mc–Carten	novel
Predicament	Jason Stutter	*Predicament*	Ronald Hugh Morrieson	novel
Cousins		*Cousins*	Patricia Grace	novel
Spinners		*Spinners*	Anthony Mc–Carten	novel
Jimmy Costello		*The Ballad of Jimmy Costello*	Tim Balme	stage play
Not Her Real Name		*Not Her Real Name*	Emily Perkins	collection of short stories
Behind the Tattooed Face		*Behind the Tattooed Face*	Heretaunga Pat Baker	novel

Notes

1. Brian McFarlane, *Novel to Film*, (Oxford: Clarendon Press, 1996), 7.
2. James Naremore, 'Introduction', *Film Adaptation*, ed. Naremore (New Brunswick, N.J.: Rutgers University Press, 2000), 10.
3. See, for example, K.O. Arvidson, 'Sons for the Return Home', *Landfall* 111 (September 1974): 256–60.
4. See Michael J. Field, *Mau: Samoa's Struggle Against New Zealand Oppression* (Wellington: Reed, 1984).
5. Roger Robinson, 'Albert Wendt: An Assessment', *Landfall* 135 (September 1980): 277.
6. Albert Wendt, *Auckland Star*, 18 October 1979, 5.
7. Paul Maunder, '*Sons for the Return Home*: An Interview with Paul Maunder', *Cinema Papers* 45 (May–June 1980): 11.
8. Ibid., 11.
9. See Whelehan's introductory chapter in *Adaptations: from text to screen, screen to text*, ed. Deborah Cartmell and Imelda Whelehan (London and New York: Routledge, 1999), 14.
10. John O'Shea, interview with author, 16 September 1985.
11. Albert Wendt, letter to author, 6 September 1985.
12. Since then only one other author has written the screenplay adaptation of his own novel: Alan Duff wrote the screenplay of *What Becomes of the Broken Hearted?* (1999), the sequel to *Once Were Warriors*.
13. Susan Buckland, 'Film-making: a people business', *Inflight* 7 (1984): 20–24.
14. *Kaleidoscope*, 18 May 1984, TVNZ Channel One (reporter Aileen O'Sullivan).
15. John Parker, 'Making *Other Halves*: our first contemporary urban film', *Metro* (February 1985): 106.
16. Sue McCauley, letter to the editor, *Metro* (April 1985): 151–52.
17. See Brian McDonnell, *The Translation of New Zealand Fiction into Film*, unpublished doctoral thesis, University of Auckland, 1986, 255–56.
18. Mark Williams, *New Outlook* (March–April 1985): 50.
19. See John Parker, 'Other Halves', *Metro* (April 1985): 151–52; Tom McWilliams, 'Whole hearted', *NZ Listener*, 9 February 1985, 29; Sandi Hall, 'Other Halves', *Broadsheet* (March 1985): 42; Wynne Colgan, 'Tough novel disappoints on screen', *New Zealand Herald*, 26 January 1985, Section 2, 7; Harvey Clark, 'Seeing how the other half lives', *Auckland Star*, 26 January 1985, B4; Nicholas Reid (alias Carl Denham), 'Uneasy, unhappy, patronising', *Zealandia*, 10 February 1985, 11.
20. For a fuller discussion of the changes made to *The Scarecrow*, see Brian McDonnell, *The Scarecrow: A film study guide* (Auckland: Longman Paul, 1982).
21. Jonathon Dowling, 'Over-the-top Mune just cannot stop performing', *New Zealand Herald*, 31 August 1985, Weekend Magazine: 3.
22. Nicholas Reid, *A Decade of New Zealand Film*: Sleeping Dogs *to* Came a Hot Friday (Dunedin: John McIndoe, 1986), 119.
23. Harvey Clark, 'A Kiwi Classic', *Auckland Star*, 24 August 1985, B4.

24. See *New Zealand Film*, 28 (April 1986): 10. The 1986 animated *Footrot Flats: The Dog's Tail/Tale*, based on Murray Ball's syndicated newspaper cartoon strip, could actually lay claim to being New Zealand most commercially successful adaptation at this point, grossing over $2 million at the local box office. See *New Zealand Film* 30 (February 1987): 3. See also Helen Martin and Sam Edwards, *New Zealand Film 1912–1996* (Auckland: Oxford University Press, 1997), 103.
25. Tom McWilliams, 'Slapstick in Hicksville', *New Zealand Listener*, 31 August 1985, 40.
26. Tom Finlayson, interview with author, 17 September 1985.
27. Donaldson was co-scriptwriter on *After the Depression* (in the television series *Winners and Losers* 1976) adapted from a Maurice Shadbolt story before co-scripting *Smash Palace* (1981); Ward co-adapted Janet Frame's novel *A State of Siege* before co-scripting *Vigil* (1984) and *The Navigator: A Mediaeval Odyssey* (1988).
28. Finlayson, interview, 17 September 1985.
29. A government budget change in 1982 eliminated tax shelter provisions for film productions but allowed any film begun prior to 5 August 1982 to have until 30 September 1984 for completion in order to qualify for the existing tax advantages.
30. Ian Mune, interview with author, 4 June 1985.

10

The Contested Nation:
DOCUMENTARY AND DISSENT

Annie Goldson and Jo Smith

Following an influential visit by John Grierson in 1940, documentary making in New Zealand underwent crucial developments during the Second World War, just as local communities consolidated a process that had begun in the 1930s of constructing their identity in specifically national terms. The genre's links to national identity and realism that date from these developments have been largely sustained, and are manifest in the primary output of documentary today, that of broadcast television. New Zealand documentary, following Grierson and the cultural nationalism of the 1940s, thus largely seeks to present the nation as a coherent social and political space, often incorporating and eliding difference and contradiction. Yet there is an alternative tradition within documentary that has resisted the general project of such nationalism. This tradition is the body of work, mainly independent and often with explicit political concerns, that has emerged from the 1970s, and which has its origins in film, rather than television.

This article will examine the emergence of alternative documentary forms within the context of earlier government documentary practices. Filmmakers such as Barry Barclay, Merata Mita, Gaylene Preston, Annie Goldson and Peter Wells have produced works that continue a vital and sustaining style of documentary that articulates real social critique, that experiments with aesthetic convention, and emphasises disruption, dissension and difference. These filmmakers reveal the nation as a contested construct, made up of peoples and viewpoints that often resist and confront prevailing and orthodox views of New Zealand society.

The Picturesque Past
New Zealand attracted local and international filmmakers before 'documentary' was named as a genre. As Mita suggests, 'Aotearoa had two remarkable attributes. The first was commonly described as New Zealand's scenic attractions, the second was the Maori—and both were eminently photogenic'.[1] Early travelling photographers and filmmakers produced single reel 'scenics' largely documenting Maori custom, local events and the landscapes. These works screened locally and internationally and were, at times, framed with a lecture from the filmmaker, a practice that highlighted their ethnographic function. The New Zealand Government

also used images of Maori and the landscape to promote the country to an international audience. The first feature-length scenic given a commercial release was the 1925 *Glorious New Zealand*, made by the Government Publicity Office, and which was screened at the New Zealand and South Seas Exhibition held in Dunedin, while the Trucolor feature *Romantic New Zealand* of 1934 was a local success in Australia as well as New Zealand.[2] While the Government used scenics to cultivate New Zealand as a brand on the international market (as well as nurture national pride) local film enthusiasts such as the journalist E. Stanhope Andrews expressed concern at the lack of diversity in New Zealand's film identity, particularly in the wake of New Zealand's involvement in the war effort.[3] The growing recognition of the function film could play in the nation's life was advanced when the New Zealand Government invited the British Grierson to stop in New Zealand as one leg in his tour of the Commonwealth.

As has been noted elsewhere, Grierson's role as a producer and writer influenced documentary worldwide.[4] Although not explicitly stated by the New Zealand or British Governments, the development of documentary (under Grierson's influence) could be seen as a vital tool for maintaining a dual sense of Empire and Nation. It is this mode of approach that is a key characteristic of New Zealand documentary making, as it is a practice based upon a settler consciousness derived from familial and economic links with Europe as well as the more pragmatic practices of everyday life in a settler state. While the links with Empire would slowly erode with each new generation of New Zealanders, as well as through changing relationships with international capital, this ambivalent dual consciousness still marks contemporary documentary practices.

1940s Cultural Nationalism

By the time that Grierson arrived in New Zealand, his notion of documentary was one that provided a creed of social interconnection and 'good propaganda'. The role of the mass media, Grierson argued, was to foster national unity and should result from a 'clericy' of intellectuals co-operating with politicians, communicating national objectives to people, and regulating and administering social life for the national good.[5] However, Grierson's prescription offered little room for social critique or any challenge to the existing establishment and indeed, his practice at 'home' and throughout the Commonwealth could be seen as an attempt to contain and, as Ian Aitken suggests, 'diminish the democratic potential unleashed by the war'.[6] Perhaps the Government Film Studio's documentary *One Hundred Crowded Years* (1940) best encapsulates Grierson's prescriptive approach. Made for the country's centennial celebrations, this film represents the pinnacle of the Government's attempt to narrate, promote and celebrate the nation through filmic means and prefigured much of what was to come in terms of Government filmmaking. *One Hundred Crowded Years* featured a stern and no-nonsense voice-over by B.W. Beeby, dramatic reenactments of significant moments in New Zealand's history (the signing of the Treaty of Waitangi in 1840; the Otago Gold Rush and the New Zealand Wars in the nineteenth century) as well as a celebratory overview of the agricultural, economic and social welfare initiatives of the government—a didactic and bellicose example of filmic propaganda.

Grierson was derisory about New Zealand's documentary efforts up to this point. Complaining about the medium's touristic tendencies, nobody, he said, would remember in it 'the face of a New Zealander'.[7] In his wake the National Film Unit (NFU) was set up, which produced a popular series of cinema shorts called the *Weekly Review*. Made up of newsreels and the occasional short documentary, the series ran for all of the 1940s, showing before features in local cinemas throughout the country. The *Weekly Review* exactly fulfilled Grierson's goal of civic education. The filmmakers, as civil servants themselves, were to work in tandem with other Government departments. During the war, the *Weekly Review* concentrated on the New Zealand war effort at home and abroad, while in the post-war period, the spirit of nation-building took over. Indeed, according to one Government list, suitable subjects for the *Weekly Review* included: the current activities of ministers; a 'meet the worker' series designed to build pride in occupation; sport; scouts and guides; community service; education subjects; the dental service; health; forestry; and selected industrial subjects.[8]

In general, the *Weekly Review* continued the white, masculine and moralising vision of the country introduced in *One Hundred Crowded Years*. Pakeha (European) men were seen as toiling hard, in tandem with the Government of the day, to build the new nation. Cultural differences amongst Pakeha were suppressed, and women, when they did appear, were shown as the grateful recipients of the efforts of state and man, manifest through Plunket and state housing.[9] Maori were also rarely glimpsed, and often treated in a patronising fashion in line with the assimilationist philosophy of the day.

This new nation or 'imagined community' to use Benedict Anderson's well-used concept, offered a rosy vision of harmonious, frugal and homogenous Pakeha families, supported by the then Labour Government in their efforts to restore calm to a culture disrupted by war.[10] The litany of subject matter of the Reviews would have pleased Grierson in the 1940s and 1950s. As stated above, by this point in his career, he lauded 'realism' and had an apparent distrust of 'fancy' filmmaking; hence his proposals had fallen on fertile ground, in that they paralleled the predominant aesthetic of realism established in New Zealand literature and painting. In summary then, at the moment of the apparent consolidation of national identity (through the 1940 celebration of the signing of the 1840 Treaty of Waitangi and the wartime effort), the Griersonian documentary was championed as the preferred form, providing an image of New Zealanders at work, at play and at war. Critically, this vision was prescriptive rather than reflective. At this point in the development of a national film culture, the New Zealand Government used documentary to narrate a particular imagined community based upon tropes of virile white masculinity and a benevolent and paternalistic form of governmentality. But while the NFU played a large part in the construction of this narrative of nationhood, the institution also served as a stepping-stone for individual filmmakers to develop their skills and to eventually produce an alternative documentary tradition that contested the nature of this imagined community.[11]

Fighting Back

An alternative tradition was evident from the beginnings of documentary, manifest through left-wing and union-based documentary. Yet, in a country the size of New Zealand, it is one that has always had to negotiate with the mainstream to obtain an audience and secure financial viability. An employee of the NFU, Cecil Holmes, was both a filmmaker and Communist, who produced a series of short newsreels and documentaries that were screened before feature films as part of the *Weekly Review* series. His short film *The Coaster* (a 1948 portrait of the trading ships that travelled the coasts of New Zealand) was deeply derivative of *Night Mail* (1936), one of the most famous films to emerge from the British Documentary Movement. Although 'pro-worker', its ideological position was not too far removed from the Labour Government's own. However, another short, *Mail Run* (1947) used the newsreel effectively as an anti-colonial polemic, consistent with Holmes' Communist beliefs and at absolute odds with the Government policy of the day. The film followed a plane delivering mail to the J-troops stationed in Japan. Using the conceit of the filmmakers 'diary', the film delivers sharp comment on the conditions of life for the poor in each of the plane's refuelling stops: including Australia, Hong Kong, Indonesia and the Philippines. When the NFU fired Holmes (largely due to his political stance) Holmes produced the militant documentary, *Fighting Back* (1949), a fiery exposé of a union lockout.

The tradition of documentary representing union struggles and perspectives has continued sporadically over the last half century, exemplified by collaborative works such as *Wildcat* (1981) and *The Bridge: The Story of Men in Dispute* (1982) all of which have strikes as their focus. Because of their dramatic quality and their ability to reveal the contradictions of capitalism, strikes have long been a favoured topic of left-wing filmmakers. Alister Barry's *Someone Else's Country* (1996), and *In A Land of Plenty* (2002), changed critical direction however, examining the consequences of the monetary reforms of the 1980s that had enforced radical and immediate change on the New Zealand populace. Although Holmes managed to sneak *Mail Run* past Government scrutineers and into the *Weekly Reviews*, the contemporary forms of documentary exhibition rely mainly upon broadcast television. Barry's work has been consistently refused airtime by television broadcasters who must balance public service mandates with the more pressing concerns of commercial viability. After producing *Someone Else's Country* and *In A Land of Plenty*, therefore, Barry undertook something of a road show, screening the documentaries in cinemas, at educational institutions and community halls and selling record numbers of video copies to a public clearly hungry for alternative perspectives.

Contested Visions in the 1970s

Independent producers and filmmakers managed to penetrate television briefly in the early 1970s, and one of the most notable results was the *Survey* series, which included Maori filmmaker Barclay's portrayal of the relationship between a friendly dolphin (Opo) and a small Northland community in *The Town That Lost a Miracle* (1972). The series also included the experimental work of Tony Williams, whose 1971 documentary *Getting Together* was an innovative take on what would have been a typical dreary subject (the inner workings of Boy Scouts, Rotary and other clubs). A second documentary, *Deciding* (1972), which traced the unsuccessful efforts of a man to find a way of preventing a factory from polluting a river, was in effect a parodic meditation on the labyrinthine workings of the public service. The tone of his documentary, again in sharp contrast to the so-called nationalist spirit celebrated in the *Weekly Reviews*, suggested a bohemianism that anticipated New Zealand's New Wave of feature films. Features such as *Sleeping Dogs* (1977), *Goodbye Pork Pie* (1980) and *Smash Palace* (1981) were to capture a sense of larrikinism that had defined a masculine style of rebellion associated with radical and hippie movements from the 1970s.

Documentary engaging with Maoridom had first emerged in the 1970s, a response to the rise of Maoritanga and a reaction against the uniformity of the Holyoake era.[12] The groundbreaking *Tangata Whenua* series, produced by John O'Shea's Pacific Films, written by historian Michael King and directed by Barclay, was broadcast nationally in 1974. In embarking on a Maori series, the filmmakers wished to explore in part why Maori called themselves Maori, rather than New Zealanders.[13] Although aspects of the then dominant cultural agenda are still evident in the series, it pitted Maori culture against New Zealand's national history in order to celebrate Maori difference. Hence, it did represent something of a break with the tendencies that had predominated in documentary making. Barclay went on to direct numerous documentaries including *The Neglected Miracle* (1985), a feature-length work on gene preservation and stewardship of genetic resources. Given today's debates on genetic modification and the threat to biodiversity, the work was prescient. His most recent feature *The Feathers of Peace* (2000), which follows the quasi-newsreel style of Peter Watkins' British produced *Battle of Culloden* (1965), tells the story of the invasion of Rekohu (known as the Chatham Islands) first by the British, then by Taranaki Maori, and the systematic massacre of the Moriori and the dispossession of their ancestral land. New Zealand school children have historically been fed a version of Moriori history that functioned as a justification for colonial occupation: hence, the political importance of *The Feathers of Peace* reverberated widely. Given Barclay's long relationship with broadcast television, he tends to have had his work readily broadcast even when it challenges some of the cherished precepts of nationhood.

Along with Barclay, Mita has also contributed to the development of a strong Maori tradition within documentary. After completing the 'strike' documentary, *The Bridge*, Mita went on to co-direct *Bastion Point—Day 507* (1978), a verité style work that documents a highly significant land occupation by Maori protestors, an event that anticipated a wave of political change. Mita also was credited as the director of the remarkable *Patu!* (1983), a documentary that depicts the huge social tensions that occurred in 1981 during the tour of the Springboks, the South African national rugby team. New Zealand, which had a strong anti-apartheid movement, has nonetheless always been a rugby-loving nation. This period of turmoil split families and communities apart, revealing a deep violence in the culture as the police were pitted against the protestors. As *Patu!* argues, the ensuing conflict, precipitated by a consideration of racism abroad, forced many New Zealanders to reflect on their own record of race relations. The film draws on historical materialist and Marxist traditions, yet with Mita taking a leading role as director, has a distinctly Maori orientation. *Patu!* was initially banned from television and showed in cinemas, and was eventually broadcast ten years after its completion.

Documentaries produced and directed by women in the 1970s also tend to challenge an easy nationalism. While the NFU employed some women as production assistants and editors, the opportunities for women to develop filmmaking skills were limited by the attitudes of the time. As Deborah Shepard has noted, when NFU production assistant and editor Judy Rymer asked to be sent on location, a NFU official responded by stating 'It would be very difficult to send you on location because you might get pregnant'.[14] It was in this conservative climate that independent films such as *Some of My Best Friends are Women* (1975), the six-part series *Women* (1976) that aired on the national broadcaster TVNZ, and Stephanie Beth's *I Want to be Joan* (1977) emerged directly from the priorities of the second-wave feminist movement. Highly polemical and strongly influenced by international trends within the women's movement, they covered a range of feminist issues from domestic abuse, reproductive rights and sexuality, to issues of media representation.

The NFU did provide opportunities for women to learn the craft of filmmaking and Rymer went on to make the eloquent documentary on Colin McCahon, *Victory Over Death* (1987), a portrait of one of New Zealand's most renowned painters. More recently, she co-directed *Cinema of Unease* (1995), a survey of New Zealand film history presented in personal fashion by Sam Neill. Thus, in summary, the 1970s' documentary tradition in New Zealand can be characterised by a left-wing, politicised practice that developed from international political movements such as feminism and anti-racist initiatives. Although these influences are evident still in the 1980s and 1990s, this latter period also saw the emergence of a more personal form of documentary practice.

22. Documenting the contested nation: Filmmakers and authorities clash in *Patu!*
Courtesy of the Ian Conrich collection of New Zealand cinema and visual culture.

Contemporary Documentary Practices

War Stories (1995), directed by Preston, continues the tradition established by 1970s feminist filmmakers of using film to articulate women's experiences. A production that gained a healthier box office than many New Zealand dramatic films, *War Stories* is effectively an oral history. Constructed of long interviews with a series of women, it appears to be minimally edited: the women speak of the pain, disruption and disillusionment that New Zealand women experienced during World War II and its aftermath. They admit to having affairs while their husbands were away; they confess the difficulties of living with men damaged by the war experience; and they speak of the sexual violence they experienced as war workers. These stories act in sharp counterpoint to the *Weekly Review*'s optimistic depiction of the noble war effort of the 1940s. Preston's insistence on politicising personal experiences is continued in her 2001 documentary, *Titless Wonders,* that tells the story of women affected by breast cancer. She also produced and co-directed the fly-on-the-wall documentary *Getting to Our Place* (1999) which observes the three-year build up to the opening of the Museum of New Zealand Te Papa Tongarewa, in Wellington, a public institution that drew much criticism for its hi-tech, populist curatorial style. The film documents the creative, commercial and political forces that collect around such a project, highlighting key figures such as CEO Cheryll Sotheran, the colourful ex-CEO Ron Trotter and Kaihautu/CEO Cliff Whiting.

Preston remains a significant figure in the development of New Zealand documentary and her influence within the film industry has led to the funding of initiatives from other New Zealand documentary makers. Indeed, *War Stories* functioned as a funding and distribution blueprint for *Punitive Damage* (1999) and Preston's presence as Executive Producer of the film gave the funders additional confidence in the project. As with *War Stories,* Goldson's *Punitive Damage* is structured around an oral testimony, this time that of Helen Todd, a New Zealand woman who successfully sued an Indonesian general in a Boston court after her son, Kamal Bamadhaj, was killed in the Dili massacre in East Timor in 1991. The film begins with the trajectory of Bamadhaj's life, following his upbringing between New Zealand and Malaysia, his school years and his growing politicisation as a university student in Australia and, finally, his death at 20 years of age. The documentary then picks up Todd's story, tracing her legal battle to obtain some accountability for Bamadhaj's murder. The film ends with Todd's provisional victory. *Punitive Damage* gained both international cinema and broadcast release, and accrued over ten awards at film festivals. Its release coincided with another bloody episode in East Timor's history, the referendum which led, eventually, to the country's independence.

Goldson has since collaborated with established gay filmmaker Peter Wells to produce the documentary *Georgie Girl* (2001). Both Wells and his one-time partner Stewart Main produced formally innovative and, at times, overtly gay documentaries beginning in the 1980s. *Newest City on the Globe* (1985) and *The Mighty Civic* (1988), for example, are decorative and fantastical pieces that celebrate a certain architectural sensibility, as seen in both the city of Napier (the Art Deco capital of the world) and of the Civic Theatre, Auckland's picture palace. Both filmmakers have also produced more personal works: Main's *God, Sreenu and Me* (2000), an essayistic work ostensibly about New Zealanders who choose to live in India, ends up being a meditation on the filmmaker's own identity, sexuality and 'journey', whilst Wells's *Pansy,* produced for TVNZ, is a film memoir, based on his experiences of growing up in the Auckland suburb of Point Chevalier.

Georgie Girl is a documentary on the life and times of Georgina Beyer, a Maori woman and the world's first transgender person to be elected into national office. The documentary screened nationally on free-to-air television in February 2002 to a third of the country's population creating a sense of what Wells describes as 'binding together in a temporal unit the whole colliding fantasy known as New Zealand'.[15] *Georgie Girl* functions as a representation of New Zealand's ambiguous status as a local market with a public sphere where the margins and the mainstream readily meet (as Wells's notion of a 'colliding fantasy' alludes to), a geopolitical circumstance that contributes to the national myth of a progressive, egalitarian society. Indeed, Beyer's own status as a marginal subject embraced by the

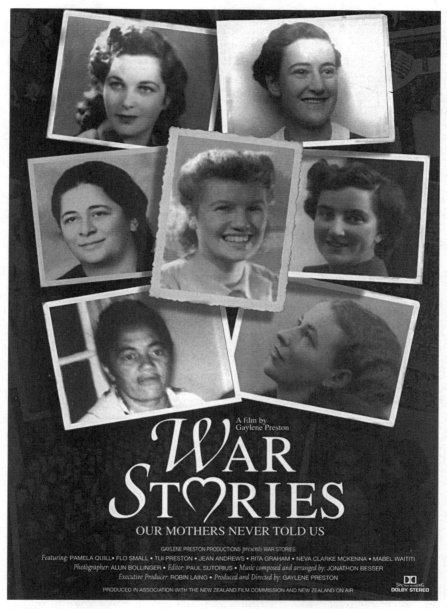

A film by
Gaylene Preston

WAR STORIES

OUR MOTHERS NEVER TOLD US

GAYLENE PRESTON PRODUCTIONS *presents* WAR STORIES
Featuring: PAMELA QUILL • FLO SMALL • TUI PRESTON • JEAN ANDREWS • RITA GRAHAM • NEVA CLARKE MCKENNA • MABEL WAITITI
Photographer: ALUN BOLLINGER • *Editor:* PAUL SUTORIUS • *Music composed and arranged by:* JONATHON BESSER
Executive Producer: ROBIN LAING • *Produced and Directed by:* GAYLENE PRESTON

PRODUCED IN ASSOCIATION WITH THE NEW ZEALAND FILM COMMISSION AND NEW ZEALAND ON AIR

DOLBY STEREO

23. Women's experience as oral history: The revisionist documentary *War Stories*.
Courtesy of the Ian Conrich collection of New Zealand cinema and visual culture.

conservative and rural Carterton electorate attests to the enduring saliency of this nationalist myth, while at the same time challenging homogeneous understandings of rural New Zealand.[16]

The film demonstrates the close links between representations of racial and sexual difference that advance a minority's cause, the representations that complement the agendas of more mainstream social regimes (be they interests of the nation state, party-political propaganda or broadcasting bodies). The complexity of this situation is embodied in the use made of archive footage from Beyer's former life in the sex and entertainment industry that is juxtaposed with contemporary images of her public life as a parliamentary representative. Commissioned by the state broadcaster TVNZ, *Georgie Girl* expresses the contradictory logic of a broadcast regime that seeks to uphold a public service duty while under the influence of a commercial imperative. As television becomes the primary site for the exhibition and funding of contemporary New Zealand documentary, the politicized filmmaker working under such conditions must negotiate the fine (and fraught) line between education and entertainment. The archive footage of *Georgie Girl* demonstrates this ambivalence in that it simultaneously provides salacious details of a subculture's community (congruent with a market logic predicated on the exploitation of sexual and racial difference) while also providing a counter-image of a New Zealand public sphere that contributes a more politicised point of view.

Conclusion

The history of an alternative tradition of documentary making in New Zealand began in film and now continues within the more ambivalent space of broadcast television. New Zealand's small local market requires some filmmakers to make strategic use of international capital to fund efforts that might reach both local and global audiences. Other strategies involve framing projects in a manner that might appeal to the government funding agencies, in effect performing a strategic form of nationalism that might appeal to the majority while also contributing a politicised point of view.[17] The placement of such a politicised or alternative tradition *within* the mainstream has both positive and negative outcomes. From a filmmaker's perspective, accessing large audiences outside one's own circle can be a pleasure and a challenge, and an alternative viewpoint can exert certain pressures on traditional film and television commissioning mechanisms. However, to reach that point, filmmakers often have to negotiate within a highly commercial media environment, with the concomitant compromises made. These compromises are formed through the ambivalent proximity of the margins to the mainstream, where state practices can take advantage of the novelty of difference provided by the alternative tradition.

To control resentment and dissent, government funding bodies have had to open up to new audiences who, in the past, have been unable to identify with the version of national consciousness and culture as offered by the NFU. Multiple identities created around a politics of gender, ethnicity and the environment means that traditional understandings of nationhood no longer work. This increasing instability has been intensified by factors such as economic restructuring, monetary deregulation, the dismantling of state enterprises and the internationalising of capital and culture. While the *Weekly Review* depicted the New Zealand nation as a homogeneous imagined community, contemporary documentary practices attempt to transform and re-write this narrative, in the process expressing the nation-state of New Zealand as what Wells refers to as a 'colliding fantasy'. The task of New Zealand's alternative documentary tradition has always been to offer a critique from *within* this nation-state that ensures that New Zealand's national imaginary remains contested, debated, challenged and unsettled.

Notes

1. Merata Mita, 'The Soul and the Image', *Film in Aotearoa New Zealand*, ed. Jonathan Dennis and Jan Bieringa (Wellington: Victoria University Press, 1996), 40.
2. Geoffrey B. Churchman, ed., *Celluloid Dreams: A Century of Film in New Zealand* (Wellington: IPL Books, 1997), 54.
3. John O'Shea cites Andrews as having a significant influence on the development of Government film practices at this time, through his personal friendship with the then Prime Minister Peter Fraser, as well as through his passion for film. See John O'Shea, 'A Charmed Life: Fragments of Memory . . . and Extracts from Conversations', *Film in Aotearoa New Zealand*, 16.
4. Joyce Nelson discusses Grierson's influence in Canada in her book, *The Colonized Eye: Rethinking the Grierson Legend* (Toronto: Between the Lines, 1988). See also Deane Williams 'Between empire and nation: Grierson in Australia' in *Screening the Past* 7 (1999) <http://www.latrobe.edu.au/screeningthepast/firstrelease/fr0799/dwfr7e.htm> for an examination of the producer's effect on the Australian documentary tradition.
5. For an in-depth discussion of the various 'phases' of Grierson's approach to documentary, see Ian Aitken's 'Grierson's Theory of Documentary Film' and 'The Critical Debates on the Documentary Film Movement', in *The Documentary Film Movement* (Edinburgh: Edinburgh University Press, 1998), 35–52.
6. Ibid., 35.
7. John Grierson, 'The Face of a New Zealander' in *'The Tin Shed': The Origins of the National Film Unit*, ed. Jonathan Dennis (The New Zealand Film Archive: Wellington, 1981), 21.
8. This list (a typewritten note) was compiled by the Prime Minister's department. It had no date but was headed *Films 1945–50*. Cited in unpublished essay 'Can the view that the "Weekly Reviews" were cut because of political bias be substantiated by fact?', David Newman, Victoria University, Wellington, 1984.

9. The Plunket Society, a 'healthy baby' movement, was founded in Dunedin in 1907 by Dr Frederick Truby King, the Superintendent of a mental hospital who was convinced he had the answer to society's ills.
10. Benedict Anderson, *Imagined Communities: Reflection on the Origins and Spread of Nationalism* (London: Verso, 1983).
11. The NFU continued to produce newsreels and documentaries until the Labour government sold it in 1990 to Avalon Television (a subsidiary of TVNZ).
12. Keith Holyoake headed the National Government from 1960 for over a decade, a period characterised by a 'steady does it' (which was the slogan of the 1960 election campaign) attitude of cautious conservatism that was popular with the electorate through the prosperous period of 1960–65 but was to be challenged with the rise of anti-Vietnam protests, falling earnings and other factors in the second half of the decade. See Michael King, *The Penguin History of New Zealand* (Auckland: Penguin Books, 2004), 449–54.
13. See Michael King, *Being Pakeha Now: Reflections and Recollections of a White Native* (Auckland: Penguin Books, 1999), 108.
14. Deborah Shepard, *Reframing Women: A History of New Zealand Film* (Auckland: HarperCollins, 2000), 68.
15. Peter Wells, 'Cosmetic: The Art of Looking Good on Television', *Landfall* 205 (May 2003): 117.
16. Carterton is a small town in the rural Wairarapa, an area north-east of the capital Wellington.
17. See Roger Horrocks, 'Strategic Nationalisms: Television Production in New Zealand', *Sites* 30 (Autumn 1995): 85–107.

3
Nation and Identity

11

'Precarious Adulthood':
COMMUNAL ANXIETIES IN 1980S FILM

Stuart Murray

By the mid 1980s, the success of New Zealand's film New Wave had resulted in the achievement of a number of significant milestones. *Sleeping Dogs* (1977) had shown that the country possessed the necessary production elements to make a feature film, *Goodbye Pork Pie* (1980) established the commercial viability of local features in terms of a national market, while *Smash Palace* (1981), *Utu* (1983) and *Vigil* (1984) were all met with critical acclaim in both national and international contexts. Writing on the emerging industry in 1982, Nick Roddick saw 'an extraordinarily high level of production values', and commented that with *Smash Palace* in particular 'the New Zealand cinema has decisively come of age'.[1] Writing again on the state of filmmaking a little later, in 1984, Roddick saw a film culture that had broken through to international recognition and was entering a 'precarious adulthood'.[2] The phrase seems particularly apt, and not simply in terms of the financing and support structures for filmmaking that are the main subject of Roddick's analysis. Even as filmmakers such as Roger Donaldson and Vincent Ward began to garner international reputations, and as the industry matured in terms of the quality of its infrastructural and thematic concerns, it nevertheless continually displayed an anxiety and precariousness that articulated issues beyond those connected to the filmmaking community alone. The precarious nature of New Zealand filmmaking in the 1980s matched that of the wider culture itself, as the nation found itself beset by challenges and crises, from within and without, that threatened many of the social orthodoxies that had defined the national space for a number of decades.

The source of the anxieties of the 1980s lay in a complex overlapping of social, political and cultural events. What Colin James has termed the 'prosperity consensus', which dominated New Zealand society from the 1950s to the 1970s, began to disintegrate. That post-war period had seen the country with less than one per cent unemployment, an economy based on the export of primary agricultural goods (such goods made up some 96 per cent of total export earnings in the 1960s—most went to Europe), and a commitment to a welfare programme providing support for all members of the population.[3] In cultural terms, post-war New Zealand still appeared comfortable with its deference to Britain on many intellectual and artistic issues, and by the late 1960s such a deferential mentality still went largely unquestioned by the majority of society. From the early 1970s onwards however, several major events radically altered this worldview. Britain's growing commitment to greater European union increasingly saw the old ties of the Commonwealth becoming anachronistic, especially those connected to commerce, and the often uninterrogated relationship with the heritage of British culture began to be eroded and replaced with a less secure apprehension of American cultural forms. Internally, in 1975 the Maori Land March (Te Matakite o Aotearoa), from Te Hapua in the far North to Wellington, dramatically reanimated the issue of land claims and the demands for compensation. In addition, in 1975 Robert Muldoon was elected Prime Minister of a National government that seemed impervious to the clear evidence of a society in transformation. In 1976 and 1977 the Ngati Whatua o Orakei (the Ngati Whatua tribe of Orakei, Auckland) and their supporters occupied land at Bastion Point in Auckland for 506 days in what was, along with the Raglan Golf Course occupation of 1978, one of the most highly visible acts of the land rights issue.[4] The television images of the protesters being evicted by police in full riot gear seemed to speak of a nation entirely different from that of ten years previously. The 1981 rugby tour of New Zealand by the South African Springbok team, taking place at a time when international sporting contact with an apartheid South Africa was discouraged, polarised the country, becoming the focus for all the unarticulated issues of race that New Zealand now found itself facing. Hand in hand with the increasing articulation of concerns over race came concomitant discussions of gender. The feminist magazine *Broadsheet*, which began publishing in 1972, became a vital outlet for those voices that sought to revise the masculine bias on which much social and political decision making was based. Muldoon's government in the early 1980s found itself presiding over not the harmonious, wealthy nation that seemed to have become the norm in recent decades, but an exhausted society that was over-regulated, inarticulate and seemingly oblivious to the very real tensions existing at its heart.

The National government was ousted in the election of 1984, and replaced by the Labour regime headed by David Lange, but for all the comfort brought to New Zealanders by the change in administration, new concerns arose. Determined to end the nation's obsequiousness to larger political powers, the Lange administration withdrew from the ANZUS military alliance with Australia and the US and voiced support for an end to nuclear testing in the Pacific. The resultant hostility from the US led to New Zealand being frozen out of certain geopolitical decision making and key trade associations, and the most poignant image of the non-nuclear campaign was that of the Greenpeace flagship *Rainbow Warrior* on its side in Auckland harbor, sunk by French security service agents in 1985 following heated diplomatic exchanges over France's nuclear testing policy. Increased self-determination, it was clear, brought with it its own set of anxieties.

The social and political events were themselves clear tears in the national fabric, but even as they acted as points of focus for public debates about the health and future of the nation, they also produced anxieties less obviously associated with the realm of the immediately social. The crises of the mid 1970s to mid 1980s triggered the full range of fears that lay in New Zealand's status as a settler community, exposing crucial doubts over the legitimacy and validity of the national project. Inherent in this was a questioning of the deep structural organisational forms of communal life: the role of the family; the place of the adult male as the normative icon of a successful society; assumptions of the 'natural' relationship between Maori and Pakeha (European), and other, immigrant, New Zealanders; the exact nature of relations between men and women; attitudes to the past and to the conception of New Zealand as a lived space. All of these became part of the precarious narratives that spoke of the nation in the 1980s, and found expression in its various cultural texts. Seen from the viewpoint of the political conflict running up to the 1984 election, the 1990 sesquicentenary of the 1840 signing of the Treaty of Waitangi—itself obviously a marker of an idea of cultural maturity—must have seemed a long way off, and more an index of confusion than a potential reminder of achievement.

The films of the period return time and again to these problems and concerns. In some cases, the features of the 1980s and early 1990s addressed the upheavals of the time directly. Merata Mita's *Bastion Point–Day 507* (1980) and *Patu!* (1983) document the Bastion Point standoff and the unrest provoked by the Springbok tour respectively, and the *Rainbow Warrior* saga was made as a drama for television, entitled *The Sinking of the Rainbow Warrior*, in 1992. The discordant sounds of New Zealand's national anthem, repeatedly played in different—sometimes atonal—forms, throughout *Patu!*, function as continual markers of the clear unease produced by the Springbok tour, and Mita's work on this documentary, and *Bastion Point–Day 507*, presented stark and graphic images of local conflict and violence before a New Zealand audience. For a nation founded on a rhetoric of cultural and social relations that were believed by much of the population to be relatively harmonious, such representations spoke of a far more contested public space, one where key events and issues affecting New Zealanders had not as yet been articulated, and where the lack of such articulation revealed the potential for quarrel and struggle.

In other features, the anxieties of the decade seem strangely overt, if in manners that seem only peripherally concerned with the specific narrative of the individual film. In Ward's *The Navigator: A Mediaeval Odyssey* (1988), a mystery nuclear submarine rises from the depths of Auckland harbour to terrify the fourteenth-century Cumbrians who have crossed the world in a dream vision to erect a cross on the spire of the tallest church in Christendom. Equally, the fears surrounding the nuclear debate are central to Geoff Murphy's *The Quiet Earth* (1985), which opens with a giant sunrise over the sea that, as the sun is about to break the horizon, suddenly seems to take the form of a vivid mushroom cloud produced by a nuclear explosion. In the film, a mystery scientific 'effect' that is controlled by the US, but which has a physical base in New Zealand, has seemingly destroyed nearly all of humanity, and it is clear that the analogy is with nuclear devastation. Ward's *Vigil*, although focused on the hardship faced by a farming family, contains an extreme version of this sense of unease and dislocation when, in the very first lines of the film, Birdie (Bill Kerr) mutters 'You know the more I think about it, the more I reckon we're heading for the South Pole—maybe the pole's coming up to us even—ice cap's shifting, coming north'. Here, in a manner that has little literal bearing on the film that follows, the idea that New Zealand is adrift frames the complexities of the characters battling the landscape in order to survive.

Vigil is in many ways a visionary work, spatially and temporally unlocated and full of Ward's powerful art-derived image making, but it is also clearly a settlement narrative, in which the difficulties of the family can be seen to mirror the idea of New Zealand as a public space in which a Pakeha community might live.[5] It is especially notions of the communal that seemed threatened by the turbulence of the period, and particularly those ideas of the public collective produced by the Pakeha majority. *The Quiet Earth* is, generically, a science fiction feature (and was heralded as 'the best science-fiction film of the 80s' by the *Los Angeles Daily News*), but the way in which it brings together its trio of effect survivors—Pakeha man, Maori man, Pakeha woman—projects much of its rumination on ideas of the end of the world in a specifically New Zealand context. New Zealand scientist Zac Hobson (Bruno Lawrence) feels guilty at his complicity in the US-led experiment which has led to the effect, but noticeably resorts to a series of empirical testing measures in order to ascertain the nature of the physical change the universe seems to have undergone. Confronted with the presence of Api (Peter Smith), who is set within the familial and tribal context of his marae (meeting place) and wharenui (meeting house), but who also through his dress also is clearly identified with a masculinity derived from Maori urban culture, Zac is thrown back upon a language of authority derived from ideas of knowledge and control. 'I'm in charge remember', Zac tells Api during a heated exchange, only for Api to reply 'Haven't you noticed? Things have changed around here. The white boss went with the rest of them—there's just you and me now'. Equally challenged by the presence of Joanne (Alison Routledge), who rejects him for Api as the film progresses, Zac becomes a symbol of a Pakeha community, especially as embodied in the figure of the adult male, guilty of complicity and unease. His antagonistic relationship with Api points to a historical past of cultural dispossession, while his unarticulated fears concerning the present speak of tensions in New Zealand's relations with the international community, as well as the country's own disparities in gender relations. 'I knew there was something wrong with that project, and I said nothing. Can you be more guilty than that?' Zac shouts to both

Api and Joanne, and in the nebulous nature of the word 'project' the cry resonates with the full range of anxieties of the period.

The troubled nature of Pakeha community, especially its potential illegitimacy, lies at the heart of *The Quiet Earth*, and in a number of other features during the decade similar forms of trouble and unease are to be found in the representation of relationships, families and communities. A predatory stranger (John Carradine) threatens a 1950s' small town in Sam Pillsbury's *The Scarecrow* (1982), raping and killing before himself being killed, and the idea of the threat from a stranger is also central to Melanie Read's psychological thriller *Trial Run* (1984), with the twist that the attacks on the central character Rosemary (Annie Whittle) turn out to be being committed by her own teenage son James (Christopher Broun), in a perverse representation of the family unit. Marital problems and family tensions are vital to John Laing's *Other Halves* (1984), in which affluent thirty-something Pakeha middle-class Liz (Lisa Harrow) leaves marriage and suburbia for a relationship with Polynesian teenager Tug (Mark Pilisi), as well as *Smash Palace* where inarticulate Al Shaw (Bruno Lawrence) seems incapable of understanding the breakdown of his marriage to Jacqui (Anna Jemison), and the consequences it will have for his family overall. In *Vigil*, the struggle to live and work on the land is matched by the tensions that come with the arrival of Ethan (Frank Whitten), a poacher, into the family of Liz (Penelope Stewart) and Toss (Fiona Kay), bereaved following the death of husband and father Justin (Gordon Shields) at the film's beginning. In particular, Toss's grief at the loss of her father, and her antagonism towards Ethan, outline an idea of trauma that accompanies the wider theme of potential settler illegitimacy. The idea of family trauma is also central to Michael Firth's *Heart of the Stag* (1984), in which farmer Robert Jackson's (Terence Cooper) abusive and incestuous relationship with daughter Cathy (Mary Regan) points to an extreme dysfunction in the kind of space—rural, agricultural, Pakeha, familial—that was often cited as an integral conceptual part of the national narrative.

Richard Riddiford's 1986 feature *Arriving Tuesday* similarly focuses upon a strained central relationship, as Monica (Judy McIntosh) and Nick (Peter Hayden) travel through the north island in a continual argumentative state. As Helen Martin has noted, the film's presentation of domestic differences also parallels shifts in national identity during the 1980s, especially in the ways in which the troubled status of Monica and Nick as a couple is contrasted with a perceived idea of a harmonious Maori community in the film.[6] Maori identity in the narrative is personified in Riki (Rawiri Paratene), who meets Monica and Nick following his decision to leave Auckland and return to his tribal roots in Northland. Riki's perceived authenticity is figured in the film as a clear point of difference to the anxieties of the Pakeha couple, and the film's invitation to consider the merits of the two cultures within the national space exemplifies the specific concern, common in the decade, with an apprehension over the validity of Pakeha community in the face of a Maori equivalent. At the conclusion of

24. Incongruous in the landscape: Ethan (left) and Toss's relationship articulates a wider instability in *Vigil*. Courtesy of the New Zealand Film Commission.

Arriving Tuesday, Monica, who has flirted with the idea of staying with Riki, returns to Nick, feeling that ultimately Riki's world is alien to her own. But the film opens a clear space to discuss the appeal of Maoritanga (Maori culture) to a worried and deracinated Pakeha majority.[7]

Arriving Tuesday may skirt the issue in terms of its full narrative, but the presence of Maori communal values as an alternative to a troubled Pakeha present was a pronounced feature across New Zealand's cultural output in the 1980s. High profile novels such as Keri Hulme's *the bone people* (1983), Witi Ihimaera's *The Matriarch* (1986) and Patricia Grace's *Potiki* (1986) brought home to a national and international audience the claim of Maoridom to the contested public space in New Zealand. Donna Awatere's political polemic *Maori Sovereignty* (1984) asserted that Pakeha identity was nonexistent other than in its desire to maintain superiority over Maori, and made a huge intellectual and political impact. Following the election victory of 1984, the Lange government's reactivation of the Waitangi Tribunal, the body charged with assessing and adjudicating on Maori land claims, made serious discussion of cultural distinctiveness a pronounced feature of the decade. And in the midst of this swirl of debate, two features made by Maori filmmakers—Barry Barclay's *Ngati* (1987) and Merata Mita's *Mauri* (1988)—offered clear outlines of Maori community, containing implicit and explicit challenges to the social and cultural formations of Pakeha society.

Both *Ngati* and *Mauri* open with scenes that stress a sense of distance between Maori and Pakeha. In *Ngati*, set in a rural coastal settlement in the late 1940s, the community gathers round the bedside of a sick boy, Ropata (Oliver Jones), as the film opens, and this harmonious coming together is contrasted through cross-cutting with the arrival in the small town of young doctor Greg Shaw (Ross Girven). Greg is initially brash and opinionated, and the contrast with the support offered to Ropata's family is clearly evident. In *Mauri*, set in the 1950s, a Pakeha doctor (Martyn Sanderson) stands by, useless and bemused, as Kara (Eva Rickard) assists at a birth. As a kuia (female elder), Kara's knowledge of Maori customs surrounding birth far outweighs that of the doctor, and his helplessness is symptomatic both of a stark cultural difference and a noticeable lack of cross-cultural understanding. Equally, in the second scene of the film, following the birth, the ceremony surrounding the burial of the placenta is interrupted by Steve (James Heyward), a young Pakeha farmer, who, despite his claims that he 'didn't mean to offend', fails to respect the nature of the ritual. In their charged sense of the differences that exist between individuals here, both scenes establish and underscore a foundational unease about cultural relations within the national community. Writing in 1992, Mita commented upon the clear differences she found between Pakeha and Maori filmmaking up to that point, seeing the national industry as largely a 'white, neurotic one' producing films that 'repeatedly fail to analyse and articulate the colonial syndrome of dislocation . . . [W]hat becomes clear in [the films of the 1970s and 1980s] is the absence of identity and how driven by repression and fear these films are'.[8]

In contrast to such neurosis and absence, *Ngati* and *Mauri* place issues of Maori communal identity at the heart of their respective narratives. The setting of both films—rural settlements some thirty to forty years before the features were shot—evokes a period of harmony before (or in *Mauri*'s case, just on the cusp of) the demographic shift that saw many Maori migrate to the cities in the 1950s and 1960s. However neither film is ultimately nostalgic, as in both a sense of coming change poses a potential threat to communal livelihood. In *Mauri*, Kara's nephew Willie (Willie Raana) visits from the city, and is warned as to who he might trust. Ignoring the warning, he is later killed. Equally, the evident desire for Maori land clearly displayed by Steve's father, Semmens (Geoff Murphy), is indicative both of a continuing policy of usurpation and theft on the part of Pakeha, as well as a pointer to a future in which Maori will increasingly find aspects of their culture under threat. In a similar vein, in *Ngati* the threatened closure of the local freezing works (the community's chief source of employment), due to the lack of business caused by some Maori farmers sending livestock to other abattoirs, potentially destabilises the entire settlement. But, in keeping with their establishment of the core values of Maori community at the heart of their respective narratives, both films articulate methods by which such threats to the nature of communal life might be overcome. In *Mauri*, Kara's emphasis on Maori custom is seen to provide the basis for collective identity, especially in the ways in which it is apprehended by her granddaughter Awatea (Rangimarie Delamere). Similarly, in *Ngati*, the young boy Tione (Michael Tibble) comes to be seen as the recipient of the community's cultural knowledge, and is—like Awatea—a guardian for the future. In addition, the film resolves the explicitly social strand of its narrative when farmer Iwi (Wi Kuki Kaa) agrees to take control of a major sheep station, thus ensuring a supply to the freezing works, which can now remain open. This clear Maori solution to a Maori problem reasserts the ability of the community to manage its own affairs, and both *Ngati* and *Mauri* close the circle of a narrativised representation of Maori community with recourse to the positive and productive values of Maori culture.[9]

For the Pakeha majority in New Zealand, the kind of confidence in cultural values displayed by *Ngati* and *Mauri* registered as a largely alien and inaccessible resource, an assertion of rights not permitted to those whose settlement history was fraught with a legacy of violence and dispossession. Indeed, *Ngati* even contains within its narrative a desired identity option that many Pakeha, anxious with guilt and insecure about their place within the nation, might have clamoured to embrace in the 1980s. Greg, the doctor who arrives from Australia in the film's opening moments, turns out (unbeknown to him) to have been born to a local Maori woman, and ends the film being instructed in Maori custom by Tione. Such a coincidental 'discovery' of indigeneity appears as a highly utopian and painless entry into a wished-for realm of communal authenticity.

But such openings of possible reciprocity are rare. More typical narratives of communal relations in the 1980s came in films like *Utu*, a dramatisation of nineteenth-century conflicts between Maori and Pakeha over land that mixes historical reflection with Hollywood inspired genre moments, or *Kingpin* (1985), in which the Maori and Polynesian inmates of a Child Welfare Training Unit impose and suffer brutalities as they deal with the consequences of their status as part of an economic underclass. Although each film differs from the other in marked respects, they share and indeed display a sense of unease about the nature of bicultural relations, and particularly how those relations take systemic form. In *Utu*'s representation of the construction of historical narrative, and *Kingpin*'s musings on the delivery of social justice, it appears that there are significant cleavages in the very fabric of the bicultural national imaginary that the Lange regime so wished to publicly assert.

The 1990 Waitangi Treaty sesquicentennial marked a natural end to the decade's public debates over the state of the nation, and was the occasion for much collective self-interrogation within New Zealand. In addition, the heady period of political change ended in the same year when, after two terms, the Labour government was replaced by a new National administration, albeit one very much different in makeup from that of Muldoon's. But in many ways the filmic representation with such concerns concluded with two of the most high profile features to emerge from the country—Jane Campion's *The Piano* (1993) and Lee Tamahori's *Once Were Warriors* (1994). Both films achieved enormous international success, both commercially and critically, and *The Piano* in particular

25. Greg (second from left) finds communal acceptance and suggests bicultural understanding in *Ngati*. Courtesy of the New Zealand Film Commission.

displayed the power of transnational associations in the making of film in New Zealand, with funding from France and Australia, and the casting of recognised Hollywood actors such as Holly Hunter and Harvey Keitel. But in the seriousness with which they portrayed issues of community within the national space both films can be seen to be continuations of the kind of fixation on the concerns of the local that had dominated the previous decade. *The Piano*'s ruminations on the issues of settlement—the competing claims of patriarchy and female agency, of Pakeha and Maori, and of the sheer struggle to live on the land—work to make the film an analysis of key foundational concepts in the establishment of modern New Zealand. For its part, *Once Were Warriors*, adapted from Alan Duff's controversial 1990 novel, completely overturned the idea of Maori community found in *Ngati* and *Mauri*. In place of the idea of a communal wholeness informed by cultural knowledge and tradition displayed by the earlier features, Tamahori's film portrayed many Maori as a social underclass largely divorced from any sense of tribal affiliation, and beset by trauma and abuse. But, for all these differences, it is important to note that the focal point on community, and the sense of the power of film to articulate communal concerns with fidelity, is in keeping with the films of the 1980s. Both the novel and film versions of *Once Were Warriors* were treated almost as social documents within New Zealand, statements of what the community had become. Such an almost narcissistic fixation with such a notion of collective self is still very much part of Roddick's 'precarious adulthood'.

Ultimately, however, such narcissism proved impossible to sustain. Post 1994, the seriousness with which film had interrogated and analysed the national imaginary reached a point of exhaustion. In its place came more irreverent conceptions of the national, films that specifically turned against the earnestness that so many 1980s features had in common. Peter Jackson had, in part, initiated such a move in the late 1980s with his paradigm shifting horror films *Bad Taste* (1988) and *Meet the Feebles* (1990), and he would follow these with *Braindead* in 1992 and the mockumentary *Forgotten Silver* (1995), which very clearly targeted and satirised a specifically nationalist version of place with its 'discovery' of Colin McKenzie, a supposedly forgotten New Zealand film director whose work on colour and sound features in the early twentieth century is presented as having predated other, international, figures.[10] Stewart Main and Peter Wells's *Desperate Remedies* (1993) turned reflections on nineteenth-century New Zealand society and the national obsession with masculinity into a high colour camp melodrama, a film which is a world away from the ideas of place that are found in the narratives of *Smash Palace* and *Vigil*. By the end of the 1990s, the films of a director such as Harry Sinclair have no interest in documenting national unease. Rather, in his *Topless Women Talk about their Lives* (1995), and *The Price of Milk* (2000) the concerns of twenty-something protagonists are played out with an attention to relationships, humour and an often flippant disregard for the various markers of the collective self that had seemed so important just a decade earlier.

In addition, the increasing diversification of the industry (in terms of the changing role of the NZFC, the escalating involvement of television and new initiatives in co-production) meant that the conditions of New Zealand filmmaking had themselves changed by the mid 1990s. Unlike the New Wave period when key figures such as Geoff Murphy and Bruno Lawrence had energised production with their own multiple commitments as writers, actors, directors and musicians, the transnational and increasingly globalised nature of filmmaking in New Zealand in the 1990s diluted the sense that a small, national creative community was producing narratives by which it defined itself and its place in the world. Films such as *Bonjour Timothy* (1995), made with money from Canada as well as from New Zealand, and *The Flight of the Albatross* (1996), a co-production between New Zealand and Germany, meant that the ways in which local filmmaking skills were being used were different from the 1980s, when it had been easy at times for the production community to feel itself somewhat embattled and isolated.

Ultimately, the anxieties over community repeatedly found in the films of the 1980s were simply new versions of an old New Zealand story. Since the development of sustained immigration and settlement in the nineteenth century, the Pakeha nation building project has been shadowed continually by fears concerning its validity and legitimacy. In terms of cultural production, such concerns were part of the slow and halting development of a literary nationalism, which finally found mature expression in the 1930s.[11] The contexts and conditions for film production that emerged out of the late 1970s saw the first period of sustained support for filmmaking, but they also manifested new forms of social and political disquiet that articulated the kind of unease that had almost become an orthodoxy in the national imaginary. Even as the country revelled in the growth of a film industry of its own, it was busy finding fresh ways of not being at home.

Notes

1. Nick Roddick, 'New Zealand Cinema: Taking Off?', *Films and Filming* 333 (June 1982): 9–10, 12.
2. Roddick, 'Kiwi Polish', *Stills* 12 (June–July 1984): 72.
3. See Colin James, *New Territory: The Transformation of New Zealand 1984–92* (Wellington: Bridget Williams Books, 1992), 6–35.
4. For an excellent discussion of the Maori activism of the period, see Ranganui Walker, *Ka Whawhai Tonu Matou/Struggle Without End* (Auckland: Penguin, 1990), 212–87.
5. For more on *Vigil*, and on Ward's filmmaking more generally, see Stephanie Rains, 'Making Strange: Journeys through the Unfamiliar in the Films of Vincent Ward', *New Zealand Filmmakers*, ed. Ian Conrich and Stuart Murray (Detroit: Wayne State University Press, 2006).
6. Helen Martin and Sam Edwards, *New Zealand Film 1912–1996* (Oxford: Oxford University Press, 1997), 124.
7. For more on the Pakeha desire to embrace Maori values during the 1980s, see Mark Williams, 'Literary Constructions of Oral Cultures', *Dirty Silence: Aspects of Language and Literature in New Zealand*, ed. Graham McGregor and Mark Williams (Auckland: Oxford University Press, 1991), 77–95.
8. Merata Mita, 'The Soul and the Image', *Film in Aotearoa New Zealand*, ed. Jonathan Dennis and Jan Bieringa (Wellington: Victoria University Press, 1992), 47.
9. It is worth noting that both films are communally made, using a number of non-professional actors (such as Rickard, who was known as a prominent activist during the cultural debates of the decade) and working closely on details of production with the communities in which they were shot in a reciprocity that is typical of Maori cultural practice. For more on this aspect of *Ngati*, see Ann Simpson, 'Haere Mai Homecoming', *Onfilm* 4, no. 4 (1987): 3–4. For more on the films of Barclay and Mita more generally, see Stuart Murray, 'Images of Dignity: The Films of Barry Barclay', and Geraldene Peters, 'Lives of Their Own: Films by Merata Mita', *New Zealand Filmmakers*, ed. Ian Conrich and Stuart Murray (Detroit: Wayne State University Press, 2007).
10. See Ian Conrich and Roy Smith, 'Fool's Gold: New Zealand's *Forgotten Silver*, Myth and National Identity', *British Review of New Zealand Studies* 11 (December 1998): 57–65, reprinted in *Docufictions: Essays on the Intersection*

of Documentary and Fictional Filmmaking, ed. Gary Rhodes and John Parris Springer (Jefferson, North Carolina: McFarlane, 2005), 230–36.

11. See Lawrence Jones, *Picking Up the Traces: The Making of a New Zealand Literary Culture 1932–1945* (Wellington: Victoria University Press, 2003), and Stuart Murray, *Never a Soul at Home: New Zealand Literary Nationalism and the 1930s* (Wellington: Victoria University Press, 1998).

12

A Waka on the Wild Side:
NATIONALISM AND ITS DISCONTENTS IN SOME RECENT NEW ZEALAND FILMS

Mark Williams

In the 1995 documentary, *Cinema of Unease*, actor Sam Neill, having left New Zealand in the late 1970s to pursue an international career,[1] presents himself returning from London to his native land. Neill's narration is both personal and national, the link between the two being provided by the burgeoning New Zealand film industry. Having left a country in which film had yet to achieve a central role in articulating national culture, Neill now finds that New Zealand has achieved a cinema able to capture the imagination of the world and to bring into being the imaginative life of New Zealanders. Neill's experience of national identity has been changed in the process: 'Now that we've produced a national cinema in this country in the last fifteen years or so, I now have a permit to dream cinematic images that are of our own place'.

In *Cinema of Unease*, personal and national narratives overlap and interpenetrate each other, as in Michael King's versions of national biography, *Being Pakeha* (1985) and *Being Pakeha Now* (1999).[2] Neill tells the tale of the tribe, a collective story in which the Pakeha (European) come into their inheritance as a people possessed of the imaginative means of self-expression, no longer exiled English yet aware that their claim to speak for the country is compromised by the competing claim of Maori. The titles of King's books hint at the source of the 'unease' in New Zealand cinema: the problem with being 'Pakeha' is that, as the very word signals, identity is still borrowed from the definitions of the other, and thus is guilty and insecure. Neill and King speak for the cultural nationalist aspirations of the Pakeha tribe, but their stories need to be couched in terms of an ongoing voyage towards *bi*cultural understanding; in the meantime, they are incomplete.

Neill uses his own story to generalise that of the Pakeha people moving towards the achievement of a condition of postcolonial maturity. It is a coming-of-age story in which nation and cinema produce each other, a story which repeats a narrative invented in the 1930s and 1940s by a group of cultural nationalists—Allen Curnow, Charles Brasch, Frank Sargeson— who believed that the making of a literary tradition would redeem New Zealand from its provincialism and its colonial dependency. *Cinema of Unease* opens with a quotation from mid-century poet and founder of the literary journal *Landfall*, Charles Brasch: 'A society can be said to have come of age when it begins to live by the light of an imaginative order of its own'.[3] Cinema here extends the cultural nationalists' programme for literature by providing an imaginative counterpart to national materialism and by bringing art into agreement with the imagery of the place, an imagery that no longer carries so achingly the taint of displacement.[4]

Dragging cultural nationalist preoccupations with it, *Cinema of Unease* occurs at a crucial point both in the development of New Zealand film and in the postcolonial reprise of the nationalist narratives of Aotearoa/New Zealand. In cinema history, this documentary arrived at the close of a period dominated by the heroic endeavors of gifted directors—Jane Campion, Lee Tamahori, Peter Jackson—who produced recognisably New Zealand films addressing an international film audience before being co-opted with varying degrees of resistance by Hollywood. Behind lay *The Piano* (1993), *Heavenly Creatures* (1994) and *Once Were Warriors* (1994); ahead lay the first serious industrialisation of cinema in New Zealand, with the filming of *The Lord of the Rings* trilogy (2001–03) bringing Hollywood capital into happy conjunction with New Zealand scenery and talent. Jackson's trilogy demonstrates the existence of a supply of world class production skills, technical expertise, and logistical support, exciting citizens with nationalist pride and politicians with the prospect of an internationally successful New Zealand-made cinema.

The late 1990s also saw a steady reorientation away from the body of ideas about national culture, government, economic and social policy, markets and globalisation inherited from the 1980s. The introduction in 1996 of a new proportional representation voting system (MMP) checking the power of the two major parties constituted a turning point in New Zealand's readjustment to the world economic order by way of market-driven 'reform' aimed at making the country more attractive to international capital. The crisis of adjustment provoked by near national bankruptcy at the close of the Robert Muldoon National government (1975–84) had produced a schizophrenic response in David Lange's incoming Labour administration (1984–90): an inward-looking cultural nationalism determined to reconfigure settler New Zealand along bicultural and postcolonial lines, coupled with a sense of entrepreneurial adventure and enlarged possibility which encouraged an unrealistic sense of the country's opportunities for global economic success.[5] Voter resistance to the bracing program of economic liberalism embraced by successive governments, Labour and National, culminated in the attempt by way of MMP to renationalise New Zealand political ideology and economic policy.

This democratisation of the voting system served to interrupt the reform process and moderate some of its harsher aspects but not to bring about the reversal desired by its supporters. The Labour government that took power in 1999 did not reintroduce substantial protections for the national economy. It did, however, speedily enlist culture in its program of economic change, shifting the terms of the debate so that nationalism and the new economy were not seen to be opposed terms, and conceiving culture as a mediating force between the two. Prime Minister Helen Clark committed her government to a transformation of the nation in which culture was to play a central role.[6] Eager to change not only the traditional ways in which New Zealand was seen but also the ways in which the nation saw itself, the new government sought to use culture to fashion a post-settler and post-pastoral society.[7] In a country intent on preserving its cultural uniqueness while 'propelling itself onto the stage of global capitalism',[8] government efforts to alter New Zealand's political imaginary have provided mixed results.

The success in 2001 of *The Lord of the Rings: The Fellowship of the Ring* at both the box office and the Academy Awards (where it won four Oscars) allowed the new government triumphantly to link its policy of supporting indigenous culture to the theme of economic transformation. A 2002 brochure celebrating the government's cultural recovery programme boasted that creative industries were 'placed at the forefront of New Zealand's economic transformation' and that the government had provided '[l]everage funding . . . to maximise opportunities for the whole nation from increased focus on New Zealand through *Lord of the Rings*'.[9] Jackson's film conspicuously endorsed the government's cultural policy. Citizenship and trade were mutually benefiting from film.

The Fellowship of the Ring generated a confidence that combined the effects in the 1980s of Keri Hulme's novel *the bone people*'s winning of the Booker Prize (the sense that New Zealand's cultural as well as its natural products might gain the admiration of the world) and victory in yachting's America's Cup (the sense that New Zealand technological innovation could triumph over size, power and capital); but translating the success of the film into a substantial local film industry, marked by its New Zealand provenance rather than merely manufactured locally by international companies, proved complicated. Anxious to attract further such projects but reluctant to do so by way of tax write-offs to international firms, the government found itself caught between a protective nationalism and its determination that New Zealanders, by virtue of their talent for innovation and their creativity, can compete globally. The government has declined to favour international over local capital by way of tax incentives, yet the fixation on *The Lord of the Rings* has perhaps blinded cultural policy setters to the difficulties of the locally funded and produced cinema industry, so acute that the Film Awards for 2002 had to be cancelled because of a lack of films available to enter.[10] Meanwhile, the American Actors' Union has argued that US-financed films should pay union wages in foreign countries, exposing the obvious limits of economic nationalism in the maintenance of a feature film industry.

The underlying problem, however, is the fundamental weakness of nationalism in New Zealand, a weakness going back to the late-colonial period when its early Pakeha manifestation emerged not as a break with imperial affiliations but as a confirmation of New Zealand's special place within empire. Pakeha nationalism has traditionally sought to define itself less by way of direct acts of filial rebellion than by maintaining muted links with the parent culture while differentiating itself from other settler cultures, especially Australia.[11] The fragility of nationalism in New Zealand is displayed in the pattern of euphoria and disappointment generated by each new phase of national endeavour, in sport, industry, social policy and cultural activity. As with the young female protagonists of so many Katherine Mansfield stories, excitement is easily generated and routinely followed by disillusionment as imaginative readiness meets an unaccommodating reality. In the early days of the Clark government there was a mood of optimism about New Zealand's capacity for self-transformation which involved an invigoration of culture, tradition and identity in concert with economic modernisation. However, such processes overlook the relative lack of historical depth of cultural capital in New Zealand. Katherine Mansfield, Janet Frame and Keri Hulme have international followings, but they are not the reason tourists come to New Zealand. *The Lord of the Rings*, certainly, attracted considerable tourist interest, demonstrating that cinema has the capacity to make 'distance look . . . our way'.[12] But an increase in tourist numbers prompted by film-disseminated imagery of sublime scenery, does not 'transform' New Zealand's traditional economy; it confirms it, the nation still figured as the site of scenic splendour.

The Clark government set itself a programme of promoting national identity by encouraging a positive sense of belonging through the arts. Film has been especially effective in projecting the country onto the main theatres of the global economy while encouraging nationalism at home. By the late 1990s, however, as cultural activities showed increasing signs of being able to achieve the desired results, younger directors and writers of New Zealand film—following a trend already established in literature— were moving away from the old forms of national self-regard. Beginning around the mid 1990s there is a break with what Jane Smith describes as the 'generic sameness' of New Zealand film, characterised by 'domestic drama with a certain edginess about history'.[13] If *The Piano*, *Once Were Warriors* and *The Lord of the Rings* remain the touchstones of recent New Zealand cinema, signifiers of the nation validated by international success, a small body of features produced between *Cinema of Unease* and *The Fellowship of the Ring*—especially, *Topless Women Talk about Their Lives* (1997), *Scarfies* (1999), *The Price of Milk* (2000), and *Stickmen* (2000)—have provided a counter-note, a demonstration that the passages between local and global need not be so fraught with the anxious over-compensations of a defensive nationalism and that a consciousness of the colonial past need not erect a prison-house of guilt.

These films showed no sign that they wished to be received as what Lee Tamahori, speaking of *Once Were Warriors*, calls 'defining document[s] of our nation'.[14] For Tamahori, in spite of *Once Were Warriors*' calculated appeal to an international audience, the film's primary audience—its stake in history—is local. As a 'defining document' it speaks to and for the nation;

it is written from the inside. In the films of the Sarkies brothers (Duncan and Robert) and Harry Sinclair, New Zealand is presented as if seen from outside, by a consciousness distanced but not alienated, observing it with wryly detached interest. There is an analogy here with the style and mood of poet Bill Manhire's immensely successful writing school at Victoria University in the 1980s and 1990s and the literary magazine, *Sport*. Cultural politics in the fiction of such new writers as Elizabeth Knox, Catherine Chidgey and Damien Wilkins were not foregrounded as they had been in the 1980s; nationalism and biculturalism were downplayed. The object was to let the culture speak by a knowing manipulation of its favourite imageries and icons that disclosed both the informing presence of international trends and local intonations.

Younger filmmakers, notably the Sarkies and Sinclair, have followed the writers of Manhire's school in seeing the nation as a repository of variously sourced signs and markers to be re-encoded rather than an intractable source of meaning to be wrestled with. *Scarfies* very obviously reworks *Shallow Grave* (1994); other films, with less cultural adroitness, have set about indigenising foreign trends—the slacker movie in Stephen Hickey's *Hopeless* (2000), Tarantino's aestheticised violence in Hamish Rothwell's *Stickmen*—as conscious adaptations of internationally marketable styles. In the 'new' New Zealand cinema of the late 1990s, anxiety about identity and location gives way to a more playful and sophisticated rendition of national themes. Andrew Horton speaks of *The Price of Milk* as signalling 'a joyous and carnivalesque departure from mainstream New Zealand cinema traditions'.[15] Horton places the film in a magic realist tradition, specifically that of Balkan director, Emir Kusturica. Just as important as the film's intelligent inscription within an international cinematic language is its ironic relation to the established language of New Zealand literature and cinema. New Zealand figures in cultural nationalist writing and painting as a landscape without lovers.[16] At the start of *The Price of Milk*, the rumpled green hills of touristic New Zealand transmogrify not into a scene of urban decay as in the opening of *Once Were Warriors*, but into a quilt under which lovers move. The land in *The Price of Milk* has plentiful lovers (and complicated infidelities), while the mythological Man Alone has been domesticated; he no longer seeks primal experiences in the wilderness, and his relations to the natural world have been so sensitised that he keeps an agoraphobic dog which inhabits a cardboard box. No longer are Maori and Pakeha the only inhabitants of the cultural landscape: the bride and bridegroom are dressed for their wedding Indian-style by the local dairy-owners. Trailing a sari, the heroine of *The Price of Milk* walks the dimpled paddocks of dairy New Zealand.

New Zealand content is a requirement of funding by the Film Commission, but in films like *Topless Women Talk about Their Lives*, *Scarfies*, and *Stickmen* its presence is invoked with a humour, irreverence and self-consciousness that have no trace of older forms of New Zealand nationalism, either Maori or Pakeha. Moreover, the sources of the humour

26. A post-national revision of New Zealand: *The Price of Milk*'s ironic and carnivalesque play on cultural orthodoxies. Courtesy of the Ian Conrich collection of New Zealand cinema and visual culture.

and irreverence frequently *are* those earlier forms. These films have not followed Campion's edgy preoccupations with the big cultural topics of the 1980s: colonial anxieties, patriarchal power, the alienation of the settler in the landscape. There is even a new sense of being at ease in the representation of race—less charged with postcolonial anxiety, more humorous. The Maori family in *The Price of Milk*, the Jacksons, are teasingly confused with childhood fairies. The unnamed kuia (Rangi Motu), in the familiar guise of old Maori ladies in New Zealand literature and film, is full of gnomic wisdom but conducts herself with a splendid and comic distance from the assigned role. The film avoids the conventional Pakeha reverence towards indigenous spirituality by translating it into a species of ironic (but not satiric) fantasy which gently pastiches the convention. This is the world of fairy-tale not reality, and knows itself as such, never taking the myths it generates for any alternative reality. Colonial history is recapitulated in the struggles over ownership of a patchwork quilt stitched with images of the land and its fauna. The quilt is swapped for a dairy herd, which must be reclaimed, but by way of heroic adventures and tests of fidelity, not by legal transaction. Irony, laconicism, and a knowing use of familiar icons and conventions characterise this slice of recent New Zealand cinema.

The Piano and *Once Were Warriors* were crucial in the development of New Zealand cinema, not simply because their successful projection of local problems of identity signalled the emergence of native-born talent able to produce films of international standing, but also because they marked the close of particular phases of cultural nationalism. Far from generating a new cinematic paradigm, they consolidated or critiqued existing national paradigms that had exhausted their potency. *The Piano* gave a postcolonial gloss to the Pakeha theme of settler displacement. Tamahori's *Once Were Warriors* toned down novelist Alan Duff's savage reply to the established conventions of Maori Renaissance writing, but nevertheless reinforced the sense of an end to the period of Maori self-representation from the 1970s to the 1990s characterised by a lyrical nostalgia on the one hand and, on the other, a fierce protest directed outwards at Pakeha power. As Jane Smith points out, the film also contests what she calls *The Piano*'s 'neo-colonial' representation of New Zealand.[17]

The main theme continually reprised in modernist New Zealand film and literature (from Charles Brasch's brooding poetry to Vincent Ward's *Vigil* [1984]) is that of the land as alienating, sublime yet dark, containing a presence which mocks the settlers, its promise of belonging endlessly deferred. In *Cinema of Unease*, Neill seems captivated by this darkly symbolist geography. New Zealand cinema's break into the modern is identified with his own generation of filmmakers—John Laing, Barry Barclay, Paul Maunder—born in the 1940s, who 'turn[ed] their backs on the picturesque, [as] they saw the landscape as a metaphor for a psychological interior and looked to the darker heart of the menacing land'. We are back in poet James K. Baxter's psychic geography, where the mountains 'crouch like tigers' and the land speaks the tormented soul of the displaced Pakeha male.[18] Neill is out of step here with a corresponding generation of writers, notably Manhire and Ian Wedde, who by the late 1960s had grown tired of the effort to 'name them hills',[19] inherited from cultural nationalism, who were interested in more knowing, ironic and playful transactions between the global and the local.

Yet Neill also shows himself alert to the ironic and subversive humour as well as to the familiar grimoire of Pakeha consciousness. In Peter Jackson and Costa Botes' brilliant mockumentary, *Forgotten Silver* (1995), he parodies the favorite myths of Pakeha New Zealand: as heroic innovators, world-first inventors, able to turn ordinary products (famously, number 8 fencing wire) to unexpected use. The film, with the participation of Harvey Weinstein and Leonard Maltin as well as Neill and other New Zealanders, opens with the supposed discovery of a treasure trove of forgotten celluloid film by Colin McKenzie, a New Zealand pioneer filmmaker. Of humble beginnings, McKenzie, we are told, was born in 1888 (the same year as Katherine Mansfield) in Geraldine (a town immortalised in Denis Glover's deadpan nationalist poem, 'Home Thoughts' [1936]). He learns technological innovation early from his job in a Timaru bicycle shop, inventing a camera capable of tracking shots, makes his own film from flax leaves and egg white, films the world's first plane flight, that of New Zealander, Richard Pearse, and invents sound and colour cinematography.

Forgotten Silver, with its fictitious protagonists and events, is a sophisticated joke directed at myths so engrained in the Pakeha psyche and so authentic in its manner of presentation (and conscription of famous overseas authorities) that its lies were believed by many when it was first screened on New Zealand television. Its humour is part of a shift away from the blokey humour of late 1970s and early 1980s New Zealand films about which Neill himself expresses embarrassment in *Cinema of Unease*. As he observes there, films like *Goodbye Pork Pie* (1980) are not art-house movies. Their sources are not Godard, but American road movies, and they suggest the anarchic freedom 'that would give grown-ups the maximum discomfort'. But Neill slips back into the mode of national unease. Even the humour he cites in New Zealand film is interpreted by way of Pakeha anxieties about parental power. It is anti-authoritarian, anarchic boys' stuff, directed especially at the father.

A wholly new style of humour is evident in *The Price of Milk*, where it appears, as Horton notes, as a difference from the 'buddy road pranks of Geoff Murphy's *Goodbye Pork Pie*, the sly social comedy of Gaylene Preston's *Ruby and Rata* (1990), and the over-the-top farcical romps of Peter Jackson's *Bad Taste* (1988) and *Braindead* (1992)'.[20] Just as important is a new tone of humour. *Scarfies*, directed by Robert Sarkies, is so highly self-conscious about the genres it inhabits that its content is transformed into something quite new. As in early Peter Jackson movies, the provincial-Gothic style is exaggerated and made the butt of humour. Unlike Jackson's films, which exult in tonal excess, *Scarfies* works by a dead-pan use of tone

27. Self-conscious and irreverent, *Scarfies'* parodic teen drama reveals a new humorous tone in New Zealand cinema. Courtesy of the New Zealand Film Commission.

that is at odds with the content. Conscripting various film genres—crime movie, film noir, psychological drama, teen scream movie—Sarkies forces them into collision with the codes of Dunedin student life: low rentals in derelict houses, rugby and the great youth music of Dunedin's Flying Nun record label. The film never indicates clearly whether we are to take it seriously or laugh at its outrageous parodies. For all its flippancy and irreverence, it insinuates its naïve students into a world like that of Sam Peckinpah's *Straw Dogs* (1971) and, for all of its refusal to behave like a serious New Zealand movie, it attends to the details of New Zealand life with almost palpable acceptance and affection. It is the sudden escalations of terror from students' games with superglue to real torture that subvert any efforts to orient the tone. *Scarfies* mocks the teen horror movie when its protagonists don spook sheets, yet is overwhelmed by a terror that comes from within, not the world of Hollywood B-grade ghosts.

The Australian novelist, Patrick White, used to refer to especially Gothic murders as 'New Zealandy'. He meant 'the despair and confusion', which he found 'under the simple, uncomplicated New Zealand surface' and expressed a lack of surprise that any New Zealander should take a gun to his neighbour.[21] The Stanley Graham story, made by Mike Newell as *Bad Blood* in 1981, is the locus classicus of the genre in which a repressed

New Zealand man does just that. One of the signs of a new direction in New Zealand cinema is the recasting of crime, freeing it from the over-compensating seriousness of guiltily postcolonial consciousness. In *Scarfies* crime is accidental, not impelled by the mechanism of repression and release (as in Frank Sargeson's classic nationalist stories) but a prank youngsters stumble into, which overwhelms them. And they are not driven beyond society into the wilderness; they return unharmed to the near confines of bourgeois life by the exercise of cunning. In *Stickmen* the urban demi-monde is glamorised and made humorous as a kind of imitation of an imitation of an international trend from the US by way of Guy Ritchie's Brit-Tarantino and his film *Lock, Stock and Two Smoking Barrels* (1998). Most significantly, Polynesian New Zealand is refurbished for the role. John Laing's 1984 film, *Other Halves*, visited Maori alienation and urbanisation in the strain of Pakeha moral self-abnegation; *Stickmen* conventionalises the exchange, discovering the cool aspects of the world of pool contests, scams, sexy Polynesians and comically menacing underworld figures. Less sophisticated in the way it inhabits genre conventions than *Scarfies*, *Stickmen* tours the rundown warehouses and pool halls of urban Wellington and features a highly stylised underground Boss, 'Daddy' (Enrico Mammarella), gay bars and comic transvestites and the usual cast of Gen X underemployed who also appear in *Hopeless*.

In *Topless Women Talk about Their Lives*, Campion's *The Piano* is the subject of both direct and indirect mockery. The film opens with a German tourist looking for the beach at Karekare on which *The Piano* was filmed, and settling for a photograph of himself at another beach. The film also follows Campion's preoccupation with marriage and land use in settler culture, but here without the guilt of Pakeha culture. Infidelity occasions light relief as well as pain. In place of Campion's super-charged Gothic atmosphere, we find a lightness of treatment which means that interpreting the emotional content is difficult, as when Prue (Willa O'Neill) asks: 'You know this marriage thing. It's serious, it's not a joke?' The long struggle to 'improve' the land by pastoral endeavor meets its bathetic conclusion in Geoff's (Andrew Binns) obsession with wool and knitting.

The Price of Milk is described by Horton as 'post-Peter Jackson',[22] but it might more tellingly be described as post-Jane Campion, breaking with *The Piano*'s seriousness and the postcolonial Gothic. Campion's film famously closes with the overwhelming symbol of cultural importation, Ada's piano, strapped to an equally potent symbol of the indigenous, a Maori waka (canoe). This ungainly relation is broken as the piano enters the immigrant's element of separation—what Allen Curnow calls the 'hulk' of oceanic space between New Zealand and England—taking Ada down with it. Faced with the choice Curnow offered the unsettled settlers in the 1940s, in the title of his 1943 poetry collection, between sailing or drowning, Ada elects to resurface and continue her sea journey.[23] But she moves this time towards a postcolonial homecoming, no longer empire's outcast or her husband's colonised subject, if not yet a fully 'indigenised'

28. The frivolity of youth: *Topless Women Talk about Their Lives* eschews traditional national angst for twenty-something concerns. Courtesy of the New Zealand Film Commission.

citizen of the new world. It is a moment rich in Pakeha self-questioning, charged with the gender politics and utopianism of the 1980s, and perhaps Peter Jackson is deflating it at the close of *The Fellowship of the Ring*, when Frodo (Elijah Wood) rescues the drowning Sam (Sean Astin) from the river and they set off together into the sublime yet dark heart of New Zealand's South Island/Middle Earth. It is difficult to know if Jackson's allusion is deliberate, but such a cheeky reference would be in character. For all the fundamentalism which marked the film's reception as a tribute both to Tolkien's fantastic realism and New Zealand's sublime nature, he is a highly self-conscious and playful filmmaker, capable of making a bad taste joke about dwarf-tossing in his most epic feature.

The humour of Harry Sinclair has a complicated relation to indigenous traditions: it is fashioned from the satirical comedy of the 1980s and 1990s in which Sinclair (along with Don McGlashan and Jennifer Ward-Lealand in the experimental performance group The Front Lawn) had a significant role; it involves an ironic yet affectionate revisiting of New Zealand icons and literary themes. It rests on a quirky stance towards cultural nationalism, which avoids and mocks the seriousness of prior treatments from Curnow to Campion, yet which attends carefully to local speech and other cultural inflections, noting the traces of the foreign in the familiar. It is self-consciously of New Zealand without trying to be 'indigenous'; it is recognisably local without excluding the international. Amit Rai's remarks on Indian film apply here: 'In India the codes of film—both within the symbology of Western aesthetics and Western technology— were appropriated, broken, and remoulded to resist, dominate, and survive. Appropriating these codes was never a matter of simply negating British domination, although it might have been represented as such. Rather it was a negotiation which existed in a space and time "of antagonistic or contradictory elements".[24] When we look at the practice of New Zealand film, we find a similar pattern of reconfiguring rather than rejecting what comes from elsewhere.

A shift in intellectual culture beginning in the mid-1980s indicated less binary and oppositional ways of confronting and dealing with the intersections of the local and the imported, national and global, popular and serious. Roger Horrocks observes the limitations of the nationalist and protectionist position when he argues that 'simple polemics against Hollywood or for national identity are not enough. This problem has an international dimension. Local film-makers trying to develop a more complex artistic and commercial strategy have more in common with maverick film-makers in the United States and other countries than with the more-market end of the New Zealand industry'.[25] In the late 1990s it is small-budget films without 'name' actors that have established a new tone, and garnered a significant number of overseas awards. If *The Fellowship of the Ring* generated a paradox inherent in the attempt to use national culture to promote economic transformation—the film's 'New Zealandness' was most apparent to New Zealanders who recognised the picture-postcard scenery and the local names in the credits but were blind to the Hollywood capital that made the film possible—Sinclair's films reinforced the paradox that critical acclaim abroad does not resolve the funding dilemma for locally produced work.

Gillian Ashurst's *Snakeskin* (2001) dramatises the penetration of local culture by American movies by way of Alice (Melanie Lynsky), an antipodean Emma Bovary, her consciousness of alienation from provincial life heightened by borrowed fantasies. Alice confesses to having learned right from wrong by watching Clint Eastwood, and seeks adventure from the big-screen movies that constitute religion in her life. In New Zealand, she laments, there are no scorpions, no gangsters, and people don't carry hand-guns: 'It seemed to me like the safest fucking country in the world, and I hated it'. Alice is allowed to realise her dreams, as the film translates South Island roads into Route 66 high adventure, complete with drugs, outlaws and pistols. Ashurst's achievement is to inhabit the conventions of the Western and the road movie without producing mere pastiche. Her purpose is to explore the way local renditions shape and transform what they borrow, producing not mere imitations but hybrid forms.

For Maori directors like Barry Barclay, the need to preserve and reflect the peculiarity and difference of the indigenous culture is pressing. In his book *Our Own Image* (1990) Barclay worries how Maori difference can be preserved and reflected in film: 'The Maori world has its own ways of talking and listening, its own humour'.[26] Yet a highly hybridised and ironic style of humour is apparent in Billie T. James's bravura performance in *Came a Hot Friday* (1985) as a Maori who thinks he is a Mexican outlaw, wearing a child's version of the 1950s' movie cowboy outfit and firing a toy pistol. James teases all those agonies about cultural hegemonies and recalls those images of Maori kids in rural areas attending the local movie house, watching the cowboy film.

Alan Duff's novel, *Once Were Warriors*, offered a grim riposte to Maori Renaissance traditionalism, while Tamahori's film reinstated the saving lure of the past. With *Came a Hot Friday*, James's subversive humour destabilises the lyrical essentialism of early Maori Renaissance film and writing by inserting Maori into more complex patterns of cultural intersection and negotiation—global and local as well as regional and national—than either source novelist, Ronald Hugh Morrieson, or director, Ian Mune, envisaged. James's Te Tainuia Kid—borrowed from Morrieson, but fabricated out of a Maori response to popular culture—anticipates shifts in the understandings of what Maoriness means that parallel shifts within a wider concept of New Zealandness. Barclay defines a Maori film as 'one made by a Maori, just as a New Zealand film (in contrast to a French or Dutch film) [is] one made by New Zealanders. Simple enough'.[27] But, as Jane Smith observes, 'there is probably no such thing as a purely New Zealand film, not when the movies that make it off the islands are launched by foreign money'.[28] *The Piano* is set in New Zealand, directed by a New Zealander and tells a New Zealand story, but was produced in Australia and financed by French interests. The limits of Barclay's definitional solution are indicated by his doubt: 'I am not sure that we could make a brown *Macbeth* here at the moment, because such work would not be "Maori"'.[29] Yet 2001 saw the release of the *Maori Merchant of Venice*, directed by Don Selwyn and produced by Te Haeata Productions.[30]

Nationalism is both limiting and enabling when applied to cinema. Depending on where one situates oneself in respect of the treacherous term 'tradition', it may mean either a prison-house of unbroken and unchanging continuity or an evolving and inclusive process of adaptation; depending on whether the nation is conceived as tribal exclusivity or hybrid mixture, it may become the vehicle of either separatism or collective belonging. A government which seeks to promote nationalism through film must steer between these conflicts and find a means of reconciling the imperatives of culture and cash. Film is one of the ways in which the Clark government envisages the arts serving economic wellbeing and nation-shaping. According to Clark, government initiatives like the Film Production Fund 'will support the expression of creative talent, . . . contribute to the development of New Zealand identity, and . . . have significant economic development spin-offs'.[31] Her own sense of the arts' mission, however, is more ambitious than this suggests. She is not merely struggling against the utilitarianism of a settler society, traditionally either indifferent to culture or seeing it as mere decoration, and thus inessential; rather, she is intent on redefining culture's utility, discovering a use that will further the transforming of the country into a post-pastoral economy and society.

But there are contradictions in the dual role envisaged for the arts. One cannot both court and control foreign capital; one cannot transform the political imaginary of the nation by relying on the traditional body of imagery constructed for tourists and prospective consumers of pastoral produce. One cannot transform the nation and the social roles available to citizens without questioning the existing terms and images of nationalism, especially the protective and defensive strain long entrenched in New Zealand. In the absence of a larger international frame of reference (culturally and intellectually New Zealand remains far more isolated and inward-looking than Australia, for example) a 'post-nationalist' New Zealand has been slow to appear. Its emergence in the writing of the Wellington School is by now unavoidable, even if its implications for existing understandings of local culture have yet to be teased out. Its more recent appearance in New Zealand film has gone largely unnoticed. If a New Zealand film industry rich, exportable and attuned to the particularities of the local is to repeat the success of the Wellington writing scene, it will need support that allows necessary funding without invoking redundant ideas of the nation. Thus far in the Clark era the 'political imaginary', far from helping to establish a new economic and social reality, has been obliged to operate with a recirculated currency of images. Fortunately, some among the younger writers and filmmakers (and Clark herself at times among the politicians) have shown themselves able to capitalise on that.

Notes

1. *Sleeping Dogs* was released in 1977; Neill then worked in Australia on *My Brilliant Career* (1979), *The Journalist* (1979), *Just Out of Reach* (1979) and *Lucinda Brayford* (1980); following the last film, he gained a role in a British movie.

2. Michael King, *Being Pakeha: An Encounter with New Zealand and the Maori Renaissance* (Auckland: Hodder & Stoughton, 1985); *Being Pakeha Now: Reflections and Recollections of a White Native* (Auckland: Penguin, 1999).

3. Charles Brasch, 'Notes', *Landfall* 32 (December 1954): 248.

4. Even the title of Neill's documentary returns to the trope of the Pakeha as displaced, homesick, anxious; the Pakeha man figures thus in Neill's role in Jane Campion's *The Piano*. Neill's own acting debut in Roger Donaldson's 1977 *Sleeping Dogs* establishes the manly existentialism of the theme.

5. Arguably, both these responses derived from the legacy of Sir Robert Muldoon's Prime Ministership (1975–84), the first generated by accumulated resentment at his support for racist sporting contacts, the latter by his populist economic nationalism.

6. Jan Bieringa and Jonathan Dennis in their 'Note on the Second Edition' of *Film in Aotearoa New Zealand* (Wellington: Victoria University Press, 1996) write: 'With the enormous social, economic and political changes of the last

decade, successive governments have completely ignored the significance of the arts or, at most, given them inadequate support' (8). Three years later Prime Minister Helen Clark signalled her intentions about the arts by also personally assuming the post of Minister of Arts, Culture and Heritage and by announcing an \$86 million payment to the sector in the new government's first budget. By encouraging creativity, the arts were expected to exert a positive influence on innovation in business and science.

7. On film, for example, the Prime Minister has argued that it is 'a very powerful medium ... able to influence the way we see ourselves and our country—and the way the rest of the world sees us too' ('Arts, culture and the role of national institutions', Address delivered to the Friends of the Turnbull Library, Wellington, 21 September 2000). Film is one of the ways in which the Clark government envisages the arts serving, in indirect ways, the economic wellbeing of the country.

8. Jane Smith, 'Knocked around in New Zealand: Postcolonialism Goes to the Movies', *Mythologies of Violence in Postmodern Media*, ed. Christopher Sharrett (Detroit: Wayne State University Press, 1999), 382.

9. 'Uniquely New Zealand: Celebrating Cultural Recovery in Aotearoa', brochure released by Judith Tizard, Associate Minister for Arts, Culture and Heritage (Autumn 2002), n.p.

10. There were four submissable films produced, and the view was taken that seven was a minimum.

11. The resistance to America is a similar act of self-definition, choosing to emphasise the benevolence of the self by comparison with an aggressively modernised culture.

12. Charles Brasch, 'The Islands', from *Disupted Ground, Poems 1939–45*, in *Charles Brasch: Collected Poems*, ed. Alan Roddick (Auckland: Oxford University Press, 1984), 17.

13. Smith, 'Knocked around in New Zealand', 381.

14. Lee Tamahori quoted by Davinia Thornley, 'White, Brown or 'Coffee?': Revisioning Race in Tamahori's *Once Were Warriors*', *Film Criticism* 25, no. 3 (Spring 2001–02): 32.

15. Andrew Horton, 'Udderly Hilarious: New Directions in New Zealand Comedy as Seen in Harry Sinclair's *The Price of Milk*', *Film Criticism* 25, no. 3 (Spring 2001–02): 59.

16. Charles Brasch wrote in 'The Silent Land' (1945) that 'Man must lie with the gaunt hills like a lover'; New Zealand's most important artist, Colin McCahon, entitled one of his paintings, 'Landscape with too few lovers'.

17. Smith, 'Knocked around in New Zealand', 386.

18. James K. Baxter, 'The Mountains', in *Collected Poems: James K. Baxter*, ed. J.E. Weir (Wellington: Oxford University Press, 1979), 9.

19. Murray Edmond, Editorial, *The Word Is Freed*, 3 (n.d.), n. p.

20. Horton, 'Udderly Hilarious': 60.

21. White writes that he 'laughed when Our Lovely Queen made her speech the other day about "this happy country" when she was in Auckland'. Patrick

White, letter to Ben Huebsch, 17 February 1963, in *Patrick White: Letters*, ed. David Marr (Sydney: Random House, 1994), 219.

22. Horton, 'Udderly Hilarious': 60.
23. See Allen Curnow, 'When the Hulk of the World' and 'Sailing or Drowning', both from the 1943 collection *Sailing or Drowning*, and both in *Allen Curnow: Selected Poems*, selected by Allen Curnow (Auckland: Penguin, 1982), 110, 60.
24. Amit Rai, 'An American Raj in Filmistan: Images of Elvis in Indian Films', *Screen* 35, no. 1 (Spring 1994): 52.
25. Roger Horrocks, 'Hollywood Colpisce Ancora/Hollywood Strikes Back', *Te Ao Marama: Il Mondo della Luce: Il Cinema della Nuova Zelanda*, ed. Jonathan Dennis and Sergio Toffetti (Turin: Le Nuove Muse, 1989), 113–14.
26. Barry Barclay, *Our Own Image* (Auckland: Longman Paul, 1990), 9.
27. Ibid., 20.
28. Smith, 'Knocked around in New Zealand', 381.
29. Barclay, *Our Own Image*, 21. See also the debate in the correspondence columns of *Onfilm* between Barry Barclay, Alan Brash and Carey Carter over the question of 'indigenous' cinema. See *Onfilm* 20, no. 3 (2003): 11; 20, no. 4 (2003): 11; 20, no. 5 (2003): 11.
30. The play was staged as a Maori production in 1990. The text was translated and published in 1946 by Pei Te Hurinui Jones. In 2000 in Auckland a conference, 'Dislocating Shakespeare', included the first ever translations of Shakespeare's poems into Maori by Merimeri Penfold, published as *Nga Waiata Aroha a Hekepia* (Love Sonnets by Shakespeare).
31. Helen Clark, 'Arts, Culture, & Public Policy: A lecture in the Winter Lecture Series on the State of the Arts', University of Auckland, 22 August 2000.

13

'He Iwi Kotahi Tatou'?:
NATIONALISM AND CULTURAL IDENTITY
IN MAORI FILM

Michelle Keown

From the beginnings of New Zealand film, and until as late as the 1970s, cinematic images of Maori people were produced almost exclusively by Pakeha or European New Zealanders. From George Tarr's *Hinemoa* (1914), the first New Zealand feature film, to more recent productions such as Jane Campion's *The Piano* (1993), Maori have been positioned in various ways vis-à-vis Pakeha cinematic constructions of 'national' identity. These have ranged, for example, from the pioneering and '(wo)man alone' myths in which Pakeha encounter a (hostile) environment from which Maori have (frequently) been strategically erased, to various myths and fantasies of colonialist subjection and control: Maori as object of scientific, ethnographic or voyeuristic scrutiny; Maori as childlike or 'ignoble savage' subject to the paternalistic or 'civilising' guidance of the European colonising culture; Maori as 'noble savage' whose culture is (according to neo-Darwinist social theory) lamentably but inevitably giving way to the dominant and 'superior' settler culture, and so on.[1] As Martin Blythe points out, the most persistent motif in (Pakeha) New Zealand films, even into the 1980s, was the cross-cultural love story, a fantasy of bi-racial integration which allegorised the 'national dilemma' faced by a settler culture attempting to lay claim to a country already occupied by an indigenous culture.[2]

From the early 1970s, however, a major cultural shift known as the 'Maori Renaissance' created a context for the emergence of a Maori perspective in New Zealand filmmaking. Maori issues came under increasing scrutiny in the 1970s, partly as a consequence of the growth of international social movements—such as the women's liberation movement, the anti-racist movement, and gay and lesbian rights movements—in the late 1960s, but also as a result of a large-scale post-war migration of Maori from rural and coastal ancestral territories into the Pakeha-dominated urban centers. As Maori writer Witi Ihimaera has pointed out, by the 1960s urbanisation had triggered a 'massive discontinuity' in Maori life, creating a new generation of urban Maori 'removed from its roots, who did not understand their language and who had not lived the culture'.[3] In response to these developments, urban Maori began to establish supra-tribal Maori organisations and urban marae (meeting areas) in an attempt to preserve traditional rituals and values. Many Maori began to resist pressure to 'integrate' into Pakeha society, viewing the process as a variation on earlier government policies of 'assimilation' whereby it was assumed that Maori would abandon their traditional cultural practices and adopt those of the Pakeha. A bicultural model—which later developed into a campaign for Maori cultural and political self-determination—was posited as a viable alternative to integrationist policies.[4] Protests were mounted throughout the 1970s (and beyond) in order to draw attention to Maori grievances regarding land claims, Maori educational and economic under-achievement, and Pakeha political and cultural hegemony.[5] Within the creative arts, Maori artists, writers and filmmakers began increasingly to challenge dominant representations of Maori culture produced by Pakeha, creating new forms which celebrated traditional practices and motifs while responding to contemporary socio-political developments. In this article, I have selected four landmark feature-length films directed by Maori for discussion within this context: Merata Mita's documentary *Patu!* (1983) and her feature film *Mauri* (1988); Barry Barclay's feature film *Ngati* (1987); and Lee Tamahori's feature film *Once Were Warriors* (1994). My discussion will focus in particular on the exploration and representation of nationalism and cultural identity, issues which have featured prominently in Maori film (and other creative arts forms) emerging from the Maori Renaissance and the cultural developments which followed.

It is important to recognise that the Maori Renaissance has been pluralistic in character, encompassing a considerable range of tribal and supra-tribal groups, each with its own specific aspirations and political strategies. Ranginui Walker, for example, has identified both 'radical' and 'conservative' elements within the Maori Renaissance, suggesting that while both elements have pursued similar objectives, their methods have often been very different in character.[6] To extend Walker's argument further, it is possible to distinguish between what might be described as Maori cultural nationalism on the one hand, and Maori political activism on the other. Maori cultural nationalism, as an intellectual movement, has emphasised the rediscovery of Maori identity through an immersion in Maori language and culture, giving rise to a process by which Maori spirituality, communalism and environmental protectionism have been posited as a positive alternative to the putative profit-oriented monomania and spiritual poverty of Pakeha culture. As cultural theorists such as Ruth Brown have noted, such ideologies have done little to ameliorate the widespread socio-economic problems faced by Maori within a Pakeha-dominated capitalist society,[7] and as anthropologist Steven Webster notes, recent State restructuring targeted towards the development of a free market economy has impacted severely on Maori, creating a paradoxical situation whereby 'Maori cultural efflorescence' is accompanied by increasing 'Maori social deterioration'.[8] The (frequently) abstracted intellectualism of the Maori cultural nationalist movement can be contrasted with a more radical or grass-roots form of Maori political nationalism which promulgates 'tino rangatiratanga' or absolute sovereignty—a phrase which has come to be identified with a variety of objectives including Maori electoral power, Maori capitalism, and revolutionary activity—through more subversive and publicly demonstrative means.[9]

While the creative art forms (such as literature and film) which have emerged from the Maori Renaissance have generally functioned in cultural nationalist terms rather than entering directly into the political milieu, an intriguing blend of the two categories is evident in Merata Mita's documentary *Patu!* (1983), which focuses on the demonstrations and protest during the 1981 Springbok Rugby Tour of New Zealand. A large proportion of the film footage comprises recordings of confrontations between anti-Tour protesters and police, and as Nicholas Reid points out, the camera, mobile and jerky in its movements, is in the thick of the action, emphasising the fact that these 'are the images of a participant, not an onlooker'.[10] The title of the film clearly signals its point of view: 'patu' means to kill, strike or punish in Maori; it is also the name of a Maori hand-held combat weapon (pictured on the film poster); and significantly, it is also the name adopted by one of the three organised protester squads at the final Test Match in Auckland. As Reid notes, the Patu squad had the highest proportion of Polynesian members, most of its marshals were women, and it was the group 'most prepared to fight with police lines'.[11] Notably, one of the many sections of Mita's film which records police violence against protesters is accompanied by the sound of a female observer (possibly Mita) wailing in a manner redolent of formal lamenting at tangi (Maori funerals). The juxtaposition serves to recontextualise the Maori anti-Tour movement as a new chapter in the history of colonial 'war' between Maori and Pakeha (with the police as representatives of colonial authority). It is significant that while Mita's footage features the activities of both Maori and Pakeha anti-Tour protesters, the documentary is edited in a way which emphasises a perceived racial and ideological divide between Maori and Pakeha, controversially implying, as Martin Blythe notes, that the 'paternalistic complacency' evinced by the Pakeha sector of the anti-Tour movement aligned its proponents with their 'antagonists—the police and the pro-Tour factions'.[12]

In exploring this cross-cultural divide, Mita's film also features a range of Maori talking heads who draw direct parallels between the racist system of apartheid in South Africa, and institutionalised racism within New Zealand culture. One individual, for example, speaks of 'our brothers' in South Africa, while Donna Awatere, author of the influential anti-colonialist text *Maori Sovereignty* (1984), is shown discussing the fact that during the Second World War, the 28th Battalion—an all-Maori battalion whose members included her father, Commander Peta Awatere—was barred from entering Cape Town when its troop-ship was anchored there. Mita herself later observes (in a voice-over) that Maori rugby players were prevented from taking part in All Blacks tours of South Africa until as late as 1961. These details lend a personal and historically grounded aspect to

CONTEMPORARY FILMS presents
MERATA MITA'S POWERFUL DOCUMENTARY

PATU!

The incredible story of the 1981 South African Rugby Tour of New Zealand
New Zealand 1983   16mm   colour   110 minutes

'. . . *a remarkable achievement covering an astonishing series of events*'   *Derek Malcolm, Guardian*

'*Riveting, disturbing and profoundly important viewing. Never has it seemed more difficult to separate a film from the issues is tackles*'   *Evening News*

'*PATU! makes you stop and think about the raw power of documentary . . .*'   *Evening Post*

M.R.A.P. Prize with special commendation from the Jury, Amiens Festival of Films against Racism 1983
International Union of Students Prize, Leipzig International Film Festival 1983
London and Wellington Film Festivals

29. The striking publicity employed by Merata Mita's political documentary *Patu!*.
Courtesy of the Ian Conrich collection of New Zealand cinema and visual culture.

the Maori anti-Tour movement which serves to render the activities of the liberal Pakeha anti-Tour protesters somewhat specious by contrast.

Mita's subversion of myths of national unity is perhaps most arrestingly conveyed through the repetition of New Zealand's national anthem, which plays at least nine times on the film soundtrack. When protesters pour onto the field at Rugby Park in Hamilton, for example, during one confrontation on the tour that led to the cancellation of a match, some of the key lines of the anthem—which is sung unaccompanied as they occupy centre field—are thrown into relief and recontextualised as the action progresses. The phrase 'make her [the country's] praises heard afar', for example, is ironically juxtaposed with the demonstrators' repeated mantra 'the whole world's watching', indicating the protesters' awareness of the international opprobrium which was drawn as a result of the New Zealand government's decision to allow the Tour to go ahead. Similarly, the phrase 'God defend our Free Land' is rendered increasingly hollow as further footage records police and army erecting barbed-wire fences around rugby fields at Palmerston North, Wellington and Auckland prior to subsequent games. As the camera zooms in on army members stringing barbed wire around the boundaries of Eden Park rugby ground in Auckland, a dolorous electronic version of the national anthem plays, as though plucked on a section of fencing wire. Apart from the obvious connotations of this juxtaposition (the 'fencing off' of the rugby ground becoming a metaphor for apartheid and other forms of racist exclusion), there are other implications here for a New Zealand audience. 'Number eight' fencing wire has become a national symbol of 'Kiwi ingenuity' and enterprise; New Zealanders jokingly pride themselves on their ability to construct almost anything out of a section of number eight wire. In the context of Mita's documentary, however, this myth—which draws upon Pakeha New Zealand's pioneering and farming heritage in particular—is emptied of its positive connotations. As Nicholas Reid notes, the increasingly 'sombre, discordant and low' timbre of the anthem's reprises represents 'a gradual disintegration of national consensus and its habitual symbols'.[13] This is no 'Godzone' (as an Auckland protester's banner emblazoned with the sardonic caption 'Garden of Eden?' aptly implies), and Mita's emphasis on national chaos and inter-racial division is underscored at the very end of the documentary, where a Maori reggae song accompanies the closing credits. The song focuses on the 1840 signing of the Treaty of Waitangi, invoking the mantra 'he iwi kotahi tatou' (we are one people)—a phrase putatively uttered by Governor Hobson during the Treaty ceremony and which has since been used to promote a myth of bicultural harmony within New Zealand—and then accusing the Pakeha of duplicitously courting Maori with a 'bible' in one hand and a 'gun' in the other. The lines are significant not only in terms of Aotearoa New Zealand's colonial history, but also in terms of the Tour itself, where the New Zealand government and police were on the one hand attempting to maintain a semblance of national stability on the international stage, while violently suppressing local dissent on the other. Mita's documentary clearly challenges 'official' narratives of the Tour, and the subversive potential of the film was recognised by police who reputedly visited Mita's house in the post-production period in an attempt to confiscate footage. Television New Zealand (TVNZ) allegedly refused to make any of its own footage available to Mita, while the New Zealand Film Commission and the Arts Council contributed a mere fraction of the film's total budget, leaving the bulk of the fundraising to a dedicated band of volunteers.[14]

Mauri (1988), Mita's second feature film, was also produced on a low budget. Mita, who directed, produced and wrote the screenplay for *Mauri*, has spoken of the difficulties faced by Maori filmmakers working within a 'white male-dominated' film industry, pointing out that in addition to facing funding and market pressures, Maori filmmakers also have the burden of 'demystifying and decolonising' the screen in order to replace colonial stereotypes with 'positive imaging' for Maori.[15] Mita has described *Mauri*—which is set in Te Mata, a small (fictional) 1950s' Maori community on the East Coast of the North Island—as a 'probing enquiry' into Maori cultural concepts, and as a 'parable about the schizophrenic existence of so many Maori in Pakeha society'.[16] The film's focus on the metaphysical is perhaps most clearly evident in the mental torture suffered by Paki (Anzac Wallace), a jail escapee who arrives in Te Mata posing as Rewi Rapana, a local-born man whom Paki has accidentally killed in a car crash. In order to make his impersonation more convincing, Paki wears a bone carving taken from Rewi's body; this violation of Maori tapu (taboo) incurs punishment in the form of a haunting by kehua or spirits, and Paki's suffering is only eased when he returns to the scene of Rewi's death, relinquishing the bone carving and asking forgiveness for his actions.

The film's preoccupation with spiritual matters is encapsulated in its very title: 'mauri' means 'life force' or 'spiritual essence' in Maori. In a memorable scene near the beginning of the film, Kara (Eva Rickard) explains to her grand-daughter Awatea (Rangimarie Delamere) that when a Maori person dies, his or her mauri leaves the body and travels to the ancestral homeland, Hawaiki. The flight of the spirit is symbolised in the image of a heron flying gracefully across the landscape, and the heron returns at the end of the film when Kara dies and Awatea waves farewell to her mauri from a hilltop on the coast. The image of the free-floating bird/spirit also evokes Rewi's liberation from mental imprisonment, allegorising Mita's argument that 'only by breaking free of colonial repression and asserting our true Maori identity can we ever gain real freedom'.[17] As actor Anzac Wallace points out, the film asserts that there is a need for Maori people to return to 'spiritual awareness' in order to save the Maori nation.[18] In this sense the film has a significance beyond its 1950s' setting: the politics of the film are clearly informed by the Maori Sovereignty movement, and the foregrounding of Maori language and ritual throughout the film functions as a celebration and reassertion of Maori culture.[19] In particular, the use of a high proportion of untranslated Maori clearly signals Mita's intention that *Mauri* was to be a film made by Maori,[20] featuring Maori, and addressed *to*

Maori; there are few concessions made here for a Pakeha (or international) audience. Indeed, Pakeha characters in the film are generally peripheral, sketchily drawn and—particularly in the case of the rabidly racist Mr. Semmens (Geoff Murphy), a local eccentric—mere caricatures, as Mita widens the inter-racial schism explored in *Patu!* and inverts the power dynamics of the colonial specular encounter by making Pakeha the objects of critical scrutiny.

While *Mauri* functions primarily as an assertion of cultural nationalism, celebrating Maori culture and ritual through a nostalgic return to an earlier period of Maori history, a number of references are also made to a contemporary political reality. For example, one of the central preoccupations of the film—the importance of tribal land to the Maori people—is lent particular contextual significance by the casting of legendary Maori land rights activist Eva Tuaiwa Hautai Rickard as Kara. The 1970s was a decade of protest over Maori land issues and, in 1978, Rickard herself led a protest occupation of the Raglan Golf Course, an amenity which had been established on Tainui Awhiro land requisitioned by the government (under the Emergency War Act during the Second World War) and never returned. The details of this and other land disputes—such as the Bastion Point affair, a high-profile case involving Ngati Whatua, whose protests were the focus of Mita's 1980 documentary *Bastion Point – Day 507*—provide an ideological backdrop for the exploration of land issues in the film. Towards the end of the film, for example, a hui (meeting) is called on the local marae in order to discuss, with Pakeha government officials, the possible establishment of a training and rehabilitation center for criminals in the area. The Pakeha officials trample on marae protocol by leaving the hui before everyone has a chance to air their views, and one of them points out that the whole hui has been little more than a 'public relations' exercise, given that the government can claim the land regardless under the (1952) Public Works Act. These details clearly have a political significance beyond the fictional confines of the film narrative, resonating for Maori across New Zealand. The issues which the community face—rural-urban drift; the loss of tribal land; the encroachment of Pakeha bureaucracy; and the emergence of Maori gang culture (encapsulated in the figure of Kara's nephew Willie [Willie Raana])—are issues which affected many rural Maori communities in the post-war period.

The setting and ideological focus of Mita's film has much in common with its immediate predecessor, Barry Barclay's *Ngati* (1987). Like Mita's film, *Ngati* is also set in a rural, North Island East Coast Maori community during the transitional post-war phase, although the date in this case is slightly earlier: 1948. Most of the filming took place in Waipiro Bay near Tokomaru, where scriptwriter Tama Poata grew up; in the film, however, the community is given a fictional name—Kapua—allowing *Ngati* (like *Mauri*) to become representative of issues affecting Maori throughout New Zealand during the post-war period. The title of the film similarly points towards its wider significance; as Poata has indicated: 'Ngāti means "tribe", so the film can easily relate to any other area, and Maori all over relate to the film'.[21] Barclay has pointed out that he made a serious attempt 'to have Maori attitudes control the film',[22] employing as many Maori as he could on the film crew as well as in the cast, and he describes the film as a 'determined attempt to say what it's like being Maori [sic]'.[23] Of Ngati Apa descent, Barclay has, since his early days as a documentary maker, been committed to Maori self-determination in filmmaking as with other areas of self-expression, and he is a founding member of Te Manu Aute, an organisation—formed in the mid-1980s—which advocates Maori sovereignty within the communications industry.[24]

The struggle for Maori self-determination is also directly incorporated into Tama Poata's screenplay. The Pakeha-owned local freezing works—upon which many members of the community depend for their livelihood—is threatened with closure, but the people of Kapua (led by local man Iwi, played by Wi Kuku Kaa) band together in response to the crisis, negotiating terms which will allow them to purchase and manage the freezing works. The resolution functions as an allegory for Maori self-determination, and Iwi's declaration, 'we will come together; we always have' sounds as a rallying cry for contemporary Maori.

In contrast to those in *Mauri*, Pakeha characters in *Ngati* are given more constructive roles within the Maori community, but their status as tauiwi (strangers) is clearly signalled near the beginning of the film when Jenny Bennett (Judy McIntosh), a Pakeha schoolteacher, leads her Maori students in a rendition of Hubert Parry's 'Jerusalem'. The hymn, with its English nationalist rhetoric, points towards the cultural schizophrenia which has putatively hampered Pakeha attempts to establish a viable sense of locally grounded identity. As is the case in *Mauri*, *Ngati* asserts, in cultural nationalist terms, that it is Maori who truly belong to the land.

Lee Tamahori's *Once Were Warriors* (1994), one of the highest grossing films in New Zealand's film history, explores an environment far removed from the tranquil rural locations in *Ngati* and *Mauri*, focusing on a community of state-housed urban Maori locked into a cycle of benefit dependency, violence and alcoholism. The film's script is an adaptation of Alan Duff's 1990 novel *Once Were Warriors*, a controversial text which, in its grim, uncompromising representation of Maori as a violent, debased and despairing socio-economic underclass, enacted an angry refutation of media constructions of a harmonious, 'bicultural' New Zealand during the 1990 sesquicentennial celebrations of the signing of the Treaty of Waitangi. As Duff observes:

In our newspapers, magazines, and the television in particular, we were inundated with this image of ourselves as one people 'joined together, hand in hand', the blaring music coupled with glossy images of sweetly smiling, teary eyed Maori and grinning Pakeha types with that look of: We're mates, the Maoris and me.[25]

Duff argues that these utopian images of bi-racial harmony mask the fact that there exists a huge socio-economic gap between Pakeha and Maori which has established a situation of virtual apartheid within New Zealand.[26] As Beth Heke, a character in the novel, observes: '[Pakeha are] like strangers . . . May as well be from another country the contact the two races have'.[27]

In the film version of *Once Were Warriors*, Pakeha and Maori are still represented as having little in the way of cross-cultural contact, but the context has shifted: while Pakeha in the film—as in the book—occupy positions of power (as judges, police, social welfare workers), they are rendered peripheral, becoming, as Gregory Waller notes, the film's 'other', rather than appearing as an object of envy or admiration, as they do in Duff's novel.[28] Similarly, while the film version of *Once Were Warriors* preserves many of the elements of Duff's original narrative, focusing on the dysfunctional Heke family headed by Maori kingpin Jake (Temuera Morrison) and his battered wife, Beth (Rena Owen), Duff's story is transformed by scriptwriter Riwia Brown in order to render the film's message a much more 'positive' one for contemporary Maori. A greater sense of hope is located in the younger generation than is evident in the book, and while the violence and brutality of Duff's narrative are still present in Tamahori's film, these darker issues are tempered with a more tangible sense of optimism, as well as a more sustained celebration of Maori culture and identity. Tamahori, of Ngati Porou descent, has spoken of his desire to film *Once Were Warriors* in a way which would emphasise its status as a 'Maori film' both within New Zealand and overseas.[29] Filters were used during filming in order to 'enrich' the brown skin tones of the Maori actors, and Tamahori made a conscious decision to downplay the influence of American popular culture on New Zealand urban Maori (youth) culture in order to create a 'look' that was 'purely New Zealand'.[30] The clothes, hairstyles and musical tastes of young urban Maori in the film are still clearly American-inflected, but there are subtle differences: the hip-hop, rap and reggae recordings featured on the soundtrack, for example, were produced mainly by Maori artists.[31] A number of the urban Maori in Tamahori's film also speak Maori; this is a significant departure from Duff's novel, where the inability to speak or understand Maori is posited as a sign of the cultural dislocation of urban Maori such as Beth, Jake and their peers.

Perhaps the most radical contrast between book and film, however, is in the representation of the gang into which Beth and Jake's son Nig (Julian Arahanga) is initiated. Both book and film posit an essential 'Maori warrior' identity which has been passed down through the generations, but in Duff's novel, contemporary Maori gang culture is represented as a debased and spurious form of Maori warriorhood, whereas Tamahori's gang members appear as a new generation of urban 'warriors' whose regalia[32] and ethos appear to resurrect a pre-colonial Maori 'fighting spirit' lacking in men of Jake's generation.[33] The name of the gang—'Toa Aotearoa'—is significant in this context: the word 'toa' can mean 'brave man' or 'warrior', rendering the gang members 'warriors of Aotearoa'. When Nig is initiated into the gang, Taka the gang leader (Calvin Tuteao) tells him: 'now you've met your new family', following up with the catch-cry: 'He whanau kotahi tatou! Toa!'—which can be translated as 'We are one family . . . Warriors!' While specific to the gang ethos, the motto also appears as a reconfiguration of the (nationalist) mantra 'he iwi kotahi tatou', suggesting a sense of group solidarity based on a pride in a shared Maori identity. Tamahori has described Toa Aotearoa as a 'taha Maori gang . . . proud of who they are and proud of their ancestry', and he has indicated that the gang was partially modelled on the Maori gang Black Power (Mana Mangu Aotearoa), a collective which has, he claims, become progressively more 'organised' and 'legitimate' since its inception in the late 1960s.[34] This is not to say, of course, that the gang is represented as an entirely positive entity in the film: at one point, for example, Nig's visually arresting (and threatening) brand of warriorhood is contrasted with the internalised (and presumably more spiritually 'authentic') warriorhood which is instilled in his younger brother Boogie (Taungaroa Emile) under the patronage of Mr Bennett, a Maori welfare officer (George Henare). Bennett rehabilitates Boogie and other young Maori incarcerated within a young offenders' institution by teaching them to draw strength from the wairua (spirits) of their warrior ancestors through performing haka (war dances) and learning about pre-colonial Maori history.

Tamahori's film, like *Mauri* and *Ngati*, explores an urban-rural dialectic, setting up an opposition between the chaos of the urban environment on one hand, and the peace and spiritual energy of 'rural Maoridom' on the other.[35] This urban–rural opposition is foregrounded from the very beginning of the film, which opens with an idyllic rural scene featuring a lake and snow-capped mountains. The scene is accorded an additional sense of cultural specificity by the soundtrack, which features traditional Maori instruments such as the koauau (flute) and the purerehua or 'bull-roarer', invoking well-established cultural nationalist connections between 'Maori spirituality' and 'the landscape'. As the camera pulls back, however, the peaceful scene is revealed as an illusion, a mere advertisement on a billboard situated next to a busy freeway, and the sound of rushing cars, accompanied by a metallic guitar riff, replaces the soothing timbre of the Maori instruments. As the film continues, this opening scene appears (in retrospect) to project that conceptions of Maori spiritual connection to the landscape have little to do with the urban environment which is the 'real' home for many contemporary Maori. A paradigmatic shift occurs towards the end of the film, however, when Beth Heke is prompted to re-establish tribal connections following the suicide of her daughter, Grace (Mamaengaroa Kerr-Bell). Grace's funeral takes place on Beth's marae, situated in a tranquil rural location, and Tamahori has pointed out that he deliberately filmed the scene in a way which emphasised the status of the marae as a communal 'place of healing'.[36] Tamahori has been accused

30. The warriors of Aotearoa: *Once Were Warriors'* urban gang culture. Courtesy of the New Zealand Film Commission.

of romanticising the marae in the film, and of promoting an 'unrealistic solution to the plight of urban Maori' through a return to a tribal source,[37] but it is important to recognise that the film does not necessarily enforce a simplistic opposition between urban hell and rural paradise: as Waller notes, the film celebrates a vital urban culture[38] which—as the situation of the gang suggests—is able to incorporate and adapt aspects of 'traditional' Maori culture (in)to a modern, contemporary context. Indeed, far from replicating the scenario of urban squalor described in Duff's novel, Tamahori's film glamorises young urban Maori featured in the narrative and, as Jonathan Dennis notes, the film's urban setting creates an aura of the 'hyper-real'.[39] The Hollywood veneer of the film—which arose from Tamahori's professed desire to make *Once Were Warriors* appealing to a wide general audience 'beyond the film festivals'—sets *Once Were Warriors* apart from its lower budget counterparts discussed above.[40]

There are other feature films with considerable Maori input which have not been discussed in this article, notably Barry Barclay's *Te Rua* (1991), a film focusing upon the recovery of taonga (tribal artifacts) from a Berlin museum; Ian Mune's *What Becomes of the Broken Hearted?* (1999), the sequel to *Once Were Warriors*; and Don Selwyn's *Maori Merchant of Venice* (2001), an adaptation of Shakespeare's play produced in Maori with English subtitles, but institutional pressures and the shortage of funding for New Zealand filmmakers in general have ensured that Maori directors have channelled their energies more into documentary, video and short filmmaking rather than full feature film projects. Training programmes mounted by Barclay, Mita and others have increased the number of Maori working within the film industry, and as filmmaker Lisa Reihana points out, there are now a growing number of Maori and Pacific Island directors creating experimental short films reflecting a 'diversity of concerns and styles'.[41] Reihana argues that these films challenge the argument that there is a recognisable 'Maori style' in filmmaking, and she points out that Maori filmmakers are now exploring connections between Maori and other Pacific Island cultures, moving beyond bicultural frameworks.[42] She also suggests, however, that given the primacy of film and video in contemporary society, Maori filmmakers have a continuing 'responsibility' and opportunity to challenge the ways in which Maori culture is perceived by both Maori and non-Maori New Zealanders.[43] This sense of responsibility has clearly motivated the directors of the four films discussed in this article; each film assesses the position of Maori in New Zealand within particular socio-historical contexts, challenging and moving beyond dominant-culture representations of Maori cultural identity in order to negotiate a space from which to articulate new forms of self and community.

Notes

1. See Martin Blythe, *Naming the Other: Images of the Maori in New Zealand Film and Television* (Metuchen, N.J. and London: Scarecrow Press, 1994); and Sam Edwards, 'Cinematic Imperialism and Maori Cultural Identity', *Illusions* 10 (1989): 17–21 for a more detailed discussion of cinematic stereotypes of Maori in Pakeha film.
2. Blythe, *Naming the Other*, 34.
3. Witi Ihimaera, 'Maori Life and Literature: A Sensory Perception', *Turnbull Library Record* 15, no. 1 (1982): 50.
4. Michael King, *Being Pakeha: An Encounter with New Zealand and the Maori Renaissance* (Auckland: Hodder and Stoughton, 1985), 104.
5. Ihimaera, 'Maori Life and Literature', 52.
6. Ranginui Walker, *Ka Whawhai Tonu Matou/Struggle Without End* (Auckland: Penguin, 1990), 243.
7. See Brown's articles 'Maori Spirituality as Pakeha Construct', *Meanjin* 48, no. 2 (1989): 252–58 and 'Contextualising Maori Writing', *New Zealand Books* 6, no. 2 (1996): 14–15 in particular for a detailed discussion of these issues.
8. Steven Webster, *Patrons of Maori Culture: Power, Theory and Ideology in the Maori Renaissance* (Dunedin: Otago University Press, 1998), 13.
9. See Walker, *Ka Whawhai Tonu Matou*, for a detailed discussion of Maori political activism during the period.
10. Nicholas Reid, *A Decade of New Zealand Film: Sleeping Dogs to Came a Hot Friday* (Dunedin: John McIndoe, 1986), 93.
11. Ibid., 93.
12. Blythe, *Naming the Other*, 267.
13. Reid, *A Decade of New Zealand Film*, 97.

14. *'Patu!* Feature Documentary Acclaimed', *New Zealand Film* 20 (May–August, 1983): 6.
15. Merata Mita, 'The Soul and the Image', *Film in Aotearoa New Zealand*, ed. Jonathan Dennis and Jan Bieringa (Wellington: Victoria University Press, 1992), 49.
16. Ibid., 49.
17. Ibid., 49.
18. 'Rimini Award for "Mauri"', *NZ Film* 36 (March 1989): 7.
19. There are, for example, several marae scenes; a sequence of Maori birth, death and marriage rituals; and widespread use of traditional Maori wind instruments (in musical sequences composed and arranged by Hirini Melbourne) throughout the film.
20. With the exception of the camera and editing crew, 90 per cent of those involved in making *Mauri* were Maori. Ann Simpson, 'From Patu to Mauri', *Onfilm* 4, no. 4 (1987): 26.
21. Barbara Cairns and Helen Martin, *Shadows on the Wall: A Study of Seven New Zealand Feature Films* (Auckland: Longman Paul, 1994), 125.
22. Barry Barclay, quoted in Rongotai Lomas, 'A First for the Maori: Ngati', *Illusions* 5 (1987): 5. Such an approach is also evident in other Barclay filmmaking projects, from the 1974 *Tangata Whenua* television documentary series (which focused on various aspects of Maori society and philosophy), to more recent productions such as his second feature film *Te Rua* (1991), and— in a wider frame— the documentary feature *The Feathers of Peace* (2000).
23. Barclay, quoted in Lomas, 'A First for the Maori', 4.
24. Barry Barclay, 'Amongst Landscapes', *Film in Aotearoa New Zealand*, ed. Jonathan Dennis and Jan Bieringa (Wellington: Victoria University Press, 1992), 127.
25. Alan Duff, *Maori: The Crisis and the Challenge* (Auckland: HarperCollins, 1993), vii.
26. Alan Duff, 'Growing up Half Caste', *Growing up Maori*, ed. Witi Ihimaera (Auckland: Tandem, 1998), 230.
27. Alan Duff, *Once Were Warriors* (Auckland: Tandem, 1994 [1990]), 43.
28. Gregory Waller, 'Embodying the Urban Maori Warrior', *Places Through the Body*, ed. Heidi J. Nast and Steve Pile (London: Routledge, 1998), 351.
29. Stuart McKenzie, 'Warrior Cast: Stuart McKenzie Talks to Lee Tamahori', *Artforum* (February 1995): 65.
30. Ibid., 65.
31. Bryan Staff, 'Initiation Rites', *Onfilm* 10, no. 8 (1993): 9.
32. The gang tattoos, for example, are based on traditional Maori moko designs, and the leather jackets and vests worn by gang members incorporate traditional Maori motifs.
33. This contrast between generations and institutions is emphasised throughout the film through cross-cutting.
34. Helen Martin, 'Lee Tamahori: *Once Were Warriors*', *The Big Picture* 5 (1995): 5.
35. McKenzie, 'Warrior Cast', 66. Both *Ngati* and *Mauri* posit the urbanised

(Pakeha) environment as a hostile entity which threatens to encroach upon rural Maoridom.

36. Ibid., 66.
37. Ibid., 66.
38. Waller, 'Embodying the Urban Maori Warrior', 352.
39. Cited in Jonathan Dennis, 'Record Box Office for Warriors in New Zealand', *NZfilm* 52 (1994): 4.
40. Martin, 'Lee Tamahori: *Once Were Warriors*', 3.
41. Lisa Reihana, 'Skinflicks: Practices in Contemporary Maori Media', *disrupted borders: An intervention in definitions of boundaries*, ed. Sunil Gupta (London: Rivers Oram Press, 1993), 77.
42. Reihana, 'Skinflicks: Practices in Contemporary Maori Media', 78.
43. Ibid., 83.

14

The Kiwi Bloke:
The Representation of Pakeha Masculinity in New Zealand Film

Russell Campbell

The opening scene of Roger Donaldson's *Sleeping Dogs* (1977), the breakthrough film of the contemporary era of New Zealand cinema, shows a morose and tearful man taking leave of his wife and children. Sensitive, vulnerable and withdrawn, the hero Smith (Sam Neill in his first major film role) seems here to represent a character type antithetical to popular conceptions of the ruggedly masculine Kiwi bloke. In the very next scene, however, a sudden change comes over him. He yells angrily at a man who has pulled his utility truck into the driveway, deliberately smashes into it, then races off in his station wagon, tires squealing. The shift upsets expectations generated in the previous scene and signals a recuperation of the traditional macho image. And yet this archetypal larrikinism[1] cannot fully cancel the impression created in the opening moments of the film, and for the rest of its trajectory *Sleeping Dogs* will seek to sustain, reiterate and somehow synthesise the oppositions, to portray Smith as *both* soft and tough, tender and violent.

This is not to argue that the reshaping of the male image which takes place in *Sleeping Dogs* and subsequent films represents a radical departure from a fixed macho norm. It is, rather, a reworking, with new emphases, of contradictions long evident in the Kiwi bloke stereotype. In his 1987 book *A Man's Country*, Jock Phillips contended that the self-image of Pakeha (European) men—he specifically excluded Maori—had been created from the intersection of two conflicting traditions, that of the frontier and that of urban respectability, the itinerant swagger versus the Protestant minister.[2] Hence the loner, the hard-drinking muscular man of the bush, could appear under another guise as the temperate good family man of the quarter-acre section. Social developments in recent decades had however—so Phillips argued—placed the traditional rough-hewn image in either of its manifestations in jeopardy: this was (the title of his final chapter) 'the bloke under siege'.

Sleeping Dogs and its successors participated in the trend of redefining Pakeha male identity which occurred during the 1970s and 1980s. The unprecedented growth of a professional urban middle class opened up, as Phillips pointed out, many new specialised occupations and reduced the relevance of a rural-based mythology.[3] The vast increase in the numbers of working women altered traditional patterns of family structure and childrearing. The anti-war and counter-culture movements of the late 1960s and early 1970s helped shift social perceptions. But perhaps the most significant influence was the critique of male values launched by the women's movement and its accompanying challenge to male prerogatives.

In 1973 Sheila Rowbotham, in *Woman's Consciousness, Man's World*, suggested that women and men were 'moving towards a new world together but development is an uneven and painful process . . . The generalisation of our consciousness of our own subordination enables them to discover a new manner of being men'.[4] The invitation to redefine male identity was taken up by theorists of men's liberation, who contended that men as well as women were oppressed by sex-role stereotyping. 'Our masculinity is our burden', wrote Christopher Wainwright in 'Male Oppression: Emotions, Sex and Work', his contribution to *Learning About Sexism in New Zealand* (1976). 'Some of us are beginning to realise that we do not know how to be passive, dependent, non-aggressive, inner oriented, emotional, empathetic, sensitive and nurturing'.[5]

But men cannot become passive and dependent without subverting the structuring of sexual difference upon which male-dominated society rests. At the historical moment at which the traditional masculine mould began to lose its appeal, the task of patriarchal ideology became twofold: on the one hand to reaffirm the validity of traditional male values, warning about the consequences of their abandonment, and on the other to show men how they could expand their possibilities, could be 'different', without relinquishing male power and the symbolism attached to it. This is the task which *Sleeping Dogs* and much of subsequent New Zealand cinema set itself.

Pakeha male identity is forged in the interstices of three paradigmatic oppositions, *on the move:settled, violent:nonviolent, loner:family man*. A powerful myth links together the first terms of the three pairs, the restless, ruggedly self-sufficient, itinerant Man Alone. This is the macho side of the Kiwi bloke stereotype, and Phillips traces the myth through the details of social history, to the footloose labourers of the nineteenth century— goldminers, gumdiggers, bushmen, navvies, shearers, always pulling out and moving on to the next job.[6] The 1984 German co-production *Among the Cinders*, in its naive recapitulation of this myth, in fact has its old gumdigger protagonist explicitly equate frontier values with the virtues of New Zealand manhood: 'Where were they [the clammy-handed bureaucrats] when men, real men, were winning this country from the wilderness?' The process of redefining male identity can be seen as a shift across the divide towards the second, settled, term of the opposition, a shift which entails great risk since it involves men adopting female-associated values. In an exploratory film such as *Sleeping Dogs* the protagonist mediates the antitheses, coming at times dangerously close to an anti-macho stance but reaffirming at crucial turning points a traditional masculinity.

31. On the lookout: The itinerant con-men Cyril and Wes assess their next scam in *Came a Hot Friday*. Courtesy of the Ian Conrich collection of New Zealand cinema and visual culture.

Smith—we never learn the first name of this quintessential average man, nor his occupation—invokes the first of the oppositions when, with no fixed destination, he hits the road, never to return to his suburban Auckland home. The pair of opposed terms *on the move:settled* is an extension of the active-male/passive-female dichotomy at the heart of patriarchal conceptualisation. In its New Zealand form rootlessness is a condition of the hero's integrity and virility, and is associated with the Pakeha's alienation from the land. The motif of criss-crossing the country underpinned such pioneering sound features as *On the Friendly Road* (1936), *Broken Barrier* (1952) and *Runaway* (1964), and survived strongly into the *Sleeping Dogs* era. Thus in *Goodbye Pork Pie* (1980), racing south in the Mini defying the law is a test of masculinity for John (Tony Barry): has he (as Gerry charges) become a half-arse, turned soft through living with a woman too long? For the younger Gerry (Kelly Johnson), traversing the country represents traditional Kiwi wanderlust infused with an anarchic Beat energy. The straight comic heroes, too, are those on the move, like the vagabond con men Cyril (Phillip Gordon) and Wes (Peter Bland) in *Came a Hot Friday* (1985). It is no accident that this film is framed by the iconic image of a car speeding across a landscape. Conversely, characters stuck in one place are suspect: the businessmen of *Skin Deep* (1978), for example, psychologically paralysed by neurotic attachment to their hick town; Stanley Graham (Jack Thompson) in *Bad Blood* (1981), chained financially to his West Coast dairy farm and becoming a lethal paranoiac; the bitter and destructive old farmer T.K. Donovan (Derek Hardwick) in *Carry Me Back* (1982); the incestuous rapist Jackson (Terence Cooper) in *Heart of the Stag* (1984).

Two films offer significant reversals of this paradigm. In *Solo* (1977) it is the female character, Judy (Lisa Peers), who is on the move, hitchhiking around New Zealand, and the male, Paul (Vincent Gil), who wants her to settle down with him. And in *Smash Palace* (1981), Al (Bruno Lawrence) is contented where he is, and the trouble is caused by the restlessness of his wife Jacqui (Anna Jemison). Of course both male protagonists, though having a fixed home, are spectacularly mobile—Paul a fire patrol pilot and flier of a restored Tiger Moth and Al a champion racing driver—and both narratives entail moving around the country, with *Smash Palace* employing the classic motif of taking to the bush on the run from the police. But the partial gender-switching, closely associated with the emphasis both films place on fatherhood, leads, in the era of 'the bloke under siege', to a revealing modification of the traditional male image.

The mediation of the opposition which occurs in *Sleeping Dogs* has Smith a reluctant man on the move. Forced out of his home by the preference of his wife Gloria (Nevan Rowe) for another man, Bullen (Ian Mune), he travels to the picturesque rural North Island district of Coromandel where he moves into a bach (holiday home) and plants a garden on a formerly uninhabited island. From here, after several months, he is uprooted and transported to Auckland by the Special Police, and it is to escape jail and threatened execution as a suspected guerrilla that he goes on the run. His subsequent movements to Rotorua and later back to the Coromandel peninsula are dictated by his status as fugitive. Thus though his actions conform outwardly to the footloose paradigm, it is clear that Smith would, by choice, lead a settled life (as the idyllic 'raindrops keep falling on my head' interlude, with a temporarily reconciled Gloria, suggests).

Such mediation is more general in New Zealand cinema's handling of the *violent:nonviolent* opposition. The good Kiwi bloke, of course, is ready to use his fists if provoked, especially in rivalry over a woman. Smith fights with Bullen at the edge of a motel pool, just as, in a rather uglier scene, Albie (Andy Anderson) attacks Stan (Frank Whitten) with a motorcycle chain in *Trespasses* (1984). But the Pakeha hero is often reluctant to resort to force. He is seldom seen, for instance, being violent with a woman, Al overpowering Jacqui in *Smash Palace* being one of few such cases.[7] Instead violence is diverted onto objects—a door (*Smash Palace*), a massage table and a mirror (*Skin Deep*), cups and a photograph (*Solo*)—in the release of pent-up frustration.

The evident ambivalence towards violence is most marked when it comes to guns, and here, when it is not being imitative, New Zealand cinema parts company with Hollywood. The Kiwi bloke is not like the American action hero, finger on the trigger. In *Heart of the Stag*, for instance, it is the villain Jackson who keeps an arsenal of firearms, and his victorious adversary Daley (Bruno Lawrence) who hunts deer with a camera. Even in films dealing with warfare, there is hesitation about the use of firearms: thus in *Utu* (1983), both Scott (Kelly Johnson) and Williamson (Bruno Lawrence) find violence unacceptable, despite the paradoxical fact that each possesses, and uses, a particularly potent weapon—Scott his Spencer repeating carbine and Williamson his homemade quadruple-barrelled shotgun.

In Smith's narrative, the question of whether to take up the gun is paramount. Scornful of Bullen and his Resistance fighters, Smith often seems a misfit in a world of war, a tortured personality with pronounced pacifist tendencies. 'Don't you ever have nightmares?' he asks the American Col. Willoughby (Warren Oates), 'Don't you ever worry about killing the wrong man?'[8] When he unhappily rejects the pistol Bullen offers him, saying 'I won't kill people', Smith comes perilously close to the edge of acceptable Kiwi male behaviour, and it is only after he reluctantly changes his mind that he proves himself a man within the traditional mould. Even so, there are doubts. In the guerrilla raid on the American troops camped at the motel, Smith is an appalled bystander, eyes closed, hands clasped over his ears to shut out the noise. His moment of truth does not come until later when, during a search, a member of the Special Police spots him crouched in a wardrobe. Smith has a split second to make his decision, to surrender or kill. He does not hesitate, shooting the man at point-blank range. The act gives Smith no satisfaction, as is clear from the ensuing sequence in which he and Bullen make their escape. Bullen is wildly jubilant, Smith subdued and bitterly sarcastic: 'You just pull the trigger and they go down . . . It's just another Special. It doesn't matter'. *Sleeping Dogs* continues its oscillation on the *violent:nonviolent* axis right up to the final scene. Smith's last gesture, prior to giving his adversaries the finger and allowing himself to be shot in the back, is to fling away his gun. But we are left in little doubt that his taking up of it was necessary, a man's destiny.

In its narrative trajectory away from domesticity, *Sleeping Dogs* also seeks to mediate the *loner:family man* opposition. There is virtually no trace of a fulfilling family relationship in Pakeha cinema of the 1970s and 1980s: for the hero it represents a dream scarcely realisable in practice. Hope for the future of a heterosexual union is projected in a few films in which couples form or get back together, like Sue (Shirley Gruar) and John in *Goodbye Pork Pie*, but such relationships are not complicated by children. As a father, the hero in New Zealand film is likely to find marriage impossible, solitude assuaged by male companionship the only viable option. In *Solo*, for example, solo father Paul has a warm, emotional relationship with his son Billy (Perry Armstrong), but cannot persuade Judy to share a life with them.

In *Smash Palace*, the affection between Al and his daughter Georgie (Greer Robson) is signalled early in the film, when she snuggles into bed beside him. After the marriage breaks up and the parents become locked in a custody battle, Al takes the lonely road of kidnapping the girl and taking off with her into the bush. A consequence of this action is Jacqui's offer, which may or may not be genuine, to return to Al and restore the family unit. But he chooses to brush aside her overtures of reconciliation, and the film remains unresolved, the final positioning of Al inside or outside the family hanging in suspense.

In *Sleeping Dogs*, too, the protagonist is poised between two modes of life, like Al ultimately finding fulfillment in neither. If Smith's affectionate reunion with Gloria feeds his hopes of reconciliation and reintegration in the family, her death soon after totally dashes them. The mediation of the antithesis here achieves a symmetry with the other two pairs of values, positioning Smith reluctantly in the camp of the macho bloke: for if he is by inclination settled, nonviolent, a family man, he is by necessity on the move, violent, a loner.

Unable to find fulfillment in marriage, the male protagonist is likely to receive support and understanding from a cobber. Mateship is an underlying thematic in much of New Zealand cinema and comes to the forefront in movies such as *Goodbye Pork Pie* (the casual relationship) and *Came a Hot Friday* (the long-term partnership). With mates there is an easy familiarity, a jokingly expressed but genuine admiration for the other's capabilities, and there is the opportunity, too, to confide one's thoughts, worries, fears: Al, for example, strolls down the street telling Ray (Keith Aberdein) of his troubles with Jacqui ('Sorry mate, it's not your problem, I know'). Mateship is cemented in shared experience of danger and anti-authoritarian behaviour—Gerry and John eluding the traffic cops in *Goodbye Pork Pie*; Wes and Cyril dodging the blasts from Sel Bishop's (Marshall Napier) shotgun in *Came a Hot Friday*. A man might even lay down his life for a friend, as Basil (Bruce Spence) does for Sam (Peter McCauley) in dispatching a pair of blackmailers in *Pallet on the Floor* (1984). Although its emotional value is seldom verbalised, mateship is often vital to the hero (whether he recognises it or not), and its rupture can assume traumatic proportions.

This is the meaning of the ending of *Smash Palace*, which discards the resolution of Al's relationship with Jacqui in favour of his resolving issues with his mate Ray, with whom she has been having an affair. After the breakup Jacqui has been painted as the guilty party, and the narrative dynamic is not towards compromise and equality in a restored marital partnership, but on the contrary a reassertion of male predominance and the sidelining of the female characters. For Al, as he now intuitively realises, the important relationship in his life is not with his wife, nor even with his daughter, but with his mate. The climax takes place in a male world of cars, cops and guns, and the threatened murder-suicide which turns instead into a practical joke (Al stops the car he and Ray are in on a railway crossing, but the oncoming train takes a different track) gives Al his revenge in a gesture which may restore their friendship, and whose homoerotic overtones cannot be ignored. With the sinking of differences

32. 'A male world of cars, cops and guns': As the police close in at the end of *Smash Palace*, Al continues to assert control with Ray (right) as his hostage. Courtesy of the Ian Conrich collection of New Zealand cinema and visual culture.

which appears to occur, the male bond is restored and the symbolic order of authority, disturbed by a woman's insubordination, re-established.

In *Sleeping Dogs*, the triangular patterning is identical. The narrative develops by the elimination of the key female character, Gloria, as an obstacle to the consummation of mateship between Smith and Bullen.[9] The rift between them is healed when Bullen is injured and they stagger through the bush together arm in arm, and as they reach the farm which is their goal there is sheer exultation in their shared achievement: 'We've beaten them Bull!', 'We did it boy!'. The joy is short-lived, of course; the Specials move in, but there is solace at the end as Bullen dies cradled in his mate's arms. Smith, who on learning of Gloria's death carried on the fight despite his desolation, can now no longer find a reason for living; his last act is to deprive his antagonists of the satisfaction of taking him alive.

In the 1970s and 1980s, New Zealand cinema did not offer action-hero models of masculinity like Clint Eastwood or Sylvester Stallone, but instead characterisations like that of Smith, attempting to hold in suspense the contradictory tendencies in the way Pakeha men pictured themselves. With a yearning for the quieter, gentler values more traditionally associated with women, for a home and family life, this hero was thrust of necessity into a world of solitary venturing, action and bloodshed. Female characters were eliminated to clear the way for the moment of male bonding which would be his fulfillment. Ultimately, in the case of *Sleeping Dogs* at least, the contradictions he represented could not be sustained or resolved, and the narrative ended in his death.

Smith and his successors became symbols of national identity, defining what it meant to be a New Zealander (contrasted significantly with the American, in *Sleeping Dogs*, and the English, in *Utu*). The heterosexual male Pakeha of British or Irish extraction was the norm, and those who did not fall into this category—women, Maori, gay men, people from other ethnic backgrounds—were the Other, inevitably subordinate figures, consigned to the periphery. Hence this characterisation, while accommodating progressive influences from, especially, the women's movement, did the work of the dominant ideology in reinforcing gender and ethnic division as cultural categories. It confirmed Pakeha men in their alienation even as they enjoyed their power.

It's no surprise that this Kiwi bloke pattern of representation emerged, because it reflected the reality of the power structure in New Zealand society. In the feature film industry, the social group of straight Pakeha men was overwhelmingly dominant. There was only one acknowledged gay director—Richard Turner, with a single film, *Squeeze* (1980) to his credit—and with the exception of Ramai Hayward's co-direction of *To Love A Maori* (1972), no women until 1984, and no Maori until 1987. But during the 1980s, the hegemony of this 'boys' own' cinema came under increasing challenge from individuals and groups such as Equity Women's Caucus, Media Women and Te Manu Aute (a collective of Maori communicators formed in 1986). The confidence of the Pakeha men working in the industry, if not their actual power, was shaken, and a crisis in the representation of the Pakeha male on screen occurred. By 1990 several of the major creators of the mythology—most noticeably Roger Donaldson and Geoff Murphy—had moved to Hollywood, while others such as John Laing and John Reid found work predominantly in television. Into the breach stepped a new generation of directors diverse in gender, ethnic background and sexual orientation, few of whom had a commitment to the figure of the heterosexual Pakeha male as paradigmatic for the nation.

At first sight Peter Jackson's *Braindead* (1992) is indicative of such change. In this comedy of the grotesque, the macho types, figures of arrogant or aggressive masculinity like the zoo official Stewart (Bill Ralston), the lecherous Uncle Les (Ian Watkin) and the bodgie[10] Void (Jed Brophy), are mercilessly pilloried and then torn limb from limb by the horde of zombies, while the hero Lionel (Timothy Balme) is a model of dutifulness and timidity—endowed, that is, with attributes traditionally associated with the feminine. But deeper reflection reveals that *Braindead* marks the continuity, rather than the ending, of a tradition. Lionel proclaims his masculinity at the moment he enters the house of carnage holding his motor mower aloft, declaring 'Party's over!' and proceeding to carve and slash his way through the amassed living dead. He goes on in the climax of

33. A threatened Lionel (Timothy Balme) finds himself forced into a physical reassertion of male authority in *Braindead*. Courtesy of the New Zealand Film Commission.

the film to vanquish the Mum Monster (Elizabeth Moody), the undead castrating matriarch (guilty of two murders in her murky past) now transformed into a frightening colossus. Rather than undermining the premises on which the Kiwi bloke as a norm of masculinity is constructed, *Braindead* retells the tale of earlier comedies and dramas such as *Skin Deep*, *Middle Age Spread* (1979) and *Among the Cinders* which gave expression to anxieties about the attainment of manhood, in families where an aggressive female—henpecking wife or domineering mother—has usurped the place of the father. Like Colin (Grant Tilly) in *Middle Age Spread*, Lionel is able to fight his way through to an assertion of male authority denied him at the outset. At the end of the film, his girlfriend Paquita (Diana Peñalver) submits to being overruled by him and they walk away to form a normal Kiwi couple, restoring the patriarchal order so disturbed by the monstrous criminality of Lionel's mum. Although *Braindead*'s parodic mode renders ambiguous much of what it represents of the nature of New Zealand life, in the structure of the narrative the archetypal norm is reproduced.

It is *Desperate Remedies* (Peter Wells and Stewart Main, 1993), however, the first feature under avowedly gay male direction since 1980, which breaks radically with the conventions of representation which generated and sustained the image of the Kiwi bloke. The film scandalously subverts the patriarchal norm, and indulges in body display and gender transposition unimaginable in the cinema of the previous decade. The narrative of this camp period drama consistently positions the lead male character Lawrence Hayes (Kevin Smith), though prominent in the action, in subordination to Dorothea (Jennifer Ward-Lealand), his employer and the object of his desire. With this couple, traditional gender roles are reversed: she selects him, hires him, gives the orders, and finally rejects him. The male here is powerless to affect the turn of events, to win the love of the woman he adores; at the end, acknowledging Dorothea's preference for her lover Anne (Lisa Chappell), he submits to her wishes and relinquishes all claim to her affection.

Part of the strangeness of the Lawrence Hayes characterisation is that it is constructed around emotions rather than actions. As theorists of masculinity have pointed out, men within patriarchal society tend to judge themselves by their success in attaining external goals, and have great difficulty relating to and articulating their emotional needs.[11] *Desperate Remedies* subverts this paradigm, since within the couple it is Lawrence who is sick with unrequited passion, Lawrence who declares his love ('You are so beautiful I ache'), Lawrence who cries out in solitary anguish after Dorothea has broken off an embrace.

The film also departs from tradition in making the male, rather than the female, the object of the gaze. At the docks, for example, Dorothea, when selecting Lawrence from among a group of new immigrants, subjects the man in the leather jacket with bared chest and smoldering good looks to a teasingly erotic contemplation. Later in the film—notably in the fight scene between Lawrence and Fraser (Cliff Curtis)—the bared torsos of the leading actors are put on display for the loving gaze of the camera, glistening with oil and sweat, hard and muscular, adorned with nipple rings or leather and chain suspenders. There are a number of other scenes, too, in which anonymous male nudity figures. It is a significant shift in perspective, since the physical attractiveness of male characters had not in the past been much dwelt upon: no doubt precisely because of its potential to open up a scenario of gay desire.[12]

While the lesbian relationship between Dorothea and Anne plays a prominent part in the film, gay male sexuality operates more at the level of subtext, particularly in the eroticisation of the bodies of the two principal males. However, the possibility of a relationship between them is once touched on in the dialogue: 'Nothing is fixed', Fraser says to Lawrence, 'We could take a ruby each and honeymoon together without the ladies'. And a short scene features explicit homosexual intercourse, evidently a transaction between a society figure and a prostitute. Although Lawrence's own heterosexuality seems insisted on in the scene in which he has sex with the aging whore Mary Anne (Bridget Armstrong), the film creates a highly charged atmosphere of eroticism and promiscuity in which sexual options are multiple and gender norms fluid. The concept of masculinity itself is placed in doubt with the absence of a consistent heterosexual orientation and a stable male power base (at the end Anne escapes retribution for ridding Dorothea of the troublesome Fraser), and the active-male/passive-female dichotomy is radically undermined. Though Lawrence might at a stretch be thought of as the new (if Victorian) version of the Kiwi bloke, by virtue of his combination of aggressiveness (in fighting Fraser) and gentleness (in courting Dorothea), the fictional world in which he operates is so little committed to the patriarchal norm that the archetype has virtually dissolved into meaninglessness.

Jane Campion's *The Piano* (1993), also pivoting on a female protagonist, holds particular interest for this study in that the woman's husband, like Smith in *Sleeping Dogs*, is played by Sam Neill. The characterisation of Stewart runs directly counter to many of the positive qualities of the Smith paradigm, with the result that the film may be seen as a feminist riposte to the Pakeha male's self-image on screen. Stewart conforms to the myth of the rugged pioneer, carving out a niche for himself in rough conditions amidst enveloping forest and none-too-friendly Maori. But he has few of the strengths of the Kiwi bloke. Stewart is ill at ease in this new land, arrogant and racist in his dealings with Maori, and frustrated in his attempts to exert authority over his recently-acquired family. Painfully awkward with women, he is unable to communicate with Ada (Holly Hunter), a problem which her muteness merely exacerbates. Diffidence is replaced by impatience and anger as he strives in bewildered fashion to elicit the affection he thinks of as a husband's right. Unable to stamp his authority on the situation, he loses his cool ('[m]asculinity is more impressive played cool', writes Andrew Tolson, 'in choice gestures and side-remarks, rather than in open boasting or violence'[13]) and his actions become more extreme. He tries to rape Ada in the undergrowth, the attempt thwarted by Victorian clothing and the timely intervention of her daughter Flora (Anna Paquin). He imprisons her in their home, and then finally wields his axe in anger against the kitchen table, her piano and, most dramatically, her finger.

The Kiwi bloke's potential for domestic violence, largely repressed in the male-created paradigm, is here exposed. The attempt to keep the wife in line is to no avail: Stewart's situation just gets worse. Not only does Ada become more alienated from him, but he begins to wonder whether he really wants her after all. In the end, listening to the voices he hears in his head—achieving, that is, a lucidity which allows him to distinguish himself from his social role—Stewart lets Ada go. The female now controls the narrative, defeating her husband in the war of wills and departing with her lover Baines (Harvey Keitel). Campion, in caricaturing the Pakeha bloke and his pretensions, has uncovered the misogyny and racism that lie beneath the surface of his proud masculine identity, but she allows him to depart with dignity, in inner dialogue with his emotions.

Thus *The Piano* dealt a death blow to the traditional Kiwi bloke. That paradigmatic figure, so important to Pakeha men's sense of self-identity, together with the hierarchical gender and ethnic positionings which the characterisation entailed, could be sustained only while a group comprising a minority of the population exerted hegemonic control over the film industry. Reflecting the waning of patriarchal power in New Zealand society, the Kiwi bloke as normative archetype largely disappeared from the screen in the mid 1990s, and an era of representation was at an end.

Subsequent films featuring a Pakeha male in a prominent role show him as enfeebled, stripped of authority and confidence.[14] Even a vicious serial killer, like Simon (Paolo Rotondo) in *The Ugly* (1997), is represented as impotent—incarcerated in a psychiatric institution, hooded, manacled, and chained at the ankles. For others, not physically restrained, it is a question of mental inhibition, of a feeling of inadequacy in a world which no longer confers traditional patriarchal privileges.

Dwight (Bryan Marshall) in *Chicken* (1996) is a washed-up middle-aged rock singer, reduced to selling takeaway chicken. Aggressively confronted by a crazed, dreadlocked animal-rights activist (played by Maori actor Cliff Curtis) at the head of an angry chanting mob—a clear analogue for the Pakeha confronted by Maori land-rights radicals—he can only stand by trembling while the protestor is felled by a diminutive karate-chopping woman. As the story develops, the despondent singer ('I'm sick to death of my whole pathetic life') decides to stage a phony fatal accident in a bizarre attempt to reinvigorate his faltering career, but though the tactic is successful, the fanciful outcome to this labored comedy carries no conviction.

In *The Ugly*, Simon's past life is revealed in a series of flashbacks: he is bullied by schoolmates, brutally beaten by his mother Evelyn (Jennifer Ward-Lealand)—who becomes his first victim—and then picked on as an adult, made the butt of practical jokes. In response he lashes out with lethal violence and, in stark contrast to the paradigmatic Kiwi bloke, has no qualms about doing so. Ant (Ian Hughes), the artistically challenged filmmaker with a breast fetish who features in the comedy *Topless Women Talk About Their Lives* (1997), would seem far removed from the psychopathic murderer, but in fact the characterisations are revealingly akin. The psychological disturbance which both he and Simon suffer from is traceable to a rupture in the patriarchal line marked by an absent father and dominant mother: they are descendants of *Braindead*'s timid Lionel, but unlike him unable to fight their way through to a restoration of masculine normality. Simon breaks his chains to become a nightmare monster; Ant catches sight of his mother topless and finally flips, stabbing the only friend who has remained loyal to him in the wake of his disastrous scriptwriting experience. Here, the world of the Kiwi bloke has become radically destabilised.

The tendency continues in *The Price of Milk* (2000), a whimsical comedy-drama of heterosexual partnership in which realism is interleaved with fantasy. Dairy farmer Rob (Karl Urban) finds himself without his herd of cows when his partner Lucinda (Danielle Cormack) swaps them to regain a prized quilt which has been stolen from her by a shadowy Maori figure. Again, as in *Chicken*, the connotations of racial conflict can hardly be ignored: the Maori who have taken possession of Rob's cows laugh at his humiliation. Rob walks out on Lucinda, but he is a shattered man, his impotence conveyed by the transformation of his voice into a high-pitched squeak. And when the couple are eventually reconciled it is on her terms, a far cry from the masculine mastery of Al in *Smash Palace*.

Savage Honeymoon (1999) is particularly significant for this study in that it comes across as a serious attempt to recuperate the image of the Kiwi bloke as lovable larrikin. Again, as in *The Price of Milk*, an unsettled male–female relationship is at the center of the narrative (both films start with the couple in bed, in sleepy embrace in the morning light). Muscular, hairy Mickey (Nicholas Eadie) incarnates rough working-class values, evoking a latter-day Bruno Lawrence as he strides around the backyard in his underpants leaving a frustrated wife behind in the bedroom. The sexy, hard-drinking biker, who has two adult children, characteristically helps a mate out by storing stolen goods, and parties riotously by burning a picket fence and throwing a gas cylinder on the flames. Yet like the other Pakeha men in this post-*Piano* string of films he is powerless to inflict his will on those around him. He is at the beck and call of his ever-present mother, and his wife Louise (Perry Piercy), who though deeply in love is unable any longer to tolerate his antics and leaves him. The truth, we discover, is that Mickey is suffering a crisis of confidence following his son's near-fatal motorcycle accident. As he tells Louise in an effort to win her back, 'I wasn't the same man you married—I was just a full-of-shit pisshead like my dad was'. *Savage Honeymoon* may grant the couple a happy reconciliation, but as in *The Price of Milk* it is the male who gives ground.

However accurate these later depictions may have been in registering changing patterns of power in New Zealand society, the characterisations did not capture the Kiwi male's imagination: the actors were forgettable and the films by and large did poorly at the local box office. In the country's cinema the male icon was now no longer Pakeha, but Maori: Temuera Morrison as Jake the Muss, battling with his violent urges in *Once Were Warriors* (1994) and *What Becomes of the Broken Hearted?* (1999), and the resulting depiction of masculinity involved distinctly different cultural traits.

This is a shortened, revised and updated version of the articles 'Smith & Co.: The Cinematic Redefinition of Pakeha Male Identity', *Illusions* (7 March 1988): 11–26 and 'Dismembering the Kiwi Bloke: Representations of Masculinity in *Braindead*, *Desperate Remedies* and *The Piano*', *Illusions* 24 (Spring 1995): 2-9.

Notes

1. *The Dictionary of New Zealand English*, ed. H.W. Orsman (Auckland: Oxford University, 1997), 438, defines 'larrikin' as 'a street rowdy or young urban hoodlum; an irresponsible vandal'. A tradition of such behaviour arose in the nineteenth century when frontier workers came to town and went on a drinking spree. See Jock Phillips, *A Man's Country?: The Image of the Pakeha*

Male—A History (Auckland: Penguin, 1987), 34–5.

2. Ibid., 80.
3. Ibid., 268–89.
4. Sheila Rowbotham, *Woman's Consciousness, Man's World* (Harmondsworth: Penguin, 1973), 43.
5. *Learning About Sexism in New Zealand*, ed. Phillida Bunkle, Stephen Levine and Christopher Wainwright (Wellington: Learmonth, 1976), 195, 194.
6. Phillips, *A Man's Country?*, 20.
7. In contrast, Pacific Islanders Sione (Uelese Petaia) in *Sons for the Return Home* (1979) and Tug (Mark Pilisi) in *Other Halves* (1984) both carry out brutal attacks on their lover.
8. *Sleeping Dogs* is obviously influenced by the Vietnam War protest movement, and its director Roger Donaldson stayed in New Zealand to avoid being drafted in Australia.
9. That Smith and Bullen were mates prior to Bullen's taking up with Gloria is only implicit in the film; the novel on which it is based, C.K. Stead's *Smith's Dream* (1971), stipulates that the two went to school together.
10. Bodgies, the New Zealand equivalent of British Teddy Boys, were members of youth street gangs in the 1950s, typically wearing slicked-back hair, leather jackets and tight jeans.
11. See, for example, Victor J. Seidler, *Rediscovering Masculinity: Reason, Language and Sexuality* (London and New York: Routledge, 1980), 8.
12. It is worth noting that the chief exceptions are *Kingpin* (1985) and *Mark II* (1987, telefeature), in which the lead actors, like Cliff Curtis in *Desperate Remedies*, are Maori or Pacific Islander. For a discussion of the repression of explicit eroticism in the act of looking at a male in mainstream cinema, see Steve Neale, 'Masculinity as Spectacle: Reflections on Men and Mainstream Cinema', *Screen* 24, no. 6 (November–December 1983): 2–16.
13. Andrew Tolson, *The Limits of Masculinity* (London: Tavistock, 1977), 43.
14. The tendency towards emasculation is, if anything, even more pronounced in films with a female protagonist, such as *Magik and Rose* (2000), *Snakeskin* (2001) and *Rain* (2001).

15

Impaired and Ill at Ease:
New Zealand's Cinematics of Disability

Angela Marie Smith

In what has been called New Zealand's 'Cinema of Unease', the nation's isolation, alienation and idiosyncracies have often been depicted in terms of physical, intellectual and psychological dysfunction.[1] Along with the centrality of disability rhetoric in New Zealanders' commentaries on their nation and their cinema, feature film representations of disability and illness indicate the importance of the disability trope for the nation's concept of itself, a dysfunctional cinematic image of the national body which is sometimes self-pitying and sometimes ironic and liberating. In considering the function of cognitive dysfunction in Ian Mune's *The End of the Golden Weather* (1991), and paralysis and brain injury in Alison Maclean's *Crush* (1992), this article contends that New Zealand's cinematics of disability offers a particularly New Zealand vision of national identity.[2]

For David Mitchell and Sharon Snyder, the central paradox of disability in cultural texts is that it functions as both a 'deterministic vehicle of characterisation for characters constructed as disabled' and a 'destabilising sign of cultural prescriptions about the body'.[3] This kind of ambivalence also characterises the use of disability to represent New Zealand identity as simultaneously a crippling conformity and a distinctive and valuable aberrance. In some of New Zealand's most resonant poetic images, the nation and its people are envisaged as metaphoric cripples. In 'I'm Older Than You, Please Listen', poet A.R.D. Fairburn declares, 'This land is a lump without leaven, / a body that has no nerves', while in his poem 'The Skeleton of the Great Moa in the Canterbury Museum, Christchurch', Allen Curnow regards 'The skeleton of the moa on iron crutches' which is 'not more fallen than I'. When Curnow famously muses, 'Not I, some child, born in a marvellous year, / Will learn the trick of standing upright here', he confirms a present sense of national evolutionary inadequacy even as he anticipates the future triumph of a New Zealand species.[4]

On the one hand, these images of physical incapacity embody the insipidity and incompleteness of New Zealand, its failure to attain a certain level of national greatness. Disability has frequently been marshalled to depict a nation that is, or feels itself, inferior to the motherland, Great Britain, or, in more recent times, to the cultural power of the United States. Witness, for example, the language used to deride the emergence of a distinctive New Zealand accent in the early twentieth century, as documented by Elizabeth Gordon: 'Defects of pronunciation were connected to defects of cognition. Those who could not speak properly could not think properly ... And the bad speech was also blamed for "many minor throat and chest disorders". . . . [T]he underlying problem was seen as a speech defect which could be remedied'.[5] New Zealandness is here presented as a physiological defect, a deviance from the British norm and ideal.

On the other hand, images of disability also embody the conservatism and conformity of a nation that, according to artistic and intellectual critics, has failed precisely in not embracing its potential difference, instead mimicking the conventions and exploitative practices of its colonial home. In this sense also, then, New Zealand is 'a body that has no nerves'. Lawrence Jones suggests that the theme preoccupying much of New Zealand's canonical literature is the failure to accomplish a distinctive national identity grounded in natural beauty and social justice.[6] Metaphors of bodily damage poignantly evoke both New Zealand's 'mutilated bush', and its history of colonial violence and persisting racism.[7] Michael King writes that colonial 'acts of confiscation—of land, of materials, of food and of culture—are the weeping sores on our body politic', and Bill Willmott refers to the 'shock' and 'trauma' experienced by Maori in the loss of their land and subsequent rapid urbanisation.[8]

When considered alongside the panoply of disabled characters in New Zealand's literary and cinematic canon, such metaphors testify to a potent relationship between national imaginings and disabled bodies and minds. New Zealand disability scholar Peter Beatson notes that images of dysfunction permeate the nation's literature of alienation, which features 'a significant cast list of impaired eccentrics, including mute, deaf, quadriplegic, psychiatrically disturbed, senile, intellectually disabled, mutilated or crippled characters in *the bone people, The Piano, Plumb, The Silent One, Crime Story, Faces in the Water, Memory, Last Summer, The Burning Boy, Pomare* and *Potiki*'.[9] Beatson suggests that in many of these texts disability offers 'a modernist metaphor for the alienated subject in a reified world'.[10] The rhetoric of literary commentary bears him out; for example, Jones contends that 'John Mulgan's *Man Alone* (1939) diagnosed the social illness that came of fighting a war with the land for profit', and quotes Bruce Mason's reference to the 'bleak and stunted lives' sketched in Frank Sargeson's short stories.[11]

Cinematic images of disability similarly communicate a national sense of isolation and insignificance. Ian Conrich and Sarah Davy note that examples of the cinematic 'Kiwi Gothic' genre often present characters as '[d]warfed by the power of the land ... fragile, eccentric or disturbed' (7), and depend on portraits of physical or psychological dysfunction to convey a sense of alienation and breakdown.[12] Thus, perhaps as a result of the omnipresence of that dwarfing land in New Zealand films, and perhaps as a result of the smallness of New Zealand and its output in the world cinematic market, these depictions of disability are frequently read as figurations of the nation itself. Commenting on *Jack Be Nimble* (1993), in which a psychologically disturbed young man carries out horrific acts of revenge for his abusive childhood, a reviewer in British newspaper *The Times* sardonically remarks, 'judging by its recent films, New Zealand is a great place to grow mad, twisted and bitter. Is this because of the isolation, the climate, the gurgling volcanic mud?'[13] Also drawing this connection between filmic images of dysfunction and the national image abroad, Raybon Kan complains that New Zealand filmmakers have 'made us look weird'.[14]

The argument might be made that such language indicates a cultural reliance upon general metaphors of grotesqueness and the Gothic, rather than an exploitation of disability *per se*. But, as Rosemarie Garland Thomson has shown, the modernist use of the grotesque to convey 'alienation and disorientation', particularly when attached to disabled characters, simultaneously aestheticises and depoliticises disability.[15] Thus, an interrogation of New Zealand film's cinematics of disability both uncovers what Thomson calls 'the sociopolitical relations that makes disability a form of cultural otherness' and insists upon a specifically New Zealand identity shaped in and through disability imagery.[16] If, as Mitchell and Snyder suggest, literary representations of disability exploit 'the materiality of metaphor', wherein '[p]hysical and cognitive anomalies promise to lend a "tangible" body to textual abstractions', the tangible and deviant body in Kiwi films is persistently attached, both within the film texts and in their reception, to the textual abstraction of the nation.[17]

The dysfunctional body or mind is salient in numerous films in New Zealand's small but growing feature film industry. In addition to the movies considered here, New Zealand feature films which foreground physically disabled or ill characters include *Heart of the Stag* (1984), *The Silent One* (1984), *The Piano* (1993), *The Whole of the Moon* (1996), and *Channelling Baby* (1999), while bodily mutilation takes centre-stage in horrors or parody-horrors such as *Death Warmed Up* (1984) and the Peter Jackson splatter-fests *Bad Taste* (1988) and *Braindead* (1992).[18] Mental illness is a central concern in films such as *Other Halves* (1984) and *An Angel At My Table* (1990) and psychologically disturbed characters feature prominently in *Bad Blood* (1981), *The Scarecrow* (1982), *Bridge to Nowhere* (1986), *Jack Be Nimble* (1993), *The Ugly* (1997) and a host of others.[19]

The exact ways in which physical and mental 'weirdness' attach to national self-conception in New Zealand film are illustrated in the different disabilities represented in *The End of the Golden Weather* and *Crush*. Both films link narratives about and images of disability to the emergence of a specific, and specifically New Zealand, identity: *The End of the Golden Weather* marking the transition of a boy into Pakeha (European) manhood; and *Crush* exploring the powerful dynamics of female sexuality and desire.

Ian Mune's film adaptation *The End of the Golden Weather* uses cognitive dysfunction or intellectual disability to delineate the formation of the kind of typical Pakeha identity described and disparaged in the cultural commentaries mentioned above. The film is based upon Bruce Mason's play of the same name, a one-man show which Mason first performed in 1960, and delightfully incorporates mythic and magical elements in telling its nostalgic story.[20] In the beachside community of Te Parenga during the 1930s, 12-year-old Geoff Crome (Stephen Fulford) spends his summer dreaming up tales of chivalrous rescue, plans concerts in which he co-opts his younger brother and sister to perform for their parents and aunt and uncle, and sees all the local eccentrics as wonderful grotesques. He is also fascinated by the ideal models of manhood he encounters: the young men who train as lifesavers, and the famous wrestler Jesse Cabot (Steve McDowell), who runs along the beach each day, arms outstretched, palms upward, bearing two huge boulders.

And then Geoff meets Firpo (Stephen Papps), a gangling, developmentally slow man, who fervently believes that he can become a 'made man' like Cabot, by entering and winning the Olympics. Geoff's Uncle Jim (Greg Johnson) and the members of Te Parenga's community mock Firpo and his ambitions, and Geoff's father (Paul Gittins) warns his son to stay away, but Geoff, whose fantasies alienate him from this stolid, conservative community, intuits a kinship with this outcast. Eager for Firpo to win a running race set up for local Olympic hopefuls—to which Firpo has been invited for the community's entertainment—Geoff sets about trying to train him.

On the big day, Firpo is mocked mercilessly on the beach, but Geoff stands by his friend. As the race begins, it seems Firpo might triumph, but towards the end he loses energy, falters and falls, taking Geoff's dreams with him. Geoff helps Firpo back to his hut, a shelter in an overgrown garden which has served as a place of refuge and fantasy for Geoff. But Firpo, desperately upset, lashes out at Geoff, accusing him of laughing at him. Frightened, Geoff flees the hut, back to the relative normalcy of the family home. Months later, we see Geoff on the beach in a winter school uniform, gazing back towards the space of past events, before walking off along the sand.

The End of the Golden Weather provides the drama of a young, imaginative boy faced with exactly the kind of conservative and suffocating society that intellectuals have criticised in New Zealand. The play, its creator asserted, was about 'the failure of romantic idealism'; Barbara Cairns and Helen Martin define 'romantic idealism' as a belief in a world in which '[t]here is a place . . . for eccentrics and non-conformists to be as they are without ridicule'.[21] The film aligns Firpo's mental eccentricity and Geoff's imaginative eccentricity, as Geoff's father exasperatedly asks, 'Why can't you just . . . just be normal?' Geoff's father thus represents the adult conformity that characterises the normative New Zealand citizen.

This conformist world is repeatedly envisioned through idealised, male, Pakeha bodies: the athletic young men who gather to race Firpo and show him up at the film's climax, and the immensely strong Cabot,

34. Training on the beach, the unathletic Firpo (right) in a display of disabled difference in *The End of the Golden Weather*. Courtesy of the New Zealand Film Commission.

'Heavyweight Champion of the British Empire'. Even Geoff's and Firpo's eccentric fantasies circulate around this vision of the 'made man', a title, according to Geoff's uncle, bestowed on 'somebody special. Somebody who's got it all going for him. Jesse Cabot would be a made man, could have just about anything he wants'. While Firpo dreams of joining the ranks of made men by winning the race and competing at the Olympics, his gawky body with its idiosyncratic movements functions as a point of contrast for the community's athletic young men. Costume underlines this opposition: the limp, one-strap black bathing suit Firpo wears everywhere is a parody of the Roman gladiator outfit worn by Cabot.

While Geoff's uncle and Te Parenga's young men find in Firpo a counterpoint to their healthy, masculine identities, Geoff's father sees in him a potential danger, one which Cairns and Martin associate with the period's eugenic denigrations of 'mental defectives' and their threat to racial purity.[22] Questioning his son about his relationship with Firpo, Mr Crome comments, 'You see, you want to be careful. You never know what they're like, these coots. You keep hanging around with people like that, before you know where you are, you're mad as they are! Loopy!' The association between this attitude to mental difference and eugenics is implicit in the speech made by Geoff's teacher, a recent British immigrant, who criticises Geoff for drawing an ideal picture of the 'Made Man' rather than attending to Wordsworth: 'This cult of brawn over brain that you're all going for can lead a country to ruin. I don't need to remind you of what's happening in

Europe'. But the teacher's conviction of British superiority—'Shakespeare! Milton! Wordsworth! All British!'—blinds him to Geoff's imaginative qualities and to the possibility of a New Zealand identity not grounded in 'brawn'. Thus, both New Zealand's worship of athleticism and its sense of cultural inferiority inhibit the emergence and validation of a national artistic and intellectual identity.

In this sense, like the New Zealand cultural commentators who deployed images of disability as signifiers of an undervalued and mistreated difference, *The End of the Golden Weather* positively presents Firpo's alternative way of seeing the world, and aligns it with Geoff's magical imaginings. Further, the film provides a certain amount of insight into and empathy with Firpo's experience, contradicting Mrs Crome's (Gabrielle Hammond) chirpy assertion, 'they say people like that are very happy', with Firpo's poignant articulation of how laughter 'takes your skin off! Leaves you all bare!', and his utter despair and rage when he loses the race. Moreover, in refusing to gloss over the realities of cognitive disability and bodily imperfection, the film embraces what might be seen as a particularly New Zealand sensibility, one which refuses a Hollywood sugar-coating.[23]

But in its conclusion, *The End of the Golden Weather* also undercuts this sympathy with Firpo, affirming his alterity and alienation, and inducting Geoff into a harder world, when he learns 'that other people don't always share his love of fantasy and belief in miracles', and 'that he and Firpo are not on the same emotional plane, and that, when provoked, Firpo is capable of lashing out'.[24] In this way, the film maintains the necessity of Geoff's separation from Firpo in order to enter the adult world. Further, any sensitivity to the complexities of disabled subjectivity is undercut by the caricature of Firpo's uncaring guardian, Mr Atkinson (Bill Johnson): wheelchair-bound, aged, loud, fussy, and cantankerous, he is an object of both fear and fun for Geoff and Firpo.

The association of bodily normalcy and conventional Pakeha masculinity is nevertheless delicately drawn in the film, particularly in a family scene that features Geoff's aunt and uncle visiting with the Crome family. The scene opens with Mr Crome and Uncle Jim hunched over the radio, which relays another wrestling-match win for Jesse Cabot. As they listen, Auntie Kass (Alison Bruce) applies lipstick, gazing into her compact mirror, while Geoff's younger sister Molly (Alexandra Marshall) carefully imitates her. Celebrating the win, Uncle Jim ponders how much Cabot must earn, and declares him a 'made man', affirming it with the expletive 'Christ!' 'Do you mind not saying "Christ"?' his wife says irritatedly. 'You bet I do!' Jim retorts. 'The guy's my hero!' In response to Jim's enthusiasm, Geoff's mother wonders in amusement 'Who needs wrestlers?':

> Jim: I need wrestlers! Jeez, if it wasn't for these wrestling broadcasts, I'd go nuts!
> Kass: Thanks, thanks a lot!

Jim: Well, you know what I mean.
Kass: Yes Jim, I know exactly what you mean.

Jim and Kass's sniping continues after the children beg their father to perform as the 'Doctor', and he leaves the room to don his costume.

Mrs Crome: I wonder who he'll choose?
Kass: Oh, not me; last time he did a hysterectomy on me. No thanks!
Jim: Gee, you're hysterical enough as it is.
Kass: No comment.

With the lights dimmed, Mr Crome returns in a black coat and bowler hat, clutching a sinister-looking black briefcase. Swooping around the room, he selects Jim as his victim/patient, and, declaring that he looks ill, sprawls him onto the dining room table. Taking out a hacksaw, he pretends to saw into Jim's stomach, and to pin back the flesh with clothes-pegs. Geoff watches in frightened fascination as his father pulls out the screaming Jim's intestines —which Geoff sees as a string of sausages —and sews Jim back together with twine. Geoff seems barely to breathe until the doctor leaves the room, flicking a stray kidney from his lapel as he goes.

The scene encapsulates the film's linkage of body image and gendered New Zealand identity. Gender oppositions around bodily presentation are established in the contrast between the men's admiration of Cabot's wrestling victory and Kass's focus on making herself conventionally attractive, as Molly imitates her. Uncle Jim conveys to Ted and Geoff the importance of the 'made man', a concept of no interest to Geoff's mother, who cannot understand the importance of wrestlers. Jim's response, affirming Cabot's heroic status and athletic prowess as a highlight of his ordinary existence, confirms the athletic male ideal as the only model of identity available to the Pakeha man in the 1930s, and hints at the conformity that stultifies other forms of expression or enjoyment.

The Doctor sequence that follows illuminates the role that Mr Crome plays in Geoff's world, suggesting that his prohibitions on Geoff's behaviour—'Why can't you just be normal?'—position him as an authority figure who physically makes and unmakes men. As a critique of normative masculine New Zealand identity, the scene presents the gaining of that identity as a surgical excision; the process of becoming a Kiwi man is presented as a violent and intrusive removal of intestines, or 'guts', in the name of health and normalcy. Importantly, the Doctor's activities are also presented as somewhat hostile to women, in Aunt Kass' reminder that he performed an imaginary hysterectomy on her, and in Jim's mocking depiction of her as 'hysterical'. In invoking 'women's problems' and the emotional instability often attributed to women's wombs, Jim aligns women with the defective bodies that cannot emulate the 'made men'. Geoff's fearful response to a scene the others greet with amusement cues us to a critical perspective in which becoming 'normal' is to be dis-abled, and which affirms the (temporary) presentation of Firpo's worldview as valid and valuable.

The End of the Golden Weather thus balances the attractions of physical and mental normalcy against a critique of a 'gutless' and inferior New Zealand that struggles to sever itself from its motherland. The national identity explored by the film is specifically white, grounded in practices of colonisation and continuing membership of a colonial Commonwealth. Alison Maclean's *Crush* similarly seeks to envisage a specifically white New Zealand identity. But where *The End of the Golden Weather* explores the persistence of British ties in the delineation of national identity, the late twentieth-century New Zealanders of *Crush* confront the destructive allure of North America; and where *The End of the Golden Weather* uses the trope of disability to engage Pakeha masculinity, *Crush*'s disability narrative interacts with a drama about female sexuality.

Set amidst the thermal mud pools of Rotorua, an iconic New Zealand location, *Crush* opens with literary critic Christina (Donogh Rees) on her way to interview a New Zealand author and former Booker Prize winner. Explicitly referencing the kinds of intellectual critiques of New Zealand society noted above, Christina tells her American friend, Lane (Marcia Gay Harden), a younger, attractive, dark-haired woman, that renowned local artist Colin McCahon described New Zealand as 'a landscape with too few lovers'. As Lane takes over driving and they wind through the countryside, Christina muses upon New Zealand's image of itself as a 'totally benign, paradisial, pre-lapsarian world' and New Zealanders' concomitant uneasiness, their 'obsession to uncover the germ of evil'. Moments later, Lane rolls and crashes the car.

While Lane is only slightly injured, we eventually discover that Christina has been badly hurt, and is in a coma at Rotorua's hospital. Instead of visiting her, Lane goes to see the author, Colin (William Zappa), and interpellates herself into his life and that of his daughter, Angela (Caitlin Bossley). She initially flirts with the tomboyish Angela, and moves on to a passionate affair with Colin. Angered by Lane's betrayal, Angela visits and befriends Christina, becoming her caretaker when she emerges from her coma, brain-damaged and partially paralysed. Angela tries to make Christina realise that Lane is the cause of her disabilities, bringing her home in a wheelchair to stay with her father and Lane. Christina appears not to remember Lane, and introduces herself: 'My name is Christina and I have head injuries. I was in a car accident in June'. But hints of her memories of her past with Lane seep out—'We used to smoke!'—and Christina jealously attacks Lane when she attempts to make love with Colin. The film builds to its climax as the foursome wander around Rotorua's thermal pools. And when Angela and Colin leave Lane and Christina alone, Christina attempts to walk, but falls. Crying, Lane hugs her, and begs 'Forgive me!' Christina responds by trying to stand and walk once again, this time succeeding, and then suddenly pushing Lane over a cliff to the rocks and water below.

35. Dangerous attraction: the American femme fatale Lane (right) manipulates and deceives New Zealand tomboy Angela in *Crush*. Courtesy of the Ian Conrich collection of New Zealand cinema and visual culture.

National dynamics structure the relationships of these women in very specific ways, positioning Angela between an idealised, attractive American image of bodily identity, and an impaired and 'freakish' New Zealand image. Christina's opening commentary positions her as an intellectual, who is both critical of and identifies with New Zealand. Christina's sly suggestion that Lane will 'fix' the lover-less nature of New Zealand establishes the sense of affectionate antagonism between the two women, with an undercurrent of jealousy, and simultaneously indicates the entwinement of a sexual and national conflict, in which Lane is presumed to be more sexual, exotic and attractive than a typical New Zealand woman. Interviewing director Alison Maclean, who notes the 'slightly archetypal' nature of her characters, Miro Bilbrough articulates the national conflict at stake: '[Lane] has the mythic scale of an American as perceived by a New Zealander. So that *Crush* is not just about Angela's crush on Lane, but about the national crush on America and the antagonism that lies at the other side of that crush'.[25] Maclean confirms this nationalistic reading: 'Yes, exactly. I think from within America, Lane is probably not a typical American at all. She's just the things that are sexy or dangerous about America personified'.[26]

After Christina's accident, the same dynamic plays out in the relationship between Lane and Angela, except that where Christina is worldly and mature, Angela is only beginning to discover her sexual identity. Lane initially takes Angela for a boy, and sets about making her over into a femme fatale in her own image, outfitting her in a slinky red dress. Again, Maclean's commentary confirms the relationship as illuminating the ambivalent relationship between New Zealand women and their vision of American female identity. Bilbrough notes that her own 'attraction and antipathy to [Lane] is cast very strongly in terms of being a woman, but also in terms of being a New Zealander. Reserve reacting to her pushyness'. Maclean avers that Lane is indeed 'predatory . . . confident . . . [d]oesn't give a fuck about what other people think of her, provocative . . . I love her for that, and I envy her'.[27]

But Angela's transformation into a pale copy of the American sexual archetype does not hold. Her continuing alienation, insecurity, and unease about her burgeoning sexuality are cast in terms of physical and psychological deviance when she comments to Lane, 'I feel like a freak sometimes'. And when Lane takes up with Colin, Angela storms off to the hospital to take up an alliance with a different role model: a badly injured and inscrutable Christina.

Christina's uncontrolled and uncontrollable body is foregrounded in a moment that parodies Lane's flirting, when Christina suddenly pulls up her shirt to flash a male nurse, whining: 'Don't you like me?'. While such an image might confirm that New Zealand women cannot emulate the seductive self-representation of the iconic American, it also emphasises the ways in which Christina's brain injury has freed her from conformity to the norms of New Zealand reserve and feminine decorum: the new Christina throws food in the hospital and belches loudly when she dines in a restaurant.[28] On an archetypal level, and read in a positive way, Christina's disability again testifies to and violates the stifling conventions that preoccupy New Zealand's sense of national identity, and asserts a more body-oriented sense of female identity, in which all aspects of bodily behaviour are embraced. Also archetypally, and read more critically, Christina's boorish behaviour illuminates, through parody, the selfish and crude underside of Lane's confidence and her treatment of other people.

Angela struggles with all these elements of her own identity and sexuality, torn between her love for her father, and her passion for and admiration of Lane. Initially seeking to foster vengeance in Christina which she can manipulate to her own ends, in order to revenge herself on Lane for her sexual betrayal, Angela also seems genuinely to connect with Christina, finding in herself a nurturing identity. But, like Geoff in *The End of the Golden Weather*, she must learn that she cannot impose her own agenda on others, and that those with cognitive disabilities do not perceive things as she does.

The conclusion of the film does not necessarily resolve things for Angela, nor provide a positive vision of Pakeha female sexuality. Maclean confirms an element of national revenge fantasy, in Bilbrough's words, 'a revenge of New Zealand on America' in the violent death of Lane: 'Yes, that was intentional. And a few Americans obviously got that point too.

I've heard second hand a few comments from Americans that they've been offended by the ending'.[29]

The conclusion affirms a conscious agency for Christina, despite her disabilities, one which Maclean has attributed to the acting of Donogh Rees: 'in the script she was more of a receptacle I think, a little more passive, more malleable and now she's this other figure in the equation. She has her own agenda going on that you don't really understand'.[30] In this sense, the film's ending offers a horrible victory for the New Zealand woman—the betrayed tomboy Angela, and the physically damaged, earthy Christina—as the beautiful Rotorua landscape, its rocks, waterfall, river and trees, absorb and consume the body of Lane. Problematically, for cinematic representations of disabled identity and of women, Christina's act confirms the malevolence and dangerousness of women, and of people with disabilities. At the same time, without eliding the disturbing resonances of the personal drama, this scene offers a grotesque vision of New Zealand's struggle for cultural identity; as allegory, it deploys the disabled figure in a cry of national defiance against both cultural domination and restrictive notions of New Zealand as cripplingly conformist. The film thus speaks back to images of the defective nation: Christina begins as the culturally cringing intellectual and concludes as the defiant, passionate, and 'walking' transgressor of moribund conventions.

Disability thus operates in both these films to portray nationally specific identities refracted through race, gender, and sexuality. The characters of Firpo and Christina both embody and speak back to New Zealand's perceived cultural inadequacies against the cultural powers of, respectively, Britain and the United States: *The End of the Golden Weather* delineates the deviant and fantastical elements marginalised in New Zealand's drive to colonial conformity and portrays the normative construction of Pakeha masculinity as itself dis-abling, while *Crush*, focusing on a triangle of female desire and a young woman's sexual awakening, allegorises New Zealand's cultural cringe as a debilitating mental and physical condition. In both films, self-pity over New Zealand's national defectiveness competes with a jubilant and ironic embrace of disability, real or perceived. But whereas in *The End of the Golden Weather* conformity seems to triumph, with Geoff's entry into Pakeha masculinity requiring Firpo's expulsion from the narrative, *Crush* imagines an alternative model of femininity and nationality, in which Christina's disability enables transgression of convention and an ironic rewriting of a defective and crippled New Zealand.

Disability is linked, in these films, to specifically Pakeha formations of identity. In noting the persistence in Pakeha New Zealand films of the theme of 'the white man or woman at odds with his/her environment, with his/her country and himself/herself', Maori filmmaker Merata Mita has suggested that 'the New Zealand film industry [is] a white, neurotic one', displacing its political guilt and anxiety into personal stories of alienation.[31] Mita's point holds, but careful readings of these disability thematics uncover the operation of national and racial politics in these apparently individualised stories of impairment. Further, consideration of films focusing upon Maori perspectives, stories and characters indicates that narratives of impairment are also used to realise and represent Maori identities: most obviously, Barry Barclay's *Ngati* (1987) employs illness to literalise the faltering health of the Maori community and to dramatise the conflict of Maori and Pakeha cultures.[32]

There is an ongoing entwinement of disability and colonisation—historical and rhetorical—in shaping New Zealand's national images. When Mita asserts that the 'acts of rebellion, insanity and misunderstood genius' that permeate the actions of white characters in Kiwi film are 'symptoms' of a 'deeper malaise', which she terms 'the colonial syndrome of dislocation', she relies upon the very rhetoric of physical and psychological dysfunction that she suggests masks New Zealand's unacknowledged history of injustice and inequality.[33] Meanwhile, speaking to disabled New Zealanders about the medicalised rhetoric that has stereotyped, excluded and disempowered them, Martin Sullivan declares: 'We have been colonised and we must begin the de-colonisation process immediately'.[34] Rhetorical constructs of colonisation and disability thus offer interlocking and powerful, if double-edged, tools in efforts to rewrite social and racial marginalisation. Consequently, disability in Kiwi film may both provide insight into a particularly New Zealand cinematic vision, and call attention to the importance of disability as a vital element in New Zealand history and self-conception.

This is a revised and shortened version of an article, 'Impaired and Ill at Ease: New Zealand's Cinematics of Disability' originally published in *Post Script* 24, no. 2–3 (Winter–Spring and Summer 2005): 65–82. My thanks to Russell Campbell, Ian Conrich and Stuart Murray for comments on draft versions of this article.

Notes

1. The term functions to define New Zealand's cinema in the documentary *Cinema of Unease: A Personal Journey by Sam Neill* (1995).
2. In keeping with recent scholarly examinations of disability, this article differentiates between 'impairment', as a physical or mental abnormality, and 'disability', as an identity or phenomenon constructed around impairment by social, cultural, political and medical discourses; see Michael Oliver, *The Politics of Disablement: A Sociological Approach* (New York: St. Martin's Press, 1990).
3. David T. Mitchell and Sharon L. Snyder, *Narrative Prosthesis: Disability And The Dependencies Of Discourse* (Ann Arbor: University of Michigan Press, 2000), 50.
4. A. R. D. Fairburn, 'I'm Older Than You, Please Listen', *Collected Poems* (Christchurch, New Zealand: Pegasus, 1966), 107; Allen Curnow, 'The Skeleton of the Great Moa in the Canterbury Museum, Christchurch',

Collected Poems 1933–1973 (Wellington: A.H. and A.W. Reed, 1974), 142.

5. Elizabeth Gordon, 'That Colonial Twang: New Zealand Speech and New Zealand Identity', *Culture and Identity in New Zealand*, ed. David Novitz and Bill Willmott (Wellington: GP Books, 1989), 82.

6. Lawrence Jones, 'Versions of the Dream: Literature and the Search for Identity', *Culture and Identity in New Zealand*, ed. David Novitz and Bill Willmott (Wellington: GP Books, 1989), 187.

7. Ibid., 191.

8. Michael King, 'Being Pakeha', *Pakeha: The Quest for Identity in New Zealand*, ed. Michael King (Auckland: Penguin Books, 1991), 10; Bill Willmott, 'Introduction: Culture and National Identity', *Culture and Identity in New Zealand*, ed. David Novitz and Bill Willmott (Wellington, GP Books, 1989), 12.

9. Peter Beatson, *The Disability Revolution in New Zealand: A Social Map* (Palmerston North, New Zealand: Massey University, 2000), 408,

10. Ibid., 409.

11. Jones, 'Versions of the Dream', 197, 196.

12. Ian Conrich and Sarah Davy, *Views from the Edge of the World: New Zealand Film* (London: Kakapo Books, 1997), 7.

13. Quoted in Conrich and Davy, *Views from the Edge of the World*, 6–7.

14. Quoted in Conrich and Davy, *Views from the Edge of the World*, 7.

15. Rosemarie Garland Thomson, *Extraordinary Bodies: Figuring Physical Disability in American Culture and Literature* (New York: Columbia University Press, 1997), 112.

16. Ibid.

17. Mitchell and Snyder, *Narrative Prosthesis*, 47–48.

18. Disability also features prominently in New Zealand short films such as Melanie Read's *Hooks and Feelers* (1983) and Brad McGann's *Possum* (1997), and in documentary films such as Gaylene Preston's *All the Way Up There* (1978) and Vincent Ward's *In Spring One Plants Alone* (1980).

19. Thanks to Ian Conrich and Russell Campbell for suggestions on this point.

20. Mune and Mason worked together on an initial film adaptation, but the project was put on hold, and Mune did not resume it until after Mason's death in 1982.

21. Barbara Cairns and Helen Martin, *Shadows on the Wall: A Study of Seven New Zealand Feature Films* (Auckland: Longman Paul, 1994), 246.

22. Ibid., 248.

23. Cairns and Martin relate an anecdote from *The End of the Golden Weather* composer Stephen McCurdy: 'When *The End of the Golden Weather* was first finished Ian was talking to some American buyer who said "But Ian, Firpo doesn't win the race! Americans aren't going to watch this picture!"', *Shadows on the Wall*, 257.

24. Cairns and Martin, *Shadows on the Wall*, 247.

25. Miro Bilbrough, 'Car Crush Views', interview with Alison Maclean, *Illusions* 21–22 (Winter 1993): 8.

26. Ibid.

27. Ibid., 8.
28. Actress Donogh Rees comments that, in her research for the role of Christina, she was confronted with the tendency of those with brain injuries to violate social convention: 'I found that a lot of things, like manners, that we take for granted, they don't have. Like looking at somebody when you talk to them; really simple things you wouldn't think were learned responses'; see Patrick Smith, 'As Luck Would Have It', *Listener*, 6 March 1993, 19.
29. Bilbrough, 'Car Crush Views', 8.
30. Ibid.
31. Merata Mita, 'The Soul and the Image', *Film in Aotearoa New Zealand*, ed. Jonathan Dennis and Jan Bieringa (Wellington: Victoria University Press, 2nd edn, 1996): 47. Similarly, Jane Smith contends that, in Jane Campion's *The Piano*, Stewart's act of violence upon (or dis-abling of) Ada 'effectively wipes out other acts of violence the film suggests, particularly the damage Old World capital inflicts upon a colonised land and people'; see Jane Smith, 'Knocked Around in New Zealand: Postcolonialism Goes to the Movies', *Mythologies of Violence in Postmodern Media*, ed. Christopher Sharrett (Detroit: Wayne State University Press, 1999), 391. *The Piano* is another film central to New Zealand's cinematics of disability, again presenting the alienation of the country's white settlers through tropes of the grotesque and the 'socially disfigured' (see Peter Cleave, *From the Depot–Takirua: Essays on the Culture of Aotearoa* [Palmerston North: Campus Press, 1998]: 64), and through impairments such as Ada's muteness and Stewart's severing of her finger. On the film's disability discourses, particularly in relation to gender, see also Caroline Molina, 'Muteness and Mutilation: The Aesthetics of Disability in Jane Campion's *The Piano*', *The Body and Physical Difference: Discourses of Disability*, ed. David Mitchell and Sharon Snyder (Ann Arbor: University of Michigan Press, 1997).
32. For a more extended analysis of *Ngati* in this light, see the previously published version of this article.
33. Mita, 'The Soul and the Image', 47. Mita's description of her own film, *Mauri* (1988), as 'a parable about the schizophrenic existence of so many Maori in Pakeha society' similarly indicates the metaphoric and material significance of disability in Maori cinematic and social identities; see Mita, 'The Soul and the Image', 49.
34. Sullivan, Martin. 'Does it Say What We Mean, Do We Mean What it Says, Do We Know What We Are Saying? Problematising the Way Disability is Conceptualised, Written and Spoken About', *New Zealand Journal of Disability Studies* 8 (2000): 45.

Filmography

New Zealand Feature and Television Films
(including related productions)

Compiled by Ian Conrich

New Zealand feature film productions are emphasised in bold.

Codes:
- M: film is missing
- F: only remnants of the film exist
- D: documentary
- A: animation
- T: movie made for television
- V: made on video / beta-sp / digi-beta / DVD
- C: New Zealand film made in collaboration with international production companies
- L: foreign film employing New Zealand locations
- R: New Zealand related story made entirely outside of New Zealand

YEAR	TITLE OF FILM	DIRECTOR	STATUS
1914	***Hinemoa***	**George Tarr**	**M**
1916	***The Test***	**Rawdon Blandford**	**M**
1916	*A Maori Maid's Love*	Raymond Longford	M/L
1916	*The Mutiny of the Bounty*	Raymond Longford	M/L
1921	*Beyond*	William Desmond Taylor	M/R
1921	*The Betrayer* (a.k.a. *The Maid of Maoriland*)	Beaumont Smith	M/L
1922	***10,000 Miles in the Southern Cross***	**George Tarr**	**F/D**
1922	***The Birth of New Zealand***	**Harrington Reynolds**	**F**
1922	***My Lady of the Cave***	**Rudall Hayward**	
1924	***Venus of the South Seas*** (a.k.a. ***Venus of the Southern Seas***)	**James R. Sullivan**	
1924	***The Romance of Sleepy Hollow***	**Henry J. Makepeace**	**M**

YEAR	TITLE OF FILM	DIRECTOR	STATUS
1925	*Rewi's Last Stand*	**Rudall Hayward**	**F**
1925	*The Adventures of Algy*	Beaumont Smith	L
1925	*Glorious New Zealand*	**(Government Publicity Office)**	**D**
1926	*Under the Southern Cross*	Gustav Pauli	M/L
1926	*The Romance of Hine-Moa*	Gustav Pauli	F/L
1927	*Carbine's Heritage*	**Edwin Coubray**	**M**
1927	*The Te Kooti Trail*	**Rudall Hayward**	
1928	*The Bush Cinderella*	**Rudall Hayward**	
1929	*Under the Southern Cross* (a.k.a. *The Devil's Pit*)	Alexander Markey & Lew Collins	L
1934	*Romantic New Zealand*	**(Filmcraft Studios)**	**D**
1935	*Down on the Farm* (New Zealand's first sound feature)	**Lee Hill & Stewart Pitt**	**F**
1935	*Hei Tiki* (a.k.a. *Primitive Passions*)	Alexander Markey	L
1936	*Phar Lap's Son?*	**A.L. Lewis**	**M**
1936	*The Wagon and the Star*	**J.J.W. Pollard**	**F**
1936	*On the Friendly Road*	**Rudall Hayward**	
1940	*Rewi's Last Stand* (a.k.a. *The Last Stand*)	**Rudall Hayward**	
1947	*Green Dolphin Street*	Victor Saville	R
1949	*The Sands of Iwo Jima*	Allan Dwan	R
1950	*British Empire Games 1950*	**(National Film Unit)**	**D**
1952	*Broken Barrier*	**John O'Shea & Roger Mirams**	
1954	*The Seekers* (a.k.a. *Land of Fury*)	Ken Annakin	L
1955	*Battle Cry*	Raoul Walsh	R
1957	*Until They Sail*	Robert Wise	L
1958	*Cinerama South Seas Adventure* (a.k.a. *South Seas Adventure*)	Francis D. Lyon	D/L
1958	*Tarawa Beachhead*	Paul Wendkos	R
1958	*The Decks Ran Red*	Andrew L. Stone	R
1961	*Two Loves* (a.k.a. *Spinster*)	Charles Walters	R
1962	*In Search of the Castaways*	Robert Stevenson	L
1964	*Quick Before it Melts*	Delbert Mann	R

Year	Title of Film	Director	Status
1964	*Runaway* (a.k.a. *Runaway Killer*)	John O'Shea	
1966	*Don't Let it Get You*	Jon O'Shea	
1969	*Nyu jirando no wakadaishô* (a.k.a. *Young Guy on Mt. Cook/ The Young Guy in New Zealand*)	Jun Fukuda	L
1972	*To Love a Maori*	Rudall & Ramai Hayward	
1973	*Rangi's Catch* (8-part children's film serial, later recut as a feature film)	Michael Forlong	C
1974	*Games '74*	John King, Sam Pillsbury, Paul Maunder & Arthur Everard	D
1975	*Test Pictures*	Geoffrey Steven	
1975	*Landfall*	Paul Maunder	T
1976	*The God Boy*	Murray Reece	T
1977	*Wild Man*	Geoff Murphy	
1977	*Off the Edge*	Mike Firth	D
1977	*Sleeping Dogs*	Roger Donaldson	
1977	*Solo*	Mike Firth	
1978	*Died in the Wool*	Brian McDuffie	T
1978	*Colour Scheme*	Peter Sharpe	T
1978	*Angel Mine*	David Blyth	
1978	*Skin Deep*	Geoff Steven	
1979	*Middle Aged Spread*	John Reid	
1979	*Sons for the Return Home*	Paul Maunder	
1980	*Squeeze*	Richard Turner	
1980	*Nambassa Festival*	Philip Howe	D
1980	*Beyond Reasonable Doubt*	John Laing	
1980	*Goodbye Pork Pie*	Geoff Murphy	
1981	*Wildcat*	Rod Prosser, Russell Campbell & Alister Barry	D
1981	*Smash Palace*	Roger Donaldson	
1981	*Pictures*	Michael Black	

Year	Title of Film	Director	Status
1981	*Race for the Yankee Zephyr* (a.k.a. *Treasure of the Yankee Zephyr*)	David Hemmings	C
1981	*Bad Blood*	Mike Newell	C
1982	*Strange Behaviour* (a.k.a. *Dead Kids*)	Michael Laughlin	C
1982	*The Scarecrow* (a.k.a. *Klynham Summer*)	Sam Pillsbury	
1982	*Brothers*	Terry Bourke	L
1982	*Battletruck* (a.k.a. *Warlords of the 21st Century*)	Harley Cokliss	
1982	*The Lost Tribe*	John Laing	
1982	*Carry Me Back*	John Reid	
1982	*Hang on a Minute Mate!*	Alan Lindsay	T
1982	*Prisoners* (film never released)	Peter Werner	C
1983	*It's Lizzie to Those Close* (a.k.a. *Lizzie*)	David Blyth	
1983	*Utu*	Geoff Murphy	
1983	*Strata*	Geoff Steven	
1983	*Patu!*	Merata Mita	D
1983	*Savage Islands* (a.k.a. *Nate and Hayes*)	Ferdinand Fairfax	
1983	*War Years* (a.k.a. *New Zealand —The War Years*)	Patrick McGuire	D
1983	*Wild Horses*	Derek Morton	
1984	*Trespasses* (a.k.a. *Omen of Evil*; orig. *Finding Katie*)	Peter Sharp	
1984	*Constance*	Bruce Morrison	
1984	*The Silent One*	Yvonne Mackay	
1984	*Merry Christmas, Mr Lawrence*	Nagisa Oshima	C
1984	*Pallet on the Floor*	Lynton Butler	
1984	*Death Warmed Up* (orig. *Brain Damaged/Doctor Death*)	David Blyth	
1984	*Among the Cinders*	Rolf Haedrich	C
1984	*Second Time Lucky*	Michael Anderson	C
1984	*The Bounty*	Roger Donaldson	C
1984	*Trial Run*	Melanie Read	

Year	Title of Film	Director	Status
1984	*Other Halves*	John Laing	
1984	*Vigil*	Vincent Ward	
1984	*Heart of the Stag*	Michael Firth	
1984	*Iris*	Tony Isaac	T/V
1984	*Mesmerized* (a.k.a. *Shocked*)	Michael Laughlin	C
1985	*Came a Hot Friday*	Ian Mune	
1985	*Should I Be Good?* (orig. *Bangkok Scam*)	Grahame McLean	
1985	*The Quiet Earth*	Geoff Murphy	
1985	*Kingpin*	Mike Walker	
1985	*Sylvia*	Michael Firth	
1985	*Leave All Fair*	John Reid	
1985	*Shaker Run*	Bruce Morrison	
1985	*Mr Wrong* (a.k.a. *Dark of the Night*)	Gaylene Preston	
1985	*The Neglected Miracle*	Barry Barclay	D/C
1985	*Restless* (a.k.a. *Hot Target*)	Denis Lewiston	
1985	*The Lie of the Land*	Grahame McLean	
1986	*Bridge to Nowhere*	Ian Mune	
1986	*Aces Go Places IV* (a.k.a. *Mad Mission IV*)	Ringo Lam	L
1986	*Dangerous Orphans*	John Laing	
1986	*Arriving Tuesday* (orig. *Monica*)	Richard Riddiford	
1986	*Queen City Rocker* (a.k.a. *Tearaway/Total Defiance*)	Bruce Morrison	
1986	*Footrot Flats: The Dog's Tail Tale*	Murray Ball	A
1986	*The Fire-Raiser*	Peter Sharp	T
1987	*Wurzel Gummidge Down Under*	James Hill	T
1987	*Mark II*	John Anderson	T/V
1987	*Ngati*	Barry Barclay	
1987	*Starlight Hotel*	Sam Pillsbury	
1987	*The Leading Edge*	Michael Firth	
1988	*Bad Taste*	Peter Jackson	
1988	*A Soldier's Tale*	Larry Parr	

Year	Title of Film	Director	Status
1988	*Illustrious Energy* (a.k.a. *Dreams of Home*)	Leon Narbey	
1988	*The Navigator: A Mediaeval Odyssey* (a.k.a. *The Navigator: An Odyssey Across Time*)	Vincent Ward	C
1988	*Mauri*	Merata Mita	
1988	*Never Say Die*	Geoff Murphy	
1988	*Send A Gorilla*	Melanie Read	
1988	*In Our Own Time*	Andrea Bosshard, Shane Loader & Jeremy Royal	D
1988	*Chill Factor*	David L. Stanton	C
1988	*The Rescue* (a.k.a. *Seals*; orig. *Seal Kids/Operation Phoenix*)	Ferdinand Fairfax	L
1988	*Midnight Run*	Martin Brest	L
1988	*Willow*	Ron Howard	L
1988	*The Grasscutter*	Ian Mune	T/C
1989	*Zilch!*	Richard Riddiford	
1989	*Champion*	Peter Sharp	T
1990	*The Rogue Stallion* (a.k.a. *Wildfire*)	Henri Safan	T/C
1990	*Mana Waka*	Merata Mita	D
1990	*Flying Fox in a Freedom Tree*	Martyn Sanderson	
1990	*Meet the Feebles* (a.k.a. *Just the Feebles*)	Peter Jackson	
1990	*User Friendly*	Gregor Nicholas	
1990	*An Angel at My Table* (shown also as a TV 3-part mini-series)	Jane Campion	
1990	*Ruby and Rata*	Gaylene Preston	
1990	*The Returning*	John Day	
1990	*The Shrimp on the Barbie* (a.k.a. *Boyfriend From Hell*)	Alan Smithie	C
1991	*Rebels in Retrospect*	Russell Campbell	D
1991	*Te Rua* (a.k.a. *The Store House/The Pit*)	Barry Barclay	
1991	*Old Scores*	Alan Clayton	C
1991	*The End of the Golden Weather*	Ian Mune	

Year	Title of Film	Director	Status
1991	*Chunuk Bair* (a.k.a. *Once on Chunuk Bair*)	**Dale G. Bradley**	
1991	*Undercover*	Yvonna Mackay	T/V
1992	*Moonrise* (a.k.a. *Grampire/ My Grandad's A Vampire/My Grandpa is a Vampire*)	**David Blyth**	
1992	*Braindead* (a.k.a. *Dead Alive*)	**Peter Jackson**	
1992	*The Sinking of the Rainbow Warrior* (a.k.a. *Rainbow Warrior*)	**Michael Tuchner**	C
1992	*Crush*	**Alison Maclean**	
1992	*Marlin Bay*	Chris Bailey	T
1992	*The Footstep Man*	**Leon Narbey**	
1992	*Alex*	**Megan Simpson**	
1993	*Typhon's People*	Yvonne Mackay	T
1993	*Absent Without Leave*	**John Laing**	
1993	*Bread and Roses* (shown also as a TV 4-part mini-series; later in 2 parts)	**Gaylene Preston**	
1993	*Desperate Remedies*	**Peter Wells & Stewart Main**	
1993	*The Piano*	**Jane Campion**	C
1993	*Jack Be Nimble*	**Garth Maxwell**	
1993	*Adrift*	Christian Duguay	L
1993	*Secrets* (a.k.a. *One Crazy Night*)	**Michael Patinson**	C
1994	*Once Were Warriors*	**Lee Tamahori**	
1994	*Heavenly Creatures*	**Peter Jackson**	
1994	*The Last Tattoo*	**John Reid**	
1994	*Hercules and the Circle of Fire*	Doug Lefler	T/C
1994	*Hercules and the Lost Kingdom*	Harley Cokeliss	T/C
1994	*Hercules in the Maze of the Minotaur*	Josh Becker	T/C
1994	*Hercules in the Underworld*	Bill L. Norton	T/C
1994	*Hercules and the Amazon Women*	Bill L. Norton	T/C
1994	*O Rugged Land of Gold*	Michael Anderson	T/C
1994	*Cops and Robbers*	**Murray Reece**	

Year	Title of Film	Director	Status
1994	*Vulcan Lane*	Mike Firth	T/V
1994	***Loaded***	**Anna Campion**	**C**
1994	***Jack Brown, Genius***	**Tony Hiles**	
1995	***War Stories Our Mothers Never Told Us***	**Gaylene Preston**	**D**
1995	***Bonjour Timothy***	**Wayne Tourell**	**C**
1996	***Flight of the Albatross***	**Werner Meyer**	**C**
1996	***Chicken***	**Grant Lahood**	
1996	***Broken English***	**Gregor Nicholas**	
1996	***Someone Else's Country***	**Alister Barry**	**D/V**
1996	***The Frighteners***	**Peter Jackson**	**C**
1996	*A Soldier's Sweetheart*	Thomas Michael Donnelly	T/L
1996	***The Whole of the Moon***	**Ian Mune**	**C**
1996	***The Offering*** (a.k.a. *Eclipse*)	**Taggart Siegel & Fran Fisher**	**C**
1996	*Christmas Oratorio*	Kjell-Ake Andersson	L
1996	*Who's Counting*	Terre Nash	D/L
1996	***Punch Me in the Stomach***	**Francine Zuckerman**	**D/C**
1997	***The Ugly***	**Scott Reynolds**	
1997	***Aberration***	**Tim Boxell**	
1997	***Saving Grace***	**Costa Botes**	
1997	*Return to Treasure Island*	Steve Lahood	T
1997	***The Road to Jerusalem***	**Bruce Morrison**	**D/V**
1997	***Topless Women Talk about Their Lives***	**Harry Sinclair**	
1997	***The Climb***	**Bob Swaim**	**C**
1998	***Memory and Desire***	**Niki Caro**	
1998	***The Lunatics' Ball***	**Michael Thorp**	
1998	***The Lost Valley*** (a.k.a. *Kiwi Safari*)	**Dale Bradley**	
1998	*Tiger Country*	John Laing	T
1998	***Heaven***	**Scott Reynolds**	
1998	*Gu cheng bielian* (a.k.a. *The Poet*)	Casey Chan Lai-Ying	L
1998	***Via Satellite***	**Anthony McCarten**	

Year	Title of Film	Director	Status
1998	*When Love Comes* (a.k.a. *When Love Comes Along*)	Garth Maxwell	
1999	*Channelling Baby*	Christine Parker	
1999	*What Becomes of the Broken Hearted?*	Ian Mune	
1999	*I'll Make You Happy*	Athina Tsoulis	
1999	*Nightmare Man*	Jim Kaufman	T/C
1999	*Betaville*	Phil Davison	V
1999	*Punitive Damage*	Annie Goldson	D
1999	*Scarfies* (a.k.a. *Crime 101*)	Robert Sarkies	
1999	*Getting to Our Place*	Gaylene Preston & Anna Cottrell	D / T / V
1999	*Savage Honeymoon*	Mark Beesley	
1999	*Uncomfortable, Comfortable*	Campbell Walker	V
1999	*Vertical Limit*	Martin Campbell	L
1999	*Campaign*	Tony Sutorius	D/V
1999	*The Shirt*	John Laing	V
1999	*Song of the Hunted*	Peter Haynes	V
1999	*Wild Blue*	Dale Bradley	
2000	*Fearless*	Charlie Haskell	T/C
2000	*Shifter*	Colin Hodson	V
2000	*The Price of Milk*	Harry Sinclair	
2000	*Magik and Rose*	Vanessa Alexander	
2000	*Exposure*	David Blyth	C
2000	*Hopeless*	Stephen Hickey	
2000	*The Feathers of Peace*	Barry Barclay	
2000	*The Irrefutable Truth About Demons* (a.k.a. *The Truth About Demons*)	Glenn Standring	
2000	*Jubilee*	Michael Hurst	
2000	*Liebesträume* (absurd dreams)	Florian Habicht	V/C
2000	*Numero Bruno*	Steve Lahood	D/T
2000	*Stickmen*	Hamish Rothwell	
2000	*Street Legal: Hit and Run*	Chris Bailey	T
2001	*Blerta Revisited*	Geoff Murphy	D

Year	Title of Film	Director	Status
2001	*Clare*	Yvonne Mackay	T/V
2001	*No One Can Hear You*	John Laing	T/C
2001	**Kid's World**	**Dale Bradley**	
2001	**Back River Road**	**Peter Tait**	V
2001	**Te Tangata Whai Rawa O Weneti: The Maori Merchant of Venice**	**Don Selwyn**	
2001	**Rain**	**Christine Jeffs**	
2001	**Snakeskin**	**Gillian Ashurst**	
2001	**Titless Wonders**	**Gaylene Preston**	D/V
2001	**Hotere**	**Merata Mita**	D
2001	**Crooked Earth**	**Sam Pillsbury**	
2001	**The Waiting Place**	**Cristobel Araus Lobos**	
2001	**Georgie Girl**	**Annie Goldson & Peter Wells**	D/V
2001	*The Other Side of Heaven*	Mitch Davis	L
2001	**Offensive Behaviour**	**Patrick Gillies**	V
2001	**When Strangers Appear** (orig. **Shearer's Breakfast**)	**Scott Reynolds**	
2001	**The Lord of the Rings: The Fellowship of the Ring**	**Peter Jackson**	C
2002	**Blessed**	**Rachel Douglas**	V
2002	*Blood Crime*	William A. Graham	T/L
2002	**Ozzie**	**Bill Tannen**	
2002	**Her Majesty**	**Mark J. Gordon**	C
2002	*Murder in Greenwich*	Tom McLoughlin	T/L
2002	**.OFF.**	**Colin Hodson**	
2002	**Family Saga**	**Jane Perkins**	D/V
2002	**Coffee, Tea or Me?**	**Brita McVeigh**	D/V
2002	**The Vector File**	**Eliot Christopher**	C
2002	*Superfire*	Steven Quale	T/L
2002	**In a Land of Plenty**	**Alister Barry**	D/V
2002	**Kung Fu Vampire Killers**	**Phil Davison**	V
2002	**Whale Rider**	**Niki Caro**	
2002	**The Lord of the Rings: The Two Towers**	**Peter Jackson**	C

Year	Title of Film	Director	Status
2003	*The Last Samurai* (a.k.a. *The Last Samurai: Bushidou*)	Edward Zwick	L
2003	*Cave-In*	Rex Piano	V
2003	*Terror Peak*	Dale Bradley	V
2003	*Jaal: The Trap*	Guddu Dhanoa	L
2003	*Gupta Versus Gordon*	Jitendra Pal	V
2003	*Te Whanau O Aotearoa— Caretakers of the Land*	Errol Wright & Abi King-Jones	D/V
2003	*The Locals*	Greg Page	
2003	*Toy Love*	Harry Sinclair	
2003	*Haunting Douglas*	Leanne Pooley	D/V
2003	*Kombi Nation*	Grant Lahood	
2003	*Why Can't I Stop This Uncontrollable Dancing*	Campbell Walker	V
2003	*Perfect Strangers*	Gaylene Preston	
2003	*Woodenhead*	Florian Habicht	V
2003	*Nemesis Game* (orig. *Paper, Scissors, Stone*)	Jesse Warn	C
2003	*Christmas*	Gregory King	V
2003	*This is Not a Love Story*	Keith Hill	V
2003	*Tongan Ninja*	Jason Stutter	
2003	*Skin and Bone*	Chris Bailey	T/V
2003	*Orphans and Angels*	Harold Brodie	V
2003	*I Think I'm Going*	Alexander Greenhough	V
2003	*For Good*	Stuart McKenzie	
2003	*Cupid's Prey*	Dale Bradley	V
2003	*The Lord of the Rings: The Return of the King*	Peter Jackson	C
2004	*Boogeyman*	Stephen Kay	L
2004	*Sheilas: 28 Years On*	Dawn Hutchesson & Annie Goldson	D/V
2004	*Giving It All Away: The Life and Times of Sir Roy McKenzie*	Paul Davidson	D/V
2004	*Murmurs*	Elric Kane, Alexander Greenhough	V
2004	*Riverworld*	Karl Skogland	L

YEAR	TITLE OF FILM	DIRECTOR	STATUS
2004	*Without a Paddle*	Stephen Brill	L
2004	*In My Father's Den*	Brad McGann	
2004	*Fracture* (orig. *Crime Story*)	Larry Parr	
2004	*Marti: The Passionate Eye*	Shirley Horrocks	D/V
2004	*1nite*	Amarbir Singh	V
2004	*Kaikohe Demolition*	Florian Habicht	D/V
2004	*Children of the Migration*	Lala Rolls	V
2004	*Big Time Love*	Gavin Butler	
2004	*Spooked*	Geoff Murphy	
2005	*Land of Our Fathers—My African Legacy*	Jennifer Bush-Daumec	D/V
2005	*The Battle of Treasure Island*	Gavin Scott	C
2005	*The Monster of Treasure Island*	Michael Hurst	C
2005	*The Mystery of Treasure Island*	Michael Hurst	C
2005	*Quiet Night In*	Christopher Banks	V
2005	*Not Only But Always*	Terry Johnson	L
2005	*April Sun*	Paul McBride	V
2005	*50 Ways of Saying Fabulous*	Stewart Main	
2005	*Tyrannical Love*	Scott Boswell	V
2005	*Futile Attraction*	Mark Prebble	V
2005	*River Queen*	Vincent Ward	C
2005	*Luella Miller*	Dane Giraud	V
2005	*Meet Me in Miami*	Eric Hannah & Iren Koster	
2005	*Antarctic Journal*	Philsung Yim	L
2005	*Memories of Tomorrow*	Amit Tripuraneni	V
2005	*Night of the Werewolf*	D. Thomas Herkes	V
2005	*Sedition*	Russell Campbell	D
2005	*The World's Fastest Indian*	Roger Donaldson	
2005	*King Kong*	Peter Jackson	C
2005	*The Chronicles of Narnia: The Lion, the Witch and the Wardrobe*	Andrew Adamson	L
2005	*Belief*	Phil Davison	V
2005	*Hidden*	Tim McLachlan	V

Year	Title of Film	Director	Status
2006	*No. 2* (a.k.a. *Naming Number Two*)	Toa Fraser	
2006	*Perfect Creature*	Glenn Standring	
2006	*Sione's Wedding* (a.k.a. *Samoan Wedding*)	Chris Graham	
2006	*Banana in a Nutshell*	Roseanna Liang	V
2006	*Squeegee Bandit*	Sandor Lau	D/V
2006	*Event 16*	Derek Pearson	V
2006	*Struggle No More*	Costa Botes	D/V
2006	*The Waimate Conspiracy*	Stefen Lewis	V
2006	*The Last Resort*	Errol Wright	V
2006	*Waves*	Li Tao	D/V
2006	*Black Sheep*	Jonathan King	
2006	*Out of the Blue*	Robert Sarkies	
2006	*{dream} preserved*	Stephen Kang	V
2007	*Stringer*	Steven Morrison	
2007	*Eagle Versus Shark*	Taika Waititi	
2007	*The Ferryman*	Chris Graham	C
2007	*Maintain*	Dean Hewison	V
2007	*Bridge to Terabithia*	Gabor Csupo	L
2007	*Me-Shee: The Water Giant*	John Henderson	L
2007	*Misspelt*	Falstaff Dowling-Mitchell & Nick Wilkinson	
2007	*The Tattooist*	Peter Burger	C
2007	*Cowboys and Communists*	Jess Feast	D/V
2007	*Men Shouldn't Sing*	Sarah A. Higginson, Michael Bell	V
2007	*When Night Falls*	Alex Galvin	V
2007	*The Devil Dared Me To*	Chris Stapp	
2007	*30 Days of Night*	David Slade	C
2007	*Dororo*	Akihiko Shiota	L
2007	*Antonello and the Architect*	Tony Hiles	D/V
2007	*A Civilised Society*	Alister Barry	D/V

YEAR	TITLE OF FILM	DIRECTOR	STATUS
2007	*¿La Verdad?*	Helen Smyth	D / C / V
2007	*You Move You Die*	Ketzal Sterling	V
2007	*Edith Collier: A Light Among Shadows*	Michael Heath	D/V
2007	*Questions for Mr Reynolds*	Shirley Horrocks	D/V
2007	*Five*	Amit Tripuraneni	V
2007	*Kissy Kissy*	Eric Kane, Alexander Greenhough	V
2007	*Land of My Ancestors*	Lala Rolls	D/V
2007	*Down By the Riverside* (orig. *Revelation 4:11*)	Brad Davison & Marama Killen	V
2007	*Break*	D.F. Mamea	V
2007	*Restoring the Mauri of Lake Omapere*	Simon Marler	D
2007	*Last of the Living*	Logan McMillan	V
2007	*The Last Magic Show* (orig. *The Magician*)	Andy Conlan	
2007	*Natural Disasters*	Eric Kane	V
2007	*We're Here to Help* (orig. *BVA/ Be Very Afraid*)	Jonothan Cullinane	
2007	*Wait Up Harriet*	Angus Benfield & Hanna Eichler	V
2007	*The Water Horse*	Jay Russell	L
2008	*10,000 B.C.*	Roland Emmerich	L
2008	*Second Hand Wedding* (orig. *Garage Sale*)	Paul Murphy	V
2008	*Rain of the Children*	Vincent Ward	
2008	*The Chronicles of Narnia: Prince Caspian*	Andrew Adamson	L
2008	*Rubbings from a Live Man*	Florian Habicht	D
2008	*A Song of Good*	Gregory King	
2008	*Apron Strings*	Sima Urale	
2008	*Jinx Sister*	Athina Tsoulis	V
2008	*Fallacy*	Gair Cook	V
2008	*Slovenia After Six*	Chantal Rayner-Burt	V

Year	Title of Film	Director	Status
2008	*Barefoot Cinema*	Gerard Smyth	D/V
2008	*The Hollow Men*	Alister Barry	D/V
2008	*The Art Star and the Sudanese Twins*	Pietra Brettkelly	D/V
2008	*Trouble is My Business*	Juliette Veber	D/V
2008	*From Street to Sky*	Bryn Evans	D/V
2008	*The Laundry Woman*	Sngmoo Lee	L
2008	*Underworld 3: Rise of the Lycans*	Patrick Tatopoulos	L
2008	*They Came From Upstairs*	John Schultz	L
2008	*The Last Great Snail Chase*	Edward Lynden-Bell	
2008	*Dean Spanley*	Toa Fraser	C
2008	*Aftershock*	Brendan Donovan, Thomas Robins	T
2008	*The Topp Twins: Untouchable Girls*	Leanne Pooley	D
2008	*Show of Hands*	Anthony McCarten	
2008	*The Strength of Water*	Armagan Ballantyne	C
2008	*Waiting for the Big Fat One*	Tony Williams	
2008	*The Vintner's Luck*	Niki Caro	C
2008	*Russian Snark*	Stephen Sinclair	
2009	*Under the Mountain*	Jonathan King	

Contributors

Russell Campbell is Senior Lecturer in Film at Victoria University of Wellington. Also a script consultant and award-winning documentary filmmaker his films include *Wildcat* (1981), *Rebels in Retrospect* (1991), and *The Suppression of Dissent in World War II New Zealand*, which was the winner of the 2005 Media Peace Award. He is a former editor of *Illusions* and has been a frequent contributor to the journal, publishing particularly in the areas of gender representation and documentary film. He has also contributed to *The Velvet Light Trap* (which he founded), *Jump Cut*, and *Quarterly Review of Film Studies*. He is the author of *Cinema Strikes Back: Radical Filmmaking in the United States, 1930–1942* (1982), and *Marked Women: Prostitutes and Prostitution in the Cinema* (2006).

Alex Cole-Baker is an active practitioner in the New Zealand film and television industry. With producing credits on four short films by 1995, including Chicago Gold Plaque winner *La Vie en Rose* (1994), she has worked freelance on a large number of projects, including commercials, documentaries, features, shorts, and drama series. Between 1991 and 1996, most of her work was as production manager or assistant director. Since 1998 she has been working predominantly as a production accountant, including on the features *Scarfies* (1999), *The Locals* (2003), *In My Father's Den* (2004), *50 Ways of Saying Fabulous* (2005), *No.2* (2006), and *The Tattooist* (2007).

Ian Conrich is the founding Director of the Centre for New Zealand Studies, Birkbeck, University of London, and Chair of the New Zealand Studies Association. He is Co-Editor of the *CNZS Bulletin of New Zealand Studies*, an Editor of the *Journal of British Cinema and Television*, an Associate Editor of *Film and Philosophy*, an advisory board member of *Studies in Australasian Cinema*, and *Interactive Media*, and a Guest Editor of the *Havard Review* (on New Zealand literature), *Asian Cinema* (on Sri Lankan Cinema) and *Post Script* (for a special issue on Australian and New Zealand Cinema). He is the author of *New Zealand Film—A Guide* (published in Polish, 2008), *New Zealand Cinema*, and *New Zealand Filmmakers in Conversation* (both forthcoming), and editor or co-editor of eleven books, including *New Zealand—A Pastoral Paradise?* (2000), *The Cinema of John Carpenter: The Technique of Terror* (2004), *Film's Musical Moments* (2006), *New Zealand Filmmakers* (2007), *New Zealand Fictions: Literature and Film* (2008), and *New Zealand National Cinema* (published in Polish, forthcoming). He has also contributed to more than 50 books and journals.

SARAH DAVY has an MA in Film Archiving. Since the late 1980s she has worked for the New Zealand Film Archive and the National Film and Television Archive (now bfi Collections). She has special interests in the history of the film archiving movement and the life and work of the New Zealand experimental artist Len Lye. The author of the booklet *A Work in Progress—Archiving Len Lye* (2001), and co-author of *Views From the Edge of the World: New Zealand Film* (1997), she has also contributed to the collection *Len Lye* (Centre Pompidou, 2000).

ANNIE GOLDSON is Associate Professor in the Film, Television and Media Studies Department at the University of Auckland. Her work has been published in a wide variety of journals including *Screen*, *Mid-West*, *Global Television*, and *Semiotext*. A documentary filmmaker, her productions include *Punitive Damage* (1999), a feature documentary that received numerous international awards, *Georgie Girl* (2001), and *Elgar's Enigma: Biography of a Concerto* (2006).

ANN HARDY is Senior Lecturer in Screen and Media Studies at the University of Waikato. She is the author of *Film, Spirituality and Hierophany* (2002). Her publications include contributions to *Jane Campion's The Piano* (2000), *Film Studies: Women in Contemporary World Cinema* (2002), *How to Study the Event Movie: The Lord of the Rings—A Case Study* (2007), the New Zealand entries for *The Women's Companion to International Film* (1990) and eight essays to the New Zealand film journal *Illusions* (1985–1999).

MICHELLE KEOWN is Lecturer in English Literature at the University of Edinburgh. She has published widely on New Zealand, Maori, and Pacific literature. She is the author of *Postcolonial Pacific Writing: Representations of the Body* (2005) and *Pacific Islands Writing: The Postcolonial Literatures of Aotearoa/New Zealand and Oceania* (2007), and is co-editor of 'New Zealand and the U.K.', a special issue of the *Journal of New Zealand Literature* (no. 21, 2003). She is a consulting editor for *Ka Mate Ka Ora* (the journal of the New Zealand Electronic Poetry Centre); a member of the editorial board for the journal *Dreadlocks in Oceania* (Fiji) and a member of the advisory board for the *CNZS Bulletin of New Zealand Studies*.

SUZETTE MAJOR held the post Lecturer in Screen and Media Studies at the University of Waikato. Previously she researched the role of marketing in New Zealand cinema and has published work in the field of marketing the arts.

BRIAN McDONNELL is Programme Co-ordinator of Media Studies at the Albany campus of Massey University in Auckland. He has published extensively on New Zealand film as well as on Hollywood Cinema. He is the author of *The Scarecrow: A Film Study Guide* (1982), *Fresh Approaches to Film* (1998), and co-author of the *Encyclopaedia of Film Noir* (2007). Between 1986 and 1994 he was the film reviewer for *North and South*; his reviews of New Zealand films have been collected in the book *On Reflection: New Zealand Film Reviews in North and South, 1986–1993* (2007).

STUART MURRAY is Senior Lecturer in Postcolonial Literatures at the University of Leeds. He is the editor of *Not On Any Map: Essays on Postcoloniality and Cultural Nationalism* (1997), and the author of *Never a Soul at Home: New Zealand Literary Nationalism and the 1930s* (1998), *Representing Autism: Culture, Narrative, Fascination* (2008), and *Images of Dignity: Barry Barclay and Fourth Cinema* (2008). He has been the guest editor of special issues of the *Journal of New Zealand Literature* and *Moving Worlds*, and has published articles on the literature and cultural history of New Zealand, Australia, Canada, the Caribbean, West Africa and Ireland. His current research is divided between work on issues of postcolonial encounter and settlement, especially in New Zealand, the Pacific and Australia, and cultural representations of disability, particularly autism.

DIANE PIVAC is the Web Projects Developer at the New Zealand Film Archive. Her publications include the booklet *Rudall Hayward's Te Kooti Trail* (2001).

NICK RODDICK has taught film and theatre at Trinity College, Dublin; French drama and film at the University of Manchester; and theatre and film at California State University, Long Beach. He has since worked as Films Editor of *Stills Magazine* in London (1982–84) and as Editor of *Cinema Papers* in Melbourne, Australia (1985–86). From 1987–88, he was Editor of the London weekly trade paper, *Screen International* and, in 1990, became founding Editor of *Moving Pictures International*. He has published several books on British and American cinema, including *A New Deal in Entertainment: Warner Brothers in the 1930s* (1983) and *British Cinema Now* (1985). For three years in the mid 1980s, he wrote the New Zealand section of the *International Film Guide*. He currently runs Split Screen, a publishing and consultancy company specialising in the international film and television business, He is also Editor of *Preview*, and a regular contributor to *Sight & Sound* and the *Evening Standard*.

ANGELA MARIE SMITH is Assistant Professor of English at the University of Utah. She has written for the journals *College Literature*, and *Post Script*, and contributed to the edited collections *The Novel and the American Left: Critical Essays on Depression-Era Fiction* (2004), *Eugenics and American*

Mass Culture in the Thirties (2004), and *Horror Zone: The Cultural Experience of Contemporary Horror Cinema* (forthcoming).

Jo SMITH is Lecturer in Media Studies, at Victoria University of Wellington. She researches in the area of postcolonial media theory, New Zealand film, and new media studies. She has contributed to *Illusions, Arena*, and the *New Zealand Journal of Media Studies*, and the article 'The Lord of the Rings in the Living Room: Changing Technologies of Cinematic Display and Reception' in the edited collection *How to Study the Event Movie: The Lord of the Rings—A Case Study* (2007).

GREGORY A. WALLER is Department Chair and Professor of Communication and Culture at Indiana University. He is the recipient of numerous academic awards, including a Fulbright Lectureship to work at the University of Waikato, between June and December 1993. He is the author of *The Stage/Screen Debate: A Study in Popular Aesthetics* (1983), *The Living and the Undead: From Stoker's Dracula to Romero's Dawn of the Dead*, (1986), *Main Street Amusements: Movies and Commercial Entertainment in a Southern City, 1896–1930* (1995), and *Moviegoing in America: A Sourcebook in the History of Film Exhibition* (2002); and editor of *American Horrors: Essays on the Modern American Horror Film*, (1987). A recent project was 'Japan-in-America: The Turn of the Twentieth Century', which included a museum exhibit sponsored by the Toshiba International Foundation.

CHRIS WATSON was, before he retired, Senior Lecturer in the School of English and Media Studies at Massey University in Palmerston North. He is president of the New Zealand Federation of Film Societies and a member of the International Film Festival Trust, which overseas the annual festivals in New Zealand's main centres. He has directed various research projects relating to censorship in New Zealand, several of which were prepared for the Broadcasting Standards Authority in Wellington and, with Roy Shuker, he is the co-author of *In the Public Good? Censorship in New Zealand* (1998).

MARK WILLIAMS is Professor in the English Programme at Victoria University of Wellington. His publications include, as author, *Leaving the Highway: Six Contemporary New Zealand Novelists* (1990), *Patrick White* (1993), and *Post-colonial Literatures in English: Southeast Asia, New Zealand and the Pacific* (1996); as co-author, *Maoriland: The Shaping of New Zealand Literature, 1880–1920* (2006); and as co-editor *Dirty Silence: Essays on Language and Literature in New Zealand* (1991), *In the Same Room: Conversations with New Zealand Writers* (1992), and *Opening the Book: New Essays on New Zealand Writing* (1995). He is also one of the editors of *An Anthology of New Zealand Poetry in English* (Oxford University Press, 1997).

Index